UNDERSTANDING PARTNERSHIP ACCOUNTING

(Second Edition)

A Guide to Investment Partnership Accounting

by Advent Software, Inc. and The Financial Services Industry Group of American Express Tax and Business Services Inc.

ADVENT

AMERICAN EXPRESS

Financial Services Industry Group

Tax & Business Services

NOTICE

ISBN: 0-931187-01-X
Part number: PARTUPA2ED
Publication date: March, 2002

Printed on Recycled Paper.

Contents

Welcome to *Understanding Partnership Accounting (Second Edition)*

Welcome to the second edition of *Understanding Partnership Accounting*, the investment partnership accounting guide from Advent Software®, Inc. and the Financial Services Industry Group in the New York office of American Express® Tax and Business Services Inc. *Understanding Partnership Accounting (Second Edition)* discusses the accounting and legal services that investment partnerships require. It also describes how investment partnerships allocate the results of their investments to the partners, including tax reallocations for performance fees, and other tax and reporting issues.

Important: This book is general in nature, and does not represent a legal or procedural guide for creating an investment partnership, nor does it endorse or suggest any practices or strategies for investment activity, or for partnership accounting. Consult the appropriate tax, legal, and investment professionals for these purposes.

About Advent Software, Inc.

Advent Software, Inc., is the world's leading provider of software solutions, data integration tools, and services for investment management professionals. The Advent Office™ suite of integrated solutions automates a wide range of investment activities, from portfolio management and partnership accounting to client relationship management, reconciliation processing, trading, and order management. Because these solutions are scalable, they are used by investment organizations of all sizes, from the single financial planner managing several million dollars, to large enterprise-wide firms with tens of billions of dollars under management. For more information about Advent Software, please visit the corporate Web site at *http://www.advent.com.*

About the Financial Services Industry Group in the New York Office of American Express Tax and Business Services Inc.

American Express is well known as one of the world's leading financial services companies, inventor of the traveler's cheque and other products to facilitate international trade and travel. The Tax and Business Services ("TBS") subsidiary of American Express is devoted to providing tax and business advisory services to individuals and corporations with sophisticated, high-level needs.

The Financial Services Industry Group in the New York office of TBS is a world leader in delivering tax and advisory services to investment partnerships, hedge funds, and broker-dealers throughout the U.S. and internationally. Its clients, numbering in the hundreds, obtain highly specialized compliance and consulting services related to all aspects of investment partnerships, including accounting, tax compliance, regulatory matters, and strategic issues. The professionals in the group are among the most highly respected practitioners in the field, many with backgrounds from the accounting firm of Goldstein Golub Kessler & Company, PC, the non-attest assets of which were acquired by American Express in July, 1998. American Express employs CPAs, but is not a licensed CPA firm.

The Financial Services Industry Group in the New York office of TBS is a user of Advent software, which it credits with increasing the efficiency of its accounting applications for partnership clients of all sizes.

Martin Lax, CPA; Stuart Kralstein, CPA; and Paul Koren, CPA, Managing Directors in the Financial Services Industry Group in the New York office of American Express Tax and Business Services Inc., contributed their technical and practical knowledge to the writing of this guide. For more information, contact Paul Koren, CPA, Managing Director, at (212) 372-1207 or *paul.m.koren@aexp.com.*

About Advent Partner

Advent Partner® is Advent Software's partnership accounting and management solution. Advent Partner helps to consistently and accurately account for a partnership's activity. Advent Partner also integrates with Axys®, which tracks the partnership's ownership in security investments. Advent Partner provides a powerful, easy-to-use Microsoft® Windows®-based graphical user interface, simple procedures, a variety of reports, direct access to Axys files and processes, and helpful utilities.

Advent Software wishes to thank the following Advent Partner team members who contributed to the research and writing of this guide: Kyle Stadt, Alternative Investments Manager; Tom McGrath, Advent Partner Senior Application Engineer; Chris Garner, Principal Writer; Geri Rebstock, Senior Technical Writer.

For more information about Advent Partner, please contact Kyle Stadt at (800) 685-7688 or *kstadt@advent.com*.

Overview of *Understanding Partnership Accounting (Second Edition)*

Understanding Partnership Accounting (Second Edition) provides conceptual information about investment partnership accounting. Where applicable, it refers to relevant U.S. tax laws, Department of Treasury regulations, and the Internal Revenue Code. This book assumes that you have a general understanding of the finance industry, accounting, and investment partnerships.

Following is a brief description of the chapters in *Understanding Partnership Accounting (Second Edition)*.

Chapter 1, Understanding Pooled Investment Structures, is new to this second edition. It starts with a brief history of investment partnerships, then provides descriptions and graphical overviews of a number of common pooled investment structures.

Chapter 2, Setting Up An Investment Partnership, describes the requirements of limited and general partners, as well as documents needed to solicit investors and form the partnership; the accounting and tax services partnerships require; and the legal considerations partnerships must address.

Chapter 3, Understanding Break Periods, explains how partners' capital contributions, withdrawals, and assignments create break periods, and how partnerships record their income and update partners' capital accounts each period.

Chapter 4, Understanding Items of Profit and Loss, has been expanded for this edition. It details how partnerships assign different kinds of income and expenses to allocation items for tax and reporting purposes. New with this second edition is a more detailed discussion of management fee schedules, including examples.

Chapter 5, Understanding Economic Allocations, describes how partnerships allocate income *pro rata* each period. It also describes non-*pro rata* allocations for hot issues, side pocket investments, and other items.

Chapter 6, Allocating Aggregate Gains, has been revised for this edition. It describes aggregate methodologies of allocating realized (capital) gains and losses, including how Advent Partner allocates Section 1256 and hot issue security gains. This edition includes a brief discussion of Aggregate with Partial Netting, and an extensive example of Assumption 4.

Chapter 7, Allocating Layered Gains, describes the tax lot layering methodology of allocating realized (capital) gains and losses, including how Advent Partner allocates Section 1256 and hot issue security gains.

Chapter 8, Reallocating/Charging Performance Fees, has been expanded for this edition. It describes the options available for structuring performance fees, including payout percentages, hurdle rates, and highwater marks, as well as how to perform a tax reallocation for performance fees. New with this second edition is a discussion of equalization methodologies that can be applied in offshore investment corporations.

Chapter 9, Contributing Securities, describes how partners can contribute securities to partnerships in lieu of cash, and how partnerships handle the built-in gains, amortization, and accrued interest associated with contributed securities.

Chapter 10, Understanding Distributions and Redemptions, explains how partnerships can deliver out securities to partners in lieu of cash, as well as Section 754 election and directed gains provisions to handle withdrawing a partner's share of appreciated securities.

Chapter 11. Understanding Tax Issues, describes other tax issues partnerships must address, including book to tax differences, wash sales, straddles, constructive sales, short sales, and UBTI.

Chapter 12, Understanding Partnership Performance, has been expanded for this edition. It explains how partnerships calculate performance, including reporting requirements, annualization, and the effects of expenses, management fees, and performance fees. Additions to this second edition include additional performance calculations and related examples.

Understanding Partnership Accounting (Second Edition) also features a glossary of terms used in partnership accounting and Advent Partner, including several new terms. For more detailed information about chapter contents, refer to the contents page at the beginning of each chapter.

Understanding the Conventions Used in This Book

Before proceeding with *Understanding Partnership Accounting (Second Edition)*, it is helpful to familiarize yourself with the conventions used throughout the book. Doing so will help avoid misunderstandings and enhance the usefulness of the documentation.

Procedural Conventions

Procedural conventions help identify procedures and tasks to be performed.

- Important procedures are always organized as a numbered set of tasks.
- Check marks indicate a checklist of general items or tasks.

Example Conventions

Most examples in this book use tables to organize information in spreadsheet format. Tables in this edition include shading to highlight information that is discussed in the example's explanatory text.

Terminology

Understanding Partnership Accounting (Second Edition) uses the following specific terminology.

Gain Profit on a securities transaction. *Understanding Partnership Accounting (Second Edition)* uses "gain" generically to refer to both profits and losses on securities transactions. Gain can be either *realized* (from closing a security position); or *unrealized* (the change in market value on a held security position).

Non-Gain Profits, losses, and expenses not attributable to the change in a security's market value. *Understanding Partnership Accounting (Second Edition)* also uses the term "income and expenses." Examples include: dividend income and expenses; interest income, expenses, and accruals; management fees; organizational expenses; investment, trade, and business expenses; and amortization and accretion.

Partnership An "investment partnership," generally a limited partnership (or sometimes a limited liability corporation) formed for investment purposes. More commonly referred to as a "hedge fund," "privately offered investment company" (by the Securities and Exchange Commission), or "securities partnership" (by the Internal Revenue Service).

Performance Fee Compensation to the general partner of an investment partnership for investment advisory services rendered. This generally is not a "fee," but rather a reallocation of a percentage of the partnership's profit for the year from the limited partners to the general partner, accomplished through shifting the partners' allocation percentages in favor of the general partner. In offshore funds, performance fee can take the form of an expense charged to the limited partner. In U.S. partnerships, performance fee may be also referred to as "performance incentive reallocation," "performance reallocation," or "incentive reallocation."

For additional terminology, see the Glossary on page page 257.

Different Types of Notes

When appropriate, notes provide additional information or warnings that may apply to you. *Understanding Partnership Accounting (Second Edition)* uses four types of notes. Each type serves a unique purpose, as defined below.

Note: A note with this format and the heading "Note" provides information that applies to some users. Notes apply to special situations. For example, a Note might explain a rule that only applies in certain specific situations.

Important: A note with this format and the heading "Important" provides information that applies to all users. This type of note provides information that is essential to the completion of a task. Unlike a Note, Important notes should not be disregarded.

Caution: A note with this format and the heading "Caution" provides important information that applies to all users. Pay special attention to these notes.

Tip: A note with this format and the heading "Tip" provides useful information that applies to most users. Although Tips are not essential to the completion of a task, they provide alternative methods, shortcuts, or special applications relating to the procedures in the text. All Tips are listed in the index under the heading "Tips."

ADVENT PARTNER

The Advent Partner logo identifies sections that provide information about Advent Partner and its functionality. These sections explain how Advent Partner automates specific partnership accounting tasks, or highlight features of the software.

How to Learn More About Advent Partner

Advent provides many resources to help you get the most out of your software. Read the following sections to find out what these resources are, and how to access them.

The Advent Partner Documentation Set

The Advent Partner documentation set contains the following guides and quick reference cards. The guides provide overview information, case studies, and references to Help (where you can find the detailed procedures). The quick reference cards are handy to keep by your desk as you work.

Title
Advent Partner 3.3 Release Notes
Using Advent Partner Release 3
Advent Partner Period Processing Quick Reference Card
Using the Geneva/Advent Partner Interface

The Advent Partner documentation set is available in the following formats.

Format	Where to Find It	Benefits
Print	In your product shipment. **Note:** To order additional printed documentation, use the Learning Products Order Form on *Advent Connection* ➤ User Documentation.	You can take printed guides anywhere you go.
Web	*Advent Connection* ➤ User Documentation.	Documentation on the Web is always current, and is ideal if you want to search for a key word or phrase.
Portable Document Format (PDF)	*Advent Connection* ➤ User Documentation.	Documentation in PDF is always current, and is ideal if you want to print selected pages, sections, chapters, or the entire document.

Advent Partner Help

As you work with Advent Partner, you can access Help for immediate access to detailed, step-by-step instructions about Advent Partner tasks.

If you have not used Help before, and you'd like to learn how it works, choose Help ➤ How to Use Help.

If you're ready to use Help, follow these steps.

1 With Advent Partner open, press F1, or select one of the following options from the Help menu.

Choose	To
Contents and Index	Display the Contents, Index, and Find tabs. ❖ Choose the Contents tab to display a table of contents for Help topics. Click on a book to see a list of topics. ❖ Choose the Index tab to see a list of index entries. Type the word you are looking for, or scroll through the list. ❖ Choose the Find tab to do a full text search of the entire Help system.
About this Window F1	Display Help about the current window, dialog box, or menu item.
How to Use Help	Display instructions on how to use Help.
Advent on the Web	Access Advent's Web sites. ❖ Go to Advent's client Web site, *Advent Connection* (*http://connection.advent.com/*) ❖ Go to Advent's corporate site (*http://www.advent.com/*)
About	Display copyright and release information for Advent Partner.

The Advent Partner Readme File

The Readme file contains any late-breaking information about that became available after the printed documentation was published. You can view the Readme file at the end of the installation process, or by following these steps.

1 Choose Start ➤ Programs ➤ Readme.

Note: If you cannot access the Readme file this way, you can use a text editor, such as Notepad, to open the file *Readme_p.wri*, which is located in your AdvPtr directory (*Example:* C:\AdvPtr\Readme_p.wri).

2 *(Optional)* To print the Readme file, choose File ➤ Print.

Advent Connection

Advent's client Web site, *Advent Connection*, gives you access to the latest technical information and support, user documentation, software updates, training, and industry news. Just point your browser to *http://connection.advent.com/*, or, from Advent Partner, choose Help ➤ Advent on the Web ➤ Advent Connection. A site search feature makes it easy for you to look up keywords, and find exactly what you need.

Note: The first time you go to *Advent Connection*, you'll be asked to set up an account. Have your Advent copy number and company information ready.

Additional Advent Resources

For more information on all of the resources available to you as an Advent client, including Technical Support, please see the *Using Advent Resources* quick reference card included in your product shipment. Or go to *Advent Connection* ➤ Advent Concierge (the red button in the upper right corner of every page).

Understanding Pooled Investment Structures

This chapter identifies and explains the functions of an investment partnership's General Partner(s) and Limited Partner(s). Then, it presents several different structures that investment partnerships can take. Each structure is defined and accompanied by a logical, graphical representation.

In This Chapter

The History of Investment Partnerships

Investment partnerships, commonly known as "hedge funds," have become a favorite medium of investment of an elite group of securities investors. Not everyone can be a hedge fund investor—finding the right hedge fund manager, and meeting that manager's standards of sophistication and minimum investment requirement, can be daunting. The number of hedge funds has also risen, from A. W. Jones's first fund 50 years ago, to more than 6,000 funds today. Investment advisors, analysts, registered representatives, and institutions continue to create new funds, offering interests to the investing public, foundations, pension funds, and others.

As originally conceived by Jones, the hedge fund truly hedged. By buying strong securities and selling short overvalued securities, Jones attempted to cushion inevitable market swings. Depending on his view of the markets, he modified his exposure, quantifying the exposure with the formula

(Long values – Short values) / Capital Invested.

Today it is not unusual to read in the business pages or in the private letters of hedge fund managers that a fund is 70%, 80%, or some other percent exposed to the market.

Early managers like Michael Steinhart followed the Jones model, but as time went on other managers used the business form of the hedge fund (that is, the investment partnership), but did not necessarily hedge. The Securities and Exchange Commission (SEC) calls these funds "privately offered investment companies," and the IRS refers to them as "securities partnerships", but the public and the industry commonly refer to these pooled investment vehicles as hedge funds, regardless of whether they hedge.

Many of the early characteristics of hedge funds have survived. Most funds organized today continue to use:

- The limited partnership structure, which takes advantage of favorable partnership tax treatment and the limitation of liability to the limited partners.
- The compensation methodology of reallocating a portion (generally 20%) of appreciation to the general partner(s).

Investment partnerships generally continue to be exempt from the Securities Acts, despite a number of regulatory initiatives, particularly after the publicity surrounding Long-Term Capital Management. Their trading activity is subject to stock exchange and SEC trading rules, however, and their offering of interests is subject to the anti-fraud provisions of the Securities Acts.

Hedge funds have changed during their history in a number of ways.

- Hedge funds can now take the form of limited liability companies (LLCs), which are taxed as partnerships, but have the limited liability of corporations.
- Originally, hedge funds paid operating expenses as incurred. With many managers now operating multiple funds, operating expenses generally are incurred by management companies related to the general partner. A fund will generally reimburse this company with a "management fee," calculated as a percentage of the fund's net assets.
- Early hedge fund managers were typically individual investment professionals. Institutions such as brokerage firms, banks, and investment advisory firms now form funds and offer them as "alternative investment programs" to their high net worth clients.
- Funds of funds, hedge funds that invests in other funds, have become more common. These entities offer investors the opportunity to diversify their investment in funds, without having to individually meet the minimum investment levels of each fund.
- Historically, a hedge fund had to limit its beneficial interests (partners) to no more than one hundred, and not offer its interests publicly, to avoid registration as a registered investment company (a mutual fund). In 1996, however, the United States Congress allowed funds to have more than 100 interests, provided their investors met more stringent acceptance standards. (For practical purposes, interests still could not exceed 499 because of conflicts with other securities statutes.)
- The number of offshore funds has grown significantly. Early managers typically formed a domestic fund and then, after achieving some success, formed an offshore fund. Today a manager often forms both the domestic and offshore funds simultaneously.

Perhaps the single most significant change in hedge funds is the sheer size of current funds. Relatively few funds operate in the multiple billions of dollars, but many funds do operate in the hundreds of millions of dollars. The increased liquidity of the investing public, the investing advantages funds offer, and the availability of technology have brought more investors to the hedge fund industry. Although still dwarfed by the mutual fund industry, the hedge fund industry continues to grow, providing wealthy individuals and institutions the opportunity to risk their capital in the pursuit of financial gain.

Investing Advantages

Pooling customers' funds in an investment partnership provides the following advantages.

- The combined assets of a number of high net worth individuals can be used to obtain more efficient and economical methods to borrow or "leverage" cash and/or securities.
- Fund managers can direct their research to a particular style of investing.
- Investors can diversify their portfolios.
- As opposed to a mutual fund, an investment partnership is much more fair in its allocation and distribution of taxable income.
- Managers' compensation is not limited to a share of commissions or a percentage of assets under management, but can be based upon a share of profits.
- Depending on the fund, pass-through income/losses may be active or passive, offering a number of approaches to tax planning.

Investment Strategies

Today, fund managers do not necessarily adhere to the "hedge" methodology, but instead choose to invest in certain segments of the investment market. The reasons for forming investment partnerships, however, remain the same. The following is a brief list of investment strategies investment partnerships may employ:

- Equity investing
- Distressed securities
- Regional securities
- High-yield fixed income
- Special situation investments
- Commodity pools
- Emerging markets
- Risk arbitrage
- Industry sector investing
- Relative value investing
- Convertible arbitrage
- Global investing
- Macro investing
- Short selling
- Market "neutral" investing

Funds can invest in publicly-traded securities, private securities of public companies, or securities of non-public companies. Funds can invest in securities traded on an established market (such as NYSE or CBOE) or with individual counterparties, as is the case in with over-the-counter options and other derivative products.

Organizing Investment Partnerships

Investment funds are typically formed as limited partnerships, comprising one or more general partners and at least one limited partner. Recently, however, some fund managers have been organizing their funds as limited liability companies (LLCs). An LLC generally provides limited liability for its members, but like a partnership is taxed at the member, rather than entity, level.

IRS regulations allow certain offshore business organizations to "check-the-box" to determine their tax classification. This eliminates the risk that the IRS will reclassify the fund's status into a corporate structure, and allows for greater flexibility in structuring complex business arrangements while maintaining limited liability. For more information about check-the-box regulations, see "Offshore Funds" on page 11.

The General Partner

The typical investment partnership is formed by individuals who have been registered representatives, traders, security analysts, mutual fund managers, or registered or non-registered investment advisors. These individuals or the company they create become the *general partner* responsible for the investment and administrative activities of the fund. The general partner:

- Solicits investments from high net worth individuals, companies, trusts, retirement plans or other partnerships, all of whom become *limited partners*.

  Note: Depending on the form of the partnership, an investor may need to be classified as an "accredited investor" or a "qualified purchaser" (see the Glossary on page 257).

- Follows a chosen style of investing described in the partnership's private placement memorandum.
- Informs the limited partners of the performance of the fund on a regular basis, usually monthly or quarterly.

In the past, many investment partnerships were structured with a corporation, limited partnership, or individual as their general partner. Currently, however, most hedge funds are formed with their general partner as an LLC.

Important: Partnerships should consult their professionals concerning the issues involved in dissolving a corporate general partner to form an LLC, or to convert a partnership (general or limited) or group of individuals into an LLC.

Important: When deciding on the structure of the entity or entities that will serve as their general partner, partnerships must consider the tax ramifications of the different types of income those entities earn. Many state and local taxing authorities have unique laws regarding how they tax these income streams. Partnerships must consult their professionals as to the issues in their locality.

Many fund managers also organize related investment advisory organizations or broker-dealers to serve clients who do not want to become limited partners in investment partnerships. Each of these organizations is subject to significant regulation by the SEC and, in some states, by a local regulatory organization. This book does not discuss the specialized services these entities require.

The Limited Partner

The limited partner is a member of the partnership that contributes capital but it is not liable for the fund's debts beyond the loss of its investment. A limited partnership must have at least one limited partner.

Understanding Pooled Investment Structures

The following sections address common pooled investment structures. They emphasize different structural and accounting characteristics.

Fund of Funds

A "fund of funds" is a investment partnership whose portfolio consists principally of investments in other investment partnerships rather than in individual securities. By investing in multiple funds, the fund of funds manager can blend the strategies of other fund managers, or pursue a limited number of strategies based on the performance of those funds and their managers. By offering these options, a fund of funds (the "investor" fund) spreads the risk of participation in any one "investee" fund and provides the limited partner investor with access to a greater number of investment styles and objectives.

Occasionally, a fund of funds' organizational documents may provide for the ability to invest directly in securities. This usually occurs when it receives securities as a distribution from one of its investee funds, and the investment generally lasts for a limited period of time.

In a fund of funds structure, the investor fund views the investee fund as an investment, and the investee fund views the investor fund as a partner. The fees that an investee fund charges to its investor funds reduce the amount of appreciation received by those that invest in the investor fund itself. Therefore, the fees the investor fund charges to its investors are typically much less than the standard 1% management fee and 20% performance fee charged by other investment partnerships.

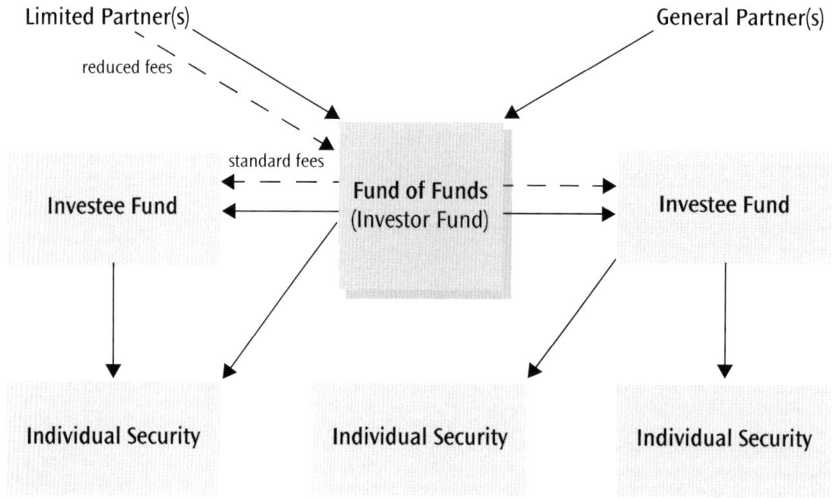

Key:
- Solid lines denote investments.
- Dashed lines denote management and performance fees; arrows point to the entity that receives the reallocated percentage.

The Commodity Futures Trading Commission (CFTC) devotes a section of it annual report to the disclosure requirements of commodity pools concerning their investments in investee funds. Regulation 4.22(c)(5) requires that for each major investee fund (those comprising 10% or more of the fund's net asset value), the fund of funds' annual report must disclose:

- ❖ The name of the investee fund.
- ❖ The value of the investor fund's investment in the investee fund.
- ❖ The net appreciation or depreciation of the investee fund.
- ❖ The amount of fees (both management and performance fee or allocation) charged by the investee fund.

These disclosures must be categorized by entity for all major investee funds. Information regarding smaller funds can be combined in the report.

The American Institute of Certified Public Accountants (AICPA) requires the disclosure of portfolio information pursuant to Statement of Position

95-2. This statement requires disclosure of the name and value of each investee fund whose value exceeds 5% of the investor fund's NAV and might, under certain circumstances, require the investor fund to disclose information about specific securities owned by the investee fund.

Fund of funds are usually not registered under the Investment Company Act of 1940. However, if a fund manager invests in investee funds that are registered as commodity pools under the Commodity Exchange Act (CEA), he or she may also have to register under the CEA as a commodity pool operator and register the fund as a commodity pool. The fund should consult its legal counsel about the requirements for registration.

Fund of Funds Accounting

The accounting for fund of funds is challenging because the investor fund's only source of financial information is its investee funds. For an investor fund to be able to accept monthly contributions or allow monthly withdrawals from its own investors, it must receive, from each of its investee funds, monthly information about appreciation, month-end value, and so on. Investee funds report information to their investor funds in different ways, however, and they generally do not provide details about sources of appreciation (such as whether it came in the form of unrealized gain, realized gain, or dividends). Further, some investee funds may calculate and report monthly increase or decrease as a change in NAV or a percentage return, rather than in dollar amounts. Other investee funds may provide information on a quarterly basis, rather than monthly, or report no information at all.

For investee funds that provide information in a form other than dollar amounts, the investor fund must derive an "appreciation" amount to be allocated among its own partners, along with the rest of the profit and loss. The reports the investor fund provides to its investors will likely show appreciation *net* of all fees paid or accruable, because without this safeguard, individual investors withdrawing from the investor fund would be overpaid, and investors contributing to the fund would pay an inflated price for their interest.

Some investee funds may charge performance fees only on realized income, or may have side pocket arrangements. The investor fund must institute procedures to compensate for all of these items in order to properly account to its own investors.

Because the investor fund treats each investment in an investee fund as an investment in a security, the investor fund must analyze the book and tax basis of its investment in each investee fund. Once the investor fund has accounted for the periodic economic income to its investors, it is faced with the challenge of allocating the components of taxable income. Generally, investee funds do not allocate taxable income to their investors on a monthly basis. The investor fund must therefore determine how to allocate items of taxable income or loss when it receives economic income monthly but taxable income annually.

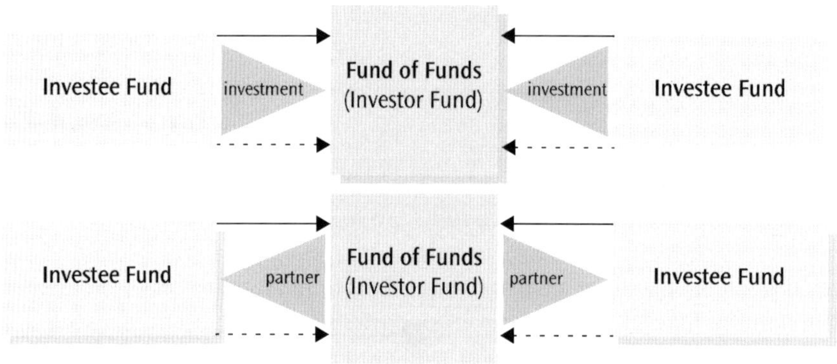

Key:
- Solid lines denote the direction of monthly appreciation.
- Dotted lines denote the direction of yearly K-1 submissions.

One way for the investor fund to account for the taxable income allocation is to use a "blended rate" method. This method calculates the percentage of each individual investor's share of economic income for the year compared to the investor fund's total economic income for the year. The investor fund then applies that percentage to all elements of the combined taxable income from all of its investee funds at the end of the year as reported on their respective Schedule K-1s. The investor fund can allocate realized gains and losses to investors using *pro rata* or aggregate methodology. For more information on aggregate methodology, refer to chapter 6, "Understanding Aggregate Methodologies" on page 110.

When an individual investor withdraws capital from the investor fund in excess of its tax basis (fully liquidating its capital account, for example), it "leaves behind" its unrealized appreciation, and the investor fund must put procedures in place to address such a situation. See chapter 10, "Understanding Distributions and Redemptions," for a discussion of various methods for doing so.

When an investor fund disposes of an investee fund, even though the investor fund has no economic income, it must record a taxable gain or loss on that disposition.

ADVENT PARTNER

You can use Advent Partner to streamline accounting for fund of funds. It lets you track fund appreciation items as well as fund tax reclassification items to be performed at year end. For more information, refer to the Advent Partner 3.2 release notes.

Offshore Funds

In addition to forming domestic limited partnerships, many fund managers form "offshore" funds (offshore of the United States). Offshore funds are usually formed as corporations, although they can also be formed as partnerships. The investors in these funds are usually nonresident aliens but may also be domestic tax-exempt organizations/investors. An investment in an offshore fund does not subject the investor to U.S. tax reporting requirements. U.S. tax-exempt organizations are generally not subject to unrelated business taxable income (UBTI) on the activities of an offshore corporation but would be taxed if the fund were a partnership. The corporate form does not pass through tax attributes from its investments to its shareholders.

Offshore funds use somewhat different terminology than U.S. investment partnerships; and some accounting principles have different applications. This table identifies the terms and principles and explains usage differences.

Term	Definition
Class	A group of investors with the same attributes. Profit and loss are divided equally among all members of the class.

Term	Definition
Gross Net Asset Value (GNAV)	The total assets of a fund, class, or series minus its total liabilities *excluding* performance fee.
GNAV per share	The GNAV of a fund, class, or series divided by the number of outstanding shares.
Highwater Net Asset Value (HNAV)	The amount that the GNAV of a class or series must exceed before a performance fee can be charged.
HNAV per share	The HNAV of a fund, class, or series divided by the number of outstanding shares.
Net Asset Value (NAV)	The total assets of a fund, class, or series minus its total liabilities *including* the impact of the performance fee.
NAV per share	The NAV of a fund, class, or series divided by the number of outstanding shares.
Offering Document	The legal document that documents the understanding between the fund's investment advisor and shareholders. Compare "private placement memorandum" in U.S. investment partnerships.
Performance Fee	Compensation made to the investment manager of an offshore fund, typically charged to shareholders as an expense. Compare "performance fee" in U.S. investment partnerships, where this compensation is generally a reallocation of a percentage of the partnership's profit from the limited partners to the general partner.
Redemption	A withdrawal of cash or securities from the fund. Compare "withdrawal" in U.S. investment partnerships.
Series	A group of shares issued when the fund receives a new or additional subscription. All subscriptions that occur at the same time belong to the same series. All shareholders in the same series pay performance fee on those shares at the same time.
Shareholder	An investor in an offshore fund. Compare "limited partner" in U.S. investment partnerships.
Subscription	A contribution of cash or securities to the fund. Compare "contribution" in U.S. investment partnerships.

The investment managers or general partners of offshore funds can be offshore corporations owned substantially by the fund manager or the manager's U.S. entity.

General Offshore Fund Accounting

Unlike funds operating entirely within the United States, offshore funds are not generally subject to U.S. taxes or reporting requirements. Prior to 1997, safe harbor practices, known as the "Ten Commandments," provided reasonable assurance that the principal office of the fund was offshore, and therefore not subject to U.S. taxation. The Taxpayer Relief Act of 1997 (1997 Act), however, eliminated the requirement that the offshore fund's principal office be located offshore to avoid U.S. taxation.

U.S. shareholders or partners of an offshore fund are taxed on their allocable share of the offshore fund's profits, even if those profits are not distributed to the U.S. person. Therefore, an offshore corporation with U.S. taxpayer shareholders must file the appropriate tax form with the IRS. An offshore corporation with U.S. taxpaying shareholders generally "checks-the-box" and elects to be treated as a partnership for U.S. tax purposes. U.S. shareholders receive a Form 1065, Schedule K-1 reporting their share of taxable income generated from the fund for the period. The offshore corporation does not issue Form 1065, Schedule K-1s or file them with the IRS for its non-U.S. shareholders.

Offshore funds provide an opportunity for the investment manager to defer taxation of performance fee and management fee, but this requires that the manager adhere to a number of strict guidelines. For example, the manager and the fund must enter into a deferred compensation agreement prior to the year in which the compensation to be deferred is earned. This agreement must also cover a fixed and specific time period.

Another key difference between investment partnerships and offshore corporations is how they calculate and charge performance fees. Investment partnerships generally allocate profit to limited partners according to their ownership percentages and reallocate performance fees from partners' capital accounts to the general partner. By contrast, offshore funds generally issue one or more classes of shares to subscribers and then charge fees to investors in proportion to their shareholdings, without regard to changes in the fund's NAV. In other words, the partner in a U.S. investment partnership incurs performance fee based on already allocated profit, but the shareholder in an offshore fund incurs performance fee based on the number of shares it holds in proportion to the total number of shares purchased. Depending on when the offshore shareholder subscribes to the fund, it may incur performance fee even if it makes no profit or takes a loss on its investment. To offset this inequity, an offshore fund may utilize a method of equalization when calculating and charging performance fee. For more information on equalization, see "Performance Fees in Offshore Funds" on page 177.

Offshore funds are typically set up in tax haven countries such as Bermuda, the Cayman Islands, the British Virgin Islands, the Netherlands Antilles, or Luxembourg, all of which grant tax holidays to the funds.

There are a number of structures an offshore fund can take, including side-by-side and master-feeder. These two structures are explained below.

Side-By-Side Offshore Fund Structure

One common offshore fund structure is known as "side-by-side". In a side-by-side structure, a U.S. partnership and an offshore fund are structured to mirror each other. The U.S. and offshore entities are distinct investing vehicles, however, and the general partner makes similar investments for both. The U.S. partnership pays taxes and follows standard partnership accounting principles, while the offshore fund may employ equalization principles to ensure that performance fee is calculated and charged fairly. For more information on equalization, see "Performance Fees in Offshore Funds" on page 177.

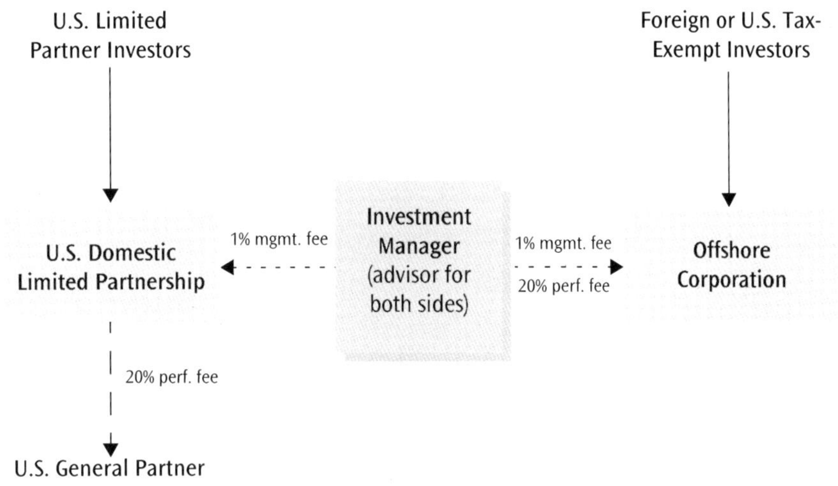

Key:
- Solid lines identify the direction of contributions/subscriptions.
- Dotted lines represent fees and identify the entity to whom the expense is charged.
- Dashed lines represent fees and identify the entity that receives the reallocation.

Master-Feeder Offshore Fund Structure

Another common type of offshore fund is the "master-feeder" structure. A master-feeder fund is a two-tiered investment structure in which investors invest their capital in a "feeder" fund, which in turn invests in a "master" fund managed by the same investment advisor. The master fund is the entity that invests in the market.

A typical master-feeder organization has one master fund with one offshore feeder and one U.S. feeder. The benefit of this organization is that it doesn't restrict the investing fund to just one type of investor (that is, tax exempt versus U.S. taxable).

Feeder funds under the same master can differ in their investor types, investment minimums, fee structure, net asset values, and other operational features.

An offshore corporation can "check the box" and elect to be taxed as a partnership for U.S. tax purposes. By investing in an offshore master-feeder fund taxed as a U.S. partnership, the U.S. limited partnership will receive "pass-through" treatment for its share of the master-feeder's income.

For a master-feeder with both U.S. and offshore feeders, there can be a number of tax-related complexities with advantages and disadvantages on both sides. The advantages include the following.

- The master-feeder structure reduces trading costs because there is no need to "split" trades into tax lots.
- The general partner's performance fee will be able to maintain the underlying fee attributes from onshore feeders.
- The fund's combined assets can be used to obtain greater financing benefits (for example, greater leverage or lower interest rates).

The disadvantages include:

- An offshore fund is generally subject to 30% withholding tax on U.S. dividends. If a fund tries to avoid such transactions, it incurs increased costs that it otherwise would not experience.
- Investing strategies may not offer advantages to all investors at all times. For example, long term capital gain is beneficial for U.S. participants but taxes are not a concern of offshore participants, so investing at the master level may create conflicts.
- Some investment types, such as REITS and mutual funds, are not appropriate for offshore investors but have no consequences for U.S. investors.
- Allocations (such as hot issue versus non-hot issue) and tax accounting can become cumbersome, negating the time savings gained from easier trade administration.

The structure of a master-feeder fund with U.S. and offshore feeders is shown below.

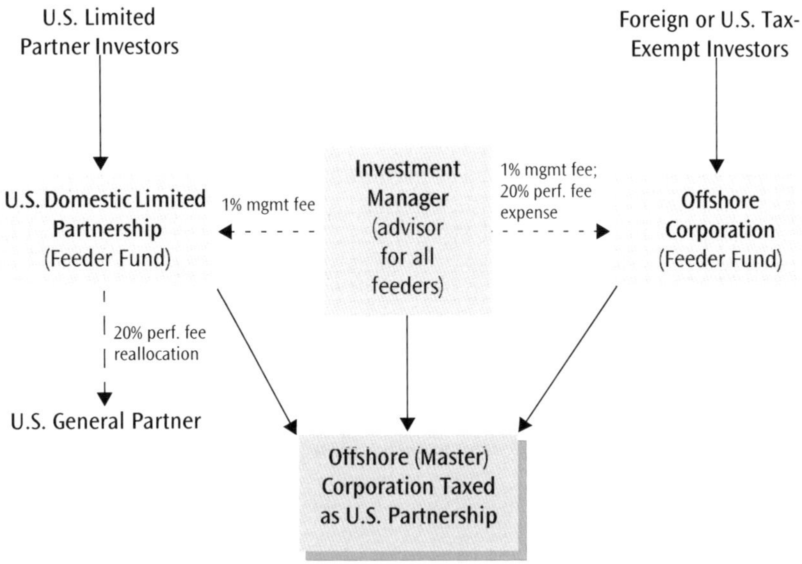

Key:
- Solid lines identify the direction of contributions/subscriptions.
- Dotted lines represent fees and identify the entity to whom the expense is charged.
- Dashed lines represent fees and identify the entity that receives the reallocation.

Private Equity and Venture Capital Funds

Private equity and venture capital (PE/VC) funds differ substantially from other investment partnerships. The securities these funds acquire are usually in privately held or newly formed public companies that need additional financing to be able to bring their products or services to market. Generally, these securities are not registered with the SEC for sale in the open market. The investment philosophy of private equity and venture capital funds is to buy and hold these securities, selling them only after a public offering takes place or in connection with the sale of the entity. In many cases, the fund does not sell the securities, but rather distributes them to its investors after they are registered by the SEC.

The securities that PE/VC funds acquire may be classified as "qualified small business stock," as defined by the Internal Revenue Code (IRC Section 1202(c)). The advantage of purchasing this type of stock is that PE/VC funds may be able to defer recognition of the resulting taxable gain when they dispose of the stock (see IRC Section 1045).

In order to protect its interest, the PE/VC fund will generally place a representative on the investee company's board of directors. The fund's only sources of information may come from board meetings and informal discussions with management.

A PE/VC fund's investments may take on different forms, such as common stock, preferred stock that may be convertible, or debt that may be convertible. These investments are usually accompanied by warrants, which are out of the money at time of issuance but are expected to appreciate over time.

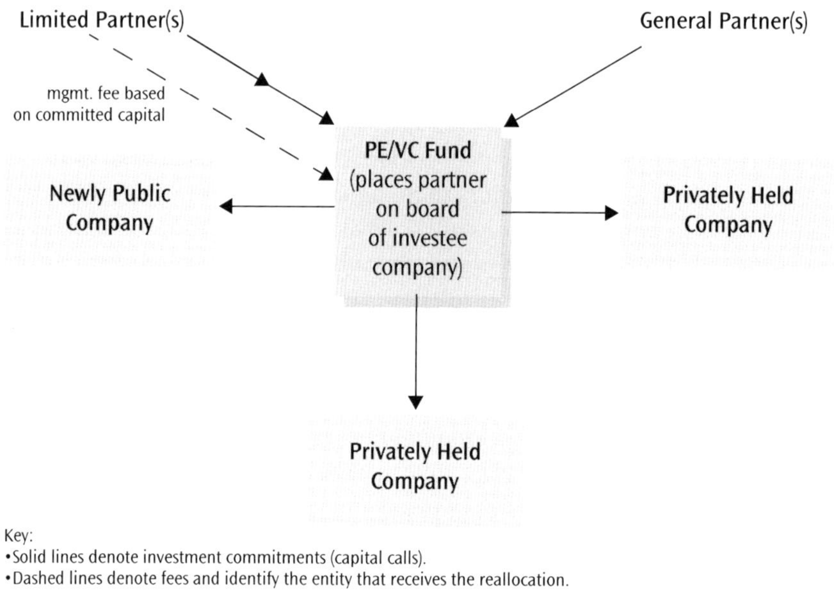

Due to the nature of the holding period for investments, most PE/VC funds are "lock-ups." This means that they include only the original partners who joined at the time the fund was formed and that these partners do not have withdrawal rights. When a fund is formed, each investor agrees to contribute a specific sum to the fund over a specific period of time, and this becomes its capital commitment. During the life of the fund, the fund manager will occasionally call a percentage of the commitment. A capital call usually occurs when the fund is contemplating a new investment, to earmark the call's proceeds for the acquisition. The capital call may also occur at predetermined dates as specified in the fund's offering documents.

A private equity / venture capital fund usually has a limited life span, with a specific date of termination. It typically calls its capital commitments during the early part of its life span; makes and nurtures its investments during the middle; and liquidates its investments at the end. Some agreements may provide for extending the life of the fund so that its investments can be liquidated in orderly fashion.

Private Equity/Venture Capital Fund Accounting

The management fee charged by the PE / VC fund manager is usually based on the aggregate of the fund's committed capital rather than its capital balance. The committed capital may be reduced for return of capital distributions that are made periodically by the fund.

The fund's performance fee or allocation may be charged only on realized appreciation that may be distributed or distributable. The agreements may also provide for some type of "clawback" provision if the fund sustains losses on later investments. These agreements might provide that the incentive be based on the aggregate profit of the fund during its lifetime. Therefore, if the fund records profit from an early investment and receives performance fees or allocations, then sustains losses on later investments, the general partners may be required to return a portion, if not all, of the performance fee or allocation originally taken. Some agreements that contain this clawback provision allow a portion of the performance fee to be placed in escrow. This mitigates the impact on the general partners and provides assurances in the event that the clawback is required.

Since there is no public market for many of their investments, most PE / VC funds do not value their investments on a periodic basis. Instead, they are valued at cost or at a value paid for in a subsequent financing; or reduced in value for a clearly evident impairment, when reports are produced. The justification for this is that because the fund is a lock-up, there can be no change in capital percentages. If the fund's general partners were to value the investments, such valuation would be in good faith. The literature describing the good faith valuation can be found in the SEC's Financial Reporting Releases at Section 404.04.

Setting Up An Investment Partnership

This chapter describes the qualifications for limited and general partners, as well as documents needed to solicit investors and form the partnership, accounting and tax services that partnerships require, and legal issues that partnerships must address.

In This Chapter

Forming an Investment Partnership

Forming a investment partnership requires the skills of many different professionals. An investment partnership must assemble the proper team early in its formation to identify and properly address all of the potential issues.

Team Required

The team required to form and manage an investment partnership consists of a general partner, an attorney, and an accountant. Additionally, most investment partnerships utilize the services of a prime broker.

- **General partner:** The general partner is the partnership's responsible party. The general partner establishes the policies that the fund will follow, and sells limited partnership interests to investors. Often, the general partner has only an idea of the kind of fund to be formed and an investment philosophy and approach. The experienced accountant and attorney then review the various issues that the general partner must address and assist in making specific determinations.
- **Attorney:** The attorney must understand the laws and regulations regarding securities, partnerships, and taxation. The attorney translates the general partner's policies into a limited partnership agreement and, if the general partner is offering limited partnership interests to more than a limited few investors, prepares an offering memorandum, a subscription document, and any other required documents. The memorandum summarizes the general partner's objectives and the important provisions of the limited partnership agreement, and identifies risks, tax, and other important legal matters. For more information, see "Investment Partnership Documentation" on page 26.
- **Accountant:** The accountant reviews the limited partnership agreement and other partnership documents to ensure that:
  - The documents express the general partner's intent.
  - The tax provisions are consistent with tax laws.

- The provisions regarding accounting and tax allocations to the fund's activity and results are objective and executable.

The accountant contributes a business person's approach to other parts of the document. After the fund commences operations, a certified public accountant (CPA) performs an annual year-end audit, and the partnership's accountant prepares or reviews all the necessary tax forms. The general partner consults the accountant during the year on accounting and tax issues. For more information, see "Accounting and Tax Issues" on page 34.

- **Prime broker:** Although an investment partnership can buy and sell securities at different brokers, it generally selects one broker (called a "prime broker") to act as custodian of the partnership's funds and securities. The prime broker:

  - Clears all of the fund's trades (whether or not the prime broker executed the trade).
  - Provides margin borrowing.
  - Provides daily, monthly, and annual reporting of the fund's activities.
  - Provides a listing of trades, a summary of open positions (including cost and market value), and a schedule of closed transactions.

  In practice, the partnership:

  - Purchases a security at a broker, and the broker delivers the security to the prime broker for payment.

    or

  - Sells a security at a broker, and the broker forwards the proceeds to the prime broker in exchange for delivery of the securities sold.

  Without the services of a prime broker, the fund must maintain separate records and reconcile the transactions for each broker it uses. Using a prime broker significantly simplifies the fund's internal accounting.

  The prime brokerage custodial accounts are known as delivery vs. payment (DVP) accounts.

ADV ENT PARTNER

Tip: If you manage your partnership's investment portfolio(s) with Axys, you can use Advent's Rex™ automated reconciliation service to reconcile with your custodians. For details, contact an Advent sales representative.

The remaining sections in this chapter discuss specific legal, tax, and accounting issues involved in creating and running an investment partnership.

Investment Company Act of 1940

Most investment partnerships avoid registration with the SEC by selling their interests under a "Regulation D" exemption under the Securities Act of 1933. To avoid registration under the Investment Company Act of 1940 (the Act), a fund can rely on exclusions provided in Section 3(c)(1) or 3(c)(7).

A fund generally qualifies for a Section 3(c)(1) exemption if it:

- Has no more than 100 beneficial interests, no more than 35 of which are "non-accredited investors."

  and

- Does not make a public offering of such interests.

A fund generally qualifies for a Section 3(c)(7) exemption if it:

- Is owned exclusively by "qualified purchasers."

  and

- Does not make a public offering of such interests.

Note: The Act does not limit the number of beneficial interests allowed in a Section 3(c)(7) fund, although there is a practical maximum of 500 beneficial interests because of certain provisions of the Securities and Exchange Act of 1934.

Section 3(c)(1) Funds

An "accredited investor" under Section 3(c)(1) is an investor who meets certain minimum net worth and earnings standards—generally, an individual who has:

- Net worth in excess of $1,000,000.

  or

- An income of $200,000 (or $300,000 joint with spouse) in each of the past two years, and can be reasonably expected to continue such earning.

General partners who accept contributions from "non-accredited investors" are subject to more significant fiduciary and disclosure responsibilities. To qualify for the Regulation D exemption, the general partner can offer no more than 35 beneficial interests to such investors. The fund's counsel should decide the issue of investor accreditation.

Section 3(c)(7) Funds

In October 1996, the National Securities Markets Improvement Act of 1996 (the 1996 Act) added Section 3(c)(7) to the Act. A fund can seek this exemption if it is owned exclusively by "qualified purchasers," defined in the 1996 Act generally as:

- Natural persons who own not less than $5 million in investments.
- Family-owned companies that own not less than $5 million in investments.
- Certain trusts.
- Any other persons (such as institutional investors) who own and invest on a discretionary basis not less than $25 million in investments.

In April 1997, the SEC adopted rules that define the term "investments," the methods of calculating the amount of investments, and beneficial ownership for the purposes of the 1996 Act. The 1996 Act also includes grandfather provisions related to converting a Section 3(c)(1) fund into a Section 3(c)(7) fund. The 1996 Act also amended certain look-through provisions (described in the section "Integration Rule" on page 26).

Note: Funds with more than 100 partners must consider certain tax issues. In particular, the IRS may consider the fund a publicly traded partnership (PTP). A fund can rely on certain exceptions, or safe harbors, to avoid PTP status. The fund should discuss issues related to the above matters with the appropriate professionals, including its counsel.

Integration Rule

The SEC's "Integration Rule" requires that, if a general partner manages several funds with the same investing style and other substantially similar characteristics, all of those funds' beneficial interests count towards the 100 interests for the funds' Section 3(c)(1) exemptions. However, a Section 3(c)(7) fund and a related Section 3(c)(1) fund are not integrated. A fund manager can have a Section 3(c)(1) fund with a similar investment style to a Section 3(c)(7) fund without counting the Section 3(c)(7) fund's investors as beneficial interests in the Section 3(c)(1) fund.

Section 3(c)(1) funds must also use a "look-through" test to determine the number of beneficial interests of the fund. The fund must count all of the beneficial interests of a limited partner as beneficial interests of the fund if the limited partner:

- Is an investment company, or would be an investment company except for its exclusion under Sections 3(c)(1) or 3(c)(7).

  and

- Has an interest that exceeds 10% of the fund's net assets.

The fund should consult counsel on this issue.

Investment Partnership Documentation

Two of the key documents required to form an investment partnership are the offering document, also known as a private placement memorandum (PPM), and the limited partnership agreement (LPA).

- The general partner uses the PPM to offer interests in the fund to potential investors.

- The LPA is the legal document that is the agreement between the general and limited partners.

The following sections describe the significant provisions of the PPM and the LPA that the partnership's accountant should review.

In addition, these documents should describe the partnership's methods for allocating profit and loss. For details, see the following chapters.

For Information About	See
Economic allocations	Chapter 5, Understanding Economic Allocations.
Tax allocations	Chapter 6, Allocating Aggregate Gains. Chapter 7, Allocating Layering Gains.
Performance-based compensation to the general partner	Chapter 8, Reallocating/Charging Performance Fees.

Investment Objective

The partnership's investment objective addresses the following considerations.

- The general partner's investment philosophy and style of investing. For example, it could state that the fund intends to:
    - Hold a diversified portfolio.
    - Hold a portfolio concentrated in one industry sector.
    - Utilize leverage.
- The types of securities that the fund may, or may not, invest in, such as:
    - Futures and forward contracts.
    - Other investment partnerships.
    - Fixed income securities.
    - Distressed securities or "junk" bonds.

- Real estate.

- The investment parameters that the general partner intends to follow, such as:
  - Limits on the percentage of the partnership's capital that the general partner can invest in one issuer.
  - The amount of leverage, if any, that the general partner can employ.
  - The amount of assets, if any, that the general partner can allocate to other investment advisers.

Description of General Partner and Related Entities

The PPM discloses to potential investors other entities the general partner owns or controls. Because the general partner is usually formed as an LLC, the PPM usually discloses the managing member of the LLC.

Many funds also have related management and investment advisory companies. The PPM also discloses these relationships, and any related fee arrangements. The potential investor must fully understand not only the structure of the fund, but also the relationship of the fund to all of its related entities.

Management Fees

Investment partnerships typically pay a fee (called a "management fee") to a management company, which is usually an entity related to the general partner. The fee is generally calculated as a percentage of each limited partner's capital (typically .75% to 2% annually), and is often collected quarterly.

The management fee generally covers the overhead expenses of the general partner, such as rent, computers, and personnel. Typically, the fund itself bears direct expenses, such as professional fees and research.

For more information about allocating management fees, see "Management Fee Items" on page 77.

Capital Contributions

The LPA should give the general partner discretion to accept contributions at any time, although the agreement can also provide for specific entry dates (for example, on the first day of any month, quarterly, or semiannually). The general partner may want to limit when limited partners can make contributions, because each time partnership interests change, the partnership must recalculate the partners' capital percentages to determine the next period's allocation. General partners should accept contributions of reasonable amounts at interim periods, however, to help increase the size of a fund.

Note: Prior to check-the-box, the general partner generally invested a minimum of 1% of the partnership's capital. This validated the partnership for tax purposes. As a result of check-the-box, this contribution is no longer required. Many general partners believe that the limited partners, and potential investors, are more likely to invest if the general partner contributes to the partnership. In many cases, the general partner has a significant amount of capital in the fund.

Contributed Securities

The LPA specifies whether the partnership accepts contributions in kind; that is, contributions of appreciated securities in lieu of (or in addition to) cash. If the LPA allows investors to contribute securities, the accountant should advise the general partner that generally, contributing securities is a taxable event, with the contributing partner subject to tax on the difference between the partner's tax basis in the securities and their fair market value on the date of the contribution. The IRS believes that the change in risk resulting from exchanging securities for a partnership interest (diversification) constitutes a taxable economic event.

The IRS provides guidance for determining when contributions diversify the partner's portfolio, triggering a taxable event. For details, see "When Are Built-In Gains Taxable?" on page 191. For general information about contributed securities, see Chapter 9, Contributing Securities.

Important: Include the appropriate professionals in any discussions regarding non-taxability of contributed securities. From an accounting viewpoint, the partnership must credit the contributing partner for the fair market value of the contributed securities, less any charges for liquidating the position (as provided for in the partnership agreement).

Capital Withdrawals

The LPA should provide for specific withdrawal dates (for example, on the last day of any month, quarterly, semiannually, or annually). The general partner limits the periods when limited partners can make withdrawals because of investment considerations.

- **Length of notice:** LPAs should provide for a reasonable period of time for the limited partners to give notice to the general partner to request a withdrawal of capital. The general partner must consider the length of time needed to liquidate positions to raise cash without adversely impacting the performance of the fund or the balance of the fund's portfolio. Generally, 30 to 60 days is considered a reasonable period of time.

- **Full withdrawals:** The LPA should permit full withdrawals from the fund only at year end, so that the partnership can have audited financial information from which to calculate a partner's capital account. Funds that permit full withdrawals do so subject to a retention amount.

  Note: A full withdrawal in the form of cash from a partnership is a taxable event to a partner, with gain or loss measured by the difference between the cash distributed to the partner and the partner's tax basis in the partnership (generally, the unrealized gains in the partner's capital account). A withdrawing partner recognizes gain or loss in the year when the partner receives the cash. If the partner receives cash for a December 31, 1998 withdrawal in January 1999, the partner recognizes gain or loss in 1999. The partnership should advise a partner who fully withdraws, in either the partner's capital letter or a supplemental memo, that the partner's withdrawal is a taxable event.

- **Retention amount:** LPAs should allow the partnership to retain 10% to 20% of a withdrawing partner's capital account balance in the fund. This amount is not subject to market risk, and is distributed to the partner after the partnership receives its audited financial statements and can verify the partner's final capital account balance. The partnership should calculate the performance reallocation paid by the withdrawing partner as of the date of the partner's withdrawal. (For details, see "Charging Performance Fees For Withdrawals" on page 161.)

Note: Many LPAs require the partnership to pay interest to the withdrawing partner on the amount retained.

- **Partial withdrawals:** Partnerships can permit partial withdrawals by a limited partner, as indicated in the LPA. The agreement generally provides that a partial withdrawal by a limited partner that reduces the partner's capital account below a certain minimum gives the general partner the right to require the partner making the withdrawal to withdraw the balance of the account.

  Note: A partial withdrawal of capital by a partner is not a taxable event to a partner unless the cash withdrawn exceeds the partner's tax basis.

- **Distributing securities:** The general partner should have the discretion to distribute either securities or cash (or a combination) to the partner making the withdrawal. The value attributed to the distributed securities is their market value at the close of business on the last day of the period.

  Note: If a partner who has a significant capital account makes a full withdrawal from a partnership, and receives appreciated securities, the partnership should distribute securities with unrealized appreciation equal to or greater than the unrealized appreciation in the partner's capital account. This way:

  - The partnership avoids liquidating a position to provide funds for the withdrawal (with the remaining partners taxed on their share of the gain realized).
  - The withdrawing partner retains the partnership's holding period on the distributed securities, and only recognizes the gain when it closes the position.

  The partnership should evaluate whether to distribute cash or securities to a partner making a partial withdrawal.

  A partnership can also liquidate a partner's capital account by distributing a short position and cash. Partnerships should discuss such transactions with the appropriate professional prior to execution.

For details about distributing securities, see "Distributing Securities" on page 205.

- **Requesting that a partner withdraw:** A general partner must have the right to request that a partner withdraw from the partnership. Generally, general partners make such requests on 30-day notice.

Valuation of Securities

Investment partnerships account for their portfolio of securities on a market-value basis (mark-to-market). The methods of valuation should follow the provisions of the LPA and conform with generally accepted accounting principles as outlined in paragraphs AAG-INV 2.27-2.34 of the AICPA's Investment Company Guide, which provides basic methods of valuing securities.

Reports to Partners

The LPA should provide for the partnership to send an annual audited financial statement to each partner along with a schedule of the partner's capital account. Some agreements state that the partnership deliver these reports, along with the related tax information, to limited partners by a specified date.

The agreement should also provide for the preparation of the partnership tax return and the forwarding of IRS Form 1065, Schedule K-1 and such other information necessary for a partner to prepare a federal and (where appropriate) state income tax return.

The LPA also generally provides for the general partner to send interim information to the partners. Such information can be in the form of a letter to limited partners, or interim financial statements. In practice, most agreements do not specify the form of interim information, and general partners typically send the letter form.

Fiscal Years

LPAs specify the year end adopted by the partnership. Investment partnerships generally adopt a calendar year, but can elect to adopt a fiscal year end. If the partnership adopts a year other than calendar, it must make enhanced tax payments (deposits) on behalf of its partners. In most cases, LPAs contain a clause that permits the general partner to adopt an appropriate year end.

Tax Elections

The LPA should contain a provision that authorizes the general partner to make all tax elections permitted by the Internal Revenue Code. This authorizes the general partner to make a number of minor elections in the ordinary conduct of the partnership's business. In addition, it authorizes the general partner to make the Section 754 election. This election increases the cost basis of securities the partnership holds by the amount of unrealized appreciation paid to a withdrawing partner.

Important: Tax accounting for the Section 754 election can be extremely complex and costly. Before a fund elects Section 754, the general partner should speak with the appropriate professional to discuss its ramifications.

ADV ENT PARTNER

For information on how Advent Partner handles Section 754 election, see "Electing Section 754" on page 209.

Directed Gains

If the partnership does not elect Section 754, the LPA usually includes a provision that allows the general partner to allocate an amount of the partnership's taxable realized gains to a withdrawing partner, equal to the amount of unrealized appreciation in the withdrawing partner's capital account. The general partner then allocates the withdrawing partner's unrealized gains to the remaining partners. For more information, see "Directing Gains" on page 212.

Caution: It is currently unclear whether directed gains satisfy the "substantial economic effect" test required of allocations by Internal Revenue Code Section 704(b). Partnerships should exercise caution in implementing directed gains.

Termination

LPAs generally provide for a specific life for the partnership. Such life should be at least 20 years, unless special circumstances make a shorter period meaningful.

LPAs typically provide for the dissolution of the partnership, or for a substitute general partner, in the event that the general partner is unable to perform its duties. The agreement also specifies that, in the event of termination, the fund's assets will be distributed in the to the following individuals in the order listed.

1. Creditors of the partnership other than creditors who are partners.
2. Creditors who are partners.
3. Partners according to their capital balance ratios.

If the partnership has more than one general partner, the agreement should provide for the continuance of the partnership when one general partner withdraws, with the right of limited partners to withdraw when they receive notice. Although not a part of the LPA, the partnership should also have an agreement covering transfers or purchases of interests between general partners (called a "buy-sell" agreement).

Other provisions may affect the accounting, tax reporting and administration of the partnership. The accountant should read the entire agreement to be sure that there are no other matters that cannot be administered or that cause conflict.

Accounting and Tax Issues

Many funds have expert internal financial personnel. In such cases, the accounting professionals and the fund's internal staff must understand their respective responsibilities. The accountants should encourage the fund to retain internal staff, when cost effective, and the internal staff should perform as many of the accounting and tax procedures as possible.

The general partner's staff may, however, consist only of administrative personnel and security analysts. If the fund does not keep internal accounting staff, its accountant controls the timing of and resources for the services that the fund requires, such as an audit and a tax return.

Investment partnerships generally require the following accounting and tax services.

Accounting services include:

- ❖ Reconciling due to/from broker balances and portfolio positions.
- ❖ Reconciling the fund's net asset value.
- ❖ Allocating the fund's profit and loss to all partners, including the general partner's performance reallocation.
- ❖ Preparing annual financial statements.

For details, see "Accounting Services" on page 36.

Tax services include:

- ❖ Allocating taxable amounts to partners.
- ❖ Notifying the partners of interim taxable amounts realized to date.
- ❖ Preparing the partnership's tax returns and Schedule K-1s (and other information needed to prepare the partners' federal or state income tax returns).

For details, see "Tax Services" on page 39.

A typical work and delivery schedule would provide for:

1 Completing interim accounting procedures and tax review in the 11th or 12th month of the year.

2 Reconciling, and calculating partners' capital accounts and tax allocations, starting the third week (or earlier, if possible) after the year end.

3 Mailing financial reports, partners' capital account letters and tax information during the third month after the year end (or earlier, if possible).

The following trial balance represents a simple investment partnership and should not be construed as complete or representative of all investment partnerships. Subsequent sections in this book refer to this trial balance.

Example: Trial Balance of Simple Fund at December 31, 1998

	Debit	Credit
Due from broker	$1,000	
Investments in securities - long	$4,000	
Unrealized gain (loss) - long securities	$1,500	
Other assets	$100	
Investments in securities - short		$1,000
Unrealized (gain) loss - short securities		$200
Partners' capital		$3,600
Realized gain (loss)		$800
Change in unrealized gain (loss)		$1,000
Interest and dividend income		$200
Short dividend expense	$70	
Management fees	$80	
Other	50	
Total	**$6,800**	**$6,800**

The following sections describe investment partnerships' accounting and tax service needs in more detail.

Accounting Services

1 **Reconciling due to/from broker balances and portfolio positions:** The broker reconciliation accounts for all cash activity within the fund, including amounts due.

- *To the broker,* for money that the fund has borrowed, such as for margin requirements.
- *From the broker,* for cash that the broker is holding on behalf of the fund.

  Note: Due to / from broker amounts are also known as debit and credit balances, respectively.

A broker reconciliation starts with the opening balance of the fund (zero for a newly formed fund), adding (and subtracting):

- Cash capital contributions (withdrawals).
- Realized gains (losses).
- Decreases (increases) in the cost of securities held at the end of a break period.
- Cash income (expense) items and any other items not recorded on either the broker statements or the fund's books and records.

The sum of these items must agree with the cash balances reported on the broker statement.

Some funds maintain general ledgers to which they reconcile. Other funds reconcile their portfolio management systems to the broker statements, or construct a general ledger (in worksheet form) from:

- Prime broker reports.
- An analysis of the cash account.
- An analysis of the broker statements for all items other than buys and sells.

Investment partnerships account for their security activity on a trade date basis (the date the trade is executed, not settled) and the prime broker's supplemental portfolio record-keeping system reports should reflect trade date accounting. Most brokers prepare their statements, however, on a settlement date basis. Equities and exchange-traded options generally settle three and one business days, respectively, after the trade. This timing difference almost always appears as the principal reconciling item element in the reconciliation of the broker's account.

Problems with the broker reconciliation often occur in:

- Accrued activities.
- Distributions of securities.
- Non-cash contributions.
- Transfers to/from other brokers to the prime broker.

2 **Reconciling the fund's net asset value:** This reconciles the client-provided NAV and the prime broker's NAV. The accountant uses the opening capital account of the fund, adding and subtracting capital contributions and withdrawals, realized and unrealized gains and losses, and income and expense items to arrive at closing capital.

3 **Allocating the fund's profit and loss to all partners, including the general partner's performance reallocation:** The process of allocating the fund's profits is too complex to describe here. For details, see the following chapters.

Chapter	Title
4	Understanding Items of Profit and Loss
5	Understanding Economic Allocations
6	Allocating Aggregate Gains
7	Allocating Layered Gains
8	Reallocating/Charging Performance Fees

4 **Preparing the fund's annual financial statements:** After reconciling the fund's activity and marking the fund's securities to market, the accountant prepares a financial statement. Generally, the fund uses the model provided in the AICPA Audit and Accounting Guide, as modified by Statement of Position 95-2. The accountant generally prepares the financial statements on the accrual basis.

Tax Services

1 **Allocating taxable amounts to partners:** A partnership's classification as a trader or investor partnership affects how it reports income and expense items for tax purposes. (For details, see "Partnership Classification" on page 41.) The partnership prepares its tax allocation schedule in the format of item J of Schedule K-1. The partnership further details each component of the "analysis of partner's capital account" to identify each tax and non-tax item.

The general partner selects a realized gain or loss allocation method (aggregate or layering) and must use it consistently unless the fund changes its trading activity and philosophy. The general partner should consult the fund's professionals before changing methods. The limited partnership agreement usually includes only general language discussing the allocation.

The partnership must allocate the unrealized gain or loss separately each period to account for partners' changing interests in the partnership over the life of each investment. Additionally, the partnership may have to make certain tax adjustments to the realized gain/loss schedule for wash sales, straddles, short sales covered but not settled at year end, and Section 1256 contracts not closed by year end. The partnership usually allocates other items of tax income and deduction using the current capital percentages.

Note: For a discussion of tax allocations, see "How Do Tax and Economic Allocations Differ?" on page 93.

The Form 1065 balance sheet and capital account reflect mark-to-market (including unrealized gains) and accrual activity. Therefore, a partner's book capital balance must agree with its capital account as reported on Schedule K-1. For the book and tax capital account balances to agree, the partnership must allocate non-tax items such as unrealized appreciation and the timing difference for dividend reporting.

Additional information, such as municipal and United States Treasury interest; Passive Foreign Investment Company (PFIC) activity; unrelated business taxable income (UBTI); state income tax information; and other information necessary for preparing income tax returns, which cannot be derived from specific information included on Schedule K-1, should be included in the "Other Information Provided by Partnership" section of Schedule K-1.

After completing the tax allocation, the accountant performs an "analytical review," comparing each tax item allocation to the economic allocation of appreciation / depreciation, and reviews significant variations with the appropriate professional.

2 Preparing or reviewing partnership tax returns and transmitting Schedule K-1 (and other information needed to prepare a partner's federal income tax return): Funds can prepare their partnership tax returns and individual partner Schedule K-1s by either:

- Retaining external accountants to prepare them, or
- Using partnership accounting and tax software such as Advent Partner.

If the fund prepares its own tax returns, it can request that its accountants review the returns and schedules.

Partnerships must file their tax returns, including extensions, in a timely manner. The IRS assesses very severe penalties, calculated by multiplying the number of months times the number of partners times a flat amount for late filings.

Investment partnerships must be on the accrual basis. They should report dividend income (except for dividends from certain mutual funds) on the cash basis, however, even though they prepare their tax returns on the accrual basis.

Partnerships should also consider whether they must file state and local tax returns and Schedule K-1s. Some partnerships are formed in one state and do business in another state. New York State and New Jersey, for example, require partnerships to file a return if a state resident is a partner in the fund, even if the fund is out of state. New York City requires a return only if the fund is located in the city.

Partnership Classification

Investment partnerships buy and sell securities. The IRS classifies taxpayers engaged in this activity as either "dealers," "traders," or "investors." Because several areas of tax law treat these taxpayers differently, and partnerships prepare partners' Schedule K-1s according to the partnership's status, investment partnerships must classify themselves as dealer, trader, or investor partnerships.

Dealers

A *dealer* is one who, like any other merchant, purchases securities and resells them to the public for a profit. In theory, the dealer's profit is the market appreciation based on cost. Dealers:

- Are required to inventory their securities.
- Are not subject to the wash sale rules.
- Treat as ordinary income any gain or loss on the sale of their inventory of securities.

Dealers are generally required to mark-to-market their dealer securities at year end. Most hedge funds should generally not be classified as dealers.

Traders and Investors

Treasury regulations recognize that buying and selling securities can constitute the carrying on of a trade or business. According to Treasury Regulation section1.471-5:

> Taxpayers who buy and sell or hold securities for investment or speculation, irrespective of whether such buying or selling constitutes the carrying on of a trade or business... are not dealers in securities within the meaning of this section.

The Internal Revenue Code and regulations, however, are silent as to what constitutes engaging in the trade or business of trading in securities. In fact, neither Treasury regulations nor the IRC defines the concept of "a trade or business."

The distinction between an entity carrying on a trade or business (a *trader*), or not (an *investor*), however, has been established in court cases. The passage most often quoted to distinguish an investment account from a trading account is from *Liang v. Comr.* (23 TC1040 (1955) acq., 1955-1 C.B. 4), where the court stated:

> ... in the former (investor), securities are purchased to be held for capital appreciation and income, usually without regard to short-term developments that would influence the price of the securities on the daily market. In a trading account, securities are bought and sold with reasonable frequency in an endeavor to catch the swings in the daily market movements and profit therefrom on a short-term basis.

That is:

- A *trader* regularly and continuously purchases and sells securities with the objective of profiting from short-term fluctuations in market values.
- An *investor* aims to realize profits from the long-term appreciation of securities or from earning interest or dividends, or both.

Intent determines trader or investor status.

- A *trader* manages its holdings to profit from swings in value resulting from subjective judgments in the market.
- An *investor* hopes to realize gains from an increase in the intrinsic value of the company issuing the security (which generally occurs over a substantially long period of time), without regard to short-term developments that influence the security's price.

This is not to say that a trader never holds a security for an extended period of time, or that an investor never holds a security for a short period of time. Rather, the taxpayer's overall activities determine its status. Also, the length of time constituting short-term versus long-term for this determination has not been established. The courts have suggested certain holding periods as being indicative of a trader, but no definitive rule exists. Instead, the courts have placed great reliance on the intent of the taxpayer.

The partnership must analyze facts and circumstances to determine whether sufficient trader status criteria exist. The partnership can make this analysis on a year-to-year basis, although the initial year's activity may set a precedent that is difficult to change. The partnership can include a statement in its LPA or offering memorandum that it intends to be a trader, but only its actual trading activity can determine its status.

Partnerships should analyze their actual trades executed during the year with the appropriate tax and legal professionals to determine their status.

Other Legal Issues

Investment partnerships must also consider the following legal issues.

For Information about	See
Whether the general partner qualifies as a registered investment advisor (RIA)	"Investment Advisers Act of 1940" on page 43.
Whether the partnership qualifies as a commodity pool	"Commodity Transactions" on page 44.
Whether the partnership's assets are considered "plan assets" under ERISA	"Investment by Pension Plans and IRAs" on page 45.
Whether the partnership must file SEC form 13D	"SEC Filings" on page 46.
Whether the partnership must charge withholding taxes to foreign partners	"Foreign Partners" on page 46.

Investment Advisers Act of 1940

General partners of hedge funds may or may not be Registered Investment Advisers (RIAs). The Investment Advisers Act of 1940 (the Advisers Act) provides generally that persons who provide investment advisory services to 15 or more clients, or who offer their services in a public manner, must register under the Act. An investment partnership is generally deemed one client.

The SEC has determined that general partners who themselves are not registered but who are principals of companies that are registered are deemed registered with respect to their activities in the fund.

In 1998, the SEC amended rule 205-3 of the Advisers Act. The amended rule provides that:

- A fund associated with a RIA can charge performance fees only to limited partners whose partnership contribution is at least $750,000, or whose net worth exceeds of $1,500,000. (These amounts were increased from $500,000 and $1,000,000, respectively.)
- General partners can receive performance fees from individual partner accounts on performance measured over a period of less than one year.

The Advisers Act also requires that a registered general partner provide quarterly information to the limited partners. General partners normally provide such information in their quarterly letters.

Finally, the Advisers Act provides that the fund may be subject to the custody rules of Treasury Regulation Section 206 (4)-2. This regulation provides for an annual surprise count (confirmation) of fund securities and cash and an audit of the adviser's financial statements.

Whether or not an investment partnership is subject to this provision is a matter of legal interpretation. As an alternative to the count and the audit, the fund can enter a "disbursement procedure agreement" with its broker(s) or other persons who hold securities or funds of the partnership. Under such an agreement, the custodian does not make payments of cash or transfer funds or securities to the general partner or related entities unless an independent representative issues an agreed-upon procedures letter (commonly known as a "Bennett" letter) to the custodian.

Commodity Transactions

If a fund trades commodities, OEX options, futures, or other similar investment items subject to the rules of the Commodity Futures Trading Commission (CFTC), the general partner may be required to register with the CFTC as a commodity pool operator. The fund then becomes a commodity pool (CP), subject to additional disclosure and reporting rules and position limits. A fund of funds investing in a partnership which is a CP is also subject to CFTC rules. The CFTC can grant an exemption to full CP reporting requirements, however. The fund's attorney should advise it as to the applicability of these rules.

Investment by Pension Plans and IRAs

Funds can accept contributions from individual retirement accounts; (IRA) pension, profit-sharing, or stock bonus plans; and governmental plans and units (retirement trusts). As a condition to admitting it to the fund, the fund should require a retirement trust to execute a representation letter that includes representations that the investment in the fund by the retirement trust has been duly authorized, and that the retirement trust has consulted counsel with respect to such investment.

The fund should consider not accepting any capital contribution if, after such capital contribution, the value of limited partnership interests in the fund held by retirement trusts would be 25% or more of the value of the total limited partnership interests in the fund.

If the limited partnership interests held by retirement trusts exceed this 25% limit (measured at the time that any partner makes a contribution to the fund), the assets of the fund are considered "plan assets" under the Employee Retirement Income Security Act of 1974 (ERISA). This may have adverse consequences for the general partners and the fiduciaries of the retirement trusts. Additionally, it forces the general partner to register as an investment adviser.

Note: Limited partner interests held exclusively by IRAs in excess of 25% do not subject the fund to the "plan assets" determination. If any other retirement accounts also hold interests in the partnership, however, the IRA accounts must be included when determining whether a fund has met the 25% limit. If the fund qualifies as "plan assets," ERISA prohibits certain transactions between the general partner and related entities.

If a fund uses leverage (margin) for its investments, partners that are tax-exempt organizations are generally subject to tax on the portion of their share of fund profits attributable to the use of leverage (debt-financed income). Such portion of their share of profits attributable to the use of leverage is taxable as UBTI under the federal income tax law. For details, see "Understanding Unrelated Business Taxable Income" on page 235.

Partnerships must withhold 20% of retirement plan distributions not directly rolled over to qualified plans. IRA withdrawals may be covered by this rule.

SEC Filings

Any person or group that acquires over 5% of any class of equity securities registered under the Securities Exchange Act of 1934 (Exchange Act) must file Form 13D within 10 days after the acquisition. If a general partner manages more than one fund, and those funds cumulatively acquire over 5% of the securities, that general partner must file Form 13D. For details, see Rule 13D-1 of the Exchange Act.

Circumstances that require a general partner to file a report on Form 13F with the SEC include:

- ❖ Its fund(s) hold securities with an aggregate fair market value of $100 million or more on the last trading day of any month of any calendar year.

  or

- ❖ It manages investments in total of $100 million or more.

The general partner must file Form 13F:

- ❖ Within 45 days after the last day of such calendar year.

  and

- ❖ Within 45 days after the last day of each of the first 3 calendar quarters of the subsequent calendar year.

Foreign Partners

If a foreign partner is a member of an investment partnership, the fund must withhold tax on certain interest income earned and dividend income. The partnership is deemed to have distributed interest and dividends to partners quarterly, when it allocates such amounts to the partners' capital accounts. Partnerships must charge the withholding taxes to the affected partner's account, and transmit the withholding to the Treasury quarterly through the depository system on Form 8109. The partnership must file Form 1042, an information return, no later than March 15 of the following year.

The Internal Revenue Code and treaties between the United States and other countries determine which items require withholding and the applicable percentage to withhold. Treaty information can be found in a service published by Matthew Bender titled "Foreign Tax and Trade Briefs."

Under the Taxpayer Relief Act of 1997, commencing January 1, 1998, foreign partners of trader partnerships are only subject to withholding on certain interest income earned and dividend income.

Prior to the 1997 Act, foreign partner investments in trader partnerships were discouraged because, for such partnerships, IRC Section 1446 required withholding at the highest effective rate, 39.6%, or 35% on a foreign partner's allocable portion of effectively connected taxable income (ECTI). For these purposes, ECTI of a trader partnership comprised all items of taxable income, including capital gains less deductible expenses. Capital losses could not be offset against ordinary income to determine ECTI.

Understanding Break Periods

This chapter describes the break period, the basic time unit of a partnership's investment and accounting activity. It details:

- ✔ How changes in partners' capital accounts define break periods.
- ✔ When partners can make capital changes.
- ✔ How partnerships record income, expenses, and gains during a break period.

In This Chapter

What Is a Break Period?

Partnerships generally allocate the profits and losses from their investments to the partners according to partners' *capital percentages* (also called "income allocation percentages") in the partnership. A partner's capital percentage is that partner's capital account balance as a percentage of the total capital of all the partners in the partnership.

A partner's capital account balance can change through:

- *Contributions,* which add more capital to the capital account, or the opening of a new capital account in the partnership. A contribution is essentially a cash flow into the partnership.
- *Withdrawals,* which withdraw capital from the capital account. A withdrawal is essentially a cash flow out of the partnership.
- *Assignments,* where a portion of the partner's interest in the partnership (including a proportionate amount of its capital account) is assigned to another partner.
- *Allocations,* where a of a portion of the partnership's appreciation is allocated to a partner.

Because partnerships allocate appreciation according to partners' capital percentages, changes in capital balances due to allocations generally do not change those percentages. Only contributions, withdrawals, and assignments can change partners' capital account balances in a way that can change their capital percentages. These three events are collectively referred to as *capital changes*.

Rather than continuously updating partners' capital accounts, partnerships usually operate in time units called *break periods*. Partnerships only record capital changes at the beginning and end of a break period; therefore, partners' capital account balances, and their capital percentages in the partnership, do not change during the period.

Capital changes "create" break periods by forcing the partnership to allocate the appreciation recorded during the period to the partners, according to their current capital percentages, before those percentages change.

Tip: A partnership must have at least one break period each year, in order to calculate the amount and character of the partners' income for tax purposes.

Understanding Capital Changes

Each period, partners can contribute capital to, or withdraw capital from, their capital accounts. They can also assign a portion of their interest in the partnership to another partner, which reassigns a proportionate amount of their capital account to that partner. Partners can make these *capital changes* before or after the partnership allocates the current period's appreciation.

- **Beginning capital changes,** made before the partnership allocates appreciation, affect partners' capital percentages (and thus their allocations) in the period when they occur. Beginning capital changes take effect on the first day of the period, before appreciation begins.
- **Ending capital changes,** made after the partnership allocates appreciation, affect partners' capital percentages (and thus their allocations) in the period after they occur. Ending capital changes take effect on the last day of the period, before the next period's appreciation begins.

The following diagram shows a time line for capital changes and allocations.

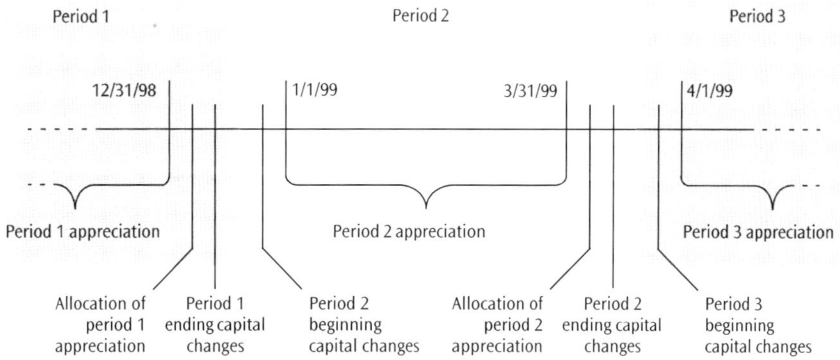

Important: Your partnership agreement should specify the actual dates when the partnership accepts contributions and withdrawals. Capital changes only take effect at the beginning or end of a break period, however.

Note: Many partnerships require that contributions take place as the first event of a break period, before appreciation begins, and that withdrawals and assignments take place as the last event of a break period, after allocations.

Understanding Capital Contributions

Partners make *contributions* to increase the amount of capital they have in the partnership, as well as their capital percentages.

In addition to contributing cash, partners can, if the partnership agreement allows, contribute capital in the form of securities. The contribution of appreciated securities can result in the recognition of gain at the time of the contribution. If the partnership:

- *Does* recognize gain on the contribution, it records the contribution at the security's fair market value on the date of contribution. This becomes the partnership's cost for purposes of realization.
- *Does not* recognize gain on the contribution, it records the contributing partner's original cost for the securities (or adjusted cost for bonds), as well as the securities' price when the partner contributes it, in order to calculate the contributing partner's portion of the securities' gain (called *built-in gain*) when the partnership sells it.

For details, see Chapter 9, Contributing Securities.

Contributions increase the partner's *tax basis* in the partnership. For details, see "Calculating Tax Basis" on page 55.

For an example of a capital contribution, see "Capital Changes: An Example" on page 55.

Understanding Capital Withdrawals

Partners make *withdrawals* to take capital out of the partnership. This also reduces the partner's capital percentage. When a partner withdraws capital from the partnership, the partner can make either a partial withdrawal (of only a portion of its capital); or a total withdrawal (of all its capital).

A partner's capital withdrawals reduce the partner's *tax basis* in the partnership. (For details, see "Calculating Tax Basis" on page 55.) If a partner withdraws capital in excess of its tax basis, the difference is attributable to the unrealized gains allocated to the partner's capital account, which generally represent the partner's share of appreciation on the securities the partnership currently holds, and therefore would constitute a capital gain to the partner.

The following sections describe the affect of withdrawing unrealized gains from the partnership, depending on the partnership's gain allocation methodology.

Allocation Methodology	See
Aggregate	"How Total Withdrawals Affect Aggregate Accounts" on page 133.
Tax lot layering	"How Withdrawals Affect Layered Gains" on page 147.

The withdrawing partner is generally taxed on withdrawal in excess of its tax basis as capital gains. If the partnership liquidates securities to pay out the withdrawing partner in cash, or when it ultimately sells the securities in which the withdrawing partner had a historical interest, the partnership allocates those taxable gains to the partners. Therefore, the partner's withdrawal effectively increases the tax burden on the remaining partners. Partnerships can minimize this effect in several ways.

Partnerships Can	For Details, See
Deliver appreciated securities to the withdrawing partner instead of cash.	"Distributing Securities" on page 205.
Elect IRC Section 754 to adjust the cost basis of securities.	"Electing Section 754" on page 209.
Include a *directed gains* provision (also called a "stuffing" or "fill up" provision) in the partnership agreement, to substitute realized gain for unrealized gain.	"Directing Gains" on page 212.

For an example of a capital withdrawal, see "Capital Changes: An Example" on page 55.

Note: Partnerships often charge performance fees to partners making capital withdrawals. This ensures that partners pay the appropriate portion of their appreciation for the performance fee. For more information, see "Charging Performance Fees For Withdrawals" on page 141.

Understanding Assignments of Interest

A partner can *assign* a portion of its interest in the partnership to another partner. When an assignment takes place, the partnership transfers from the assigning partner to the receiving partner a proportionate amount of each of the following.

- *Capital account balance*
- *Tax basis*
- Unrealized gain/loss (that is, historical interest in securities' gain/loss), as either:
  - *Layered unrealized gain/loss.* (For details, see "How Assignments of Interest Affect Layered Gains" on page 148.)

  or

  - *Aggregate account balance.* (For details, see "How Assignments Affect Aggregate Accounts" on page 136.)

For an example of an assignment of interest, see "Capital Changes: An Example" on page 55.

Note: Partnerships often charge performance fees to partners making assignments of interest. This ensures that partners pay the appropriate portion of their appreciation for the performance fee. For more information, see "Charging Performance Fees For Assignments" on page 161. Partnerships usually do *not* charge a performance fee for assignments between two "partner" accounts controlled by the same investor (*Example*: From a personal account to a trust account).

Capital Changes: An Example

Example: Four partners each begin with a capital balance of $100.

Partner	Capital Balance	Capital Percentage
A	$100	25%
B	$100	25%
C	$100	25%
D	$100	25%
Total	**$400**	**100%**

During the break period, the partnership earns $100 in appreciation. At the end of the period, the partners make the following capital changes.

- Partner A contributes $50 to the partnership.
- Partner B withdraws $25 from the partnership.
- Partner C assigns 30% of its interest in the partnership to Partner D (30% X $125 = $38).

The partners' new capital account balances and capital percentages are:

Partner	Beginning Capital		Allocation of Appreciation	Ending Capital Change	Ending Capital	
	Balance	Percent			Balance	Percent
A	$100	25%	+$25	+$50 contribution	$175	33%
B	$100	25%	+$25	-$25 withdrawal	$100	19%
C	$100	25%	+$25	-$38 assignment	$87	17%
D	$100	25%	+$25	+$38 assignment	$163	31%
Total	**$400**	**100%**	**$100**	**$25**	**$525**	**100%**

Calculating Tax Basis

A partner's tax basis in the partnership is the net of the partner's contributions and withdrawals, plus or minus all taxable profit/loss that the partnership has allocated to the partner. A partner needs its tax basis, however, to calculate the gain or loss it incurs upon receiving its withdrawal from the partnership.

Example: On January 1, a partner contributes capital of $500,000. During the course of the year:

- The partner withdraws $50,000, but later contributes $100,000.
- The partnership allocates the partner $150,000 of taxable income and realized gain (net of expenses and performance fees).

On December 31, the partner's tax basis in the partnership is $700,000 ($500,000 – $50,000 + $100,000 + $150,000).

In Advent Partner, the Partners' Capital Balances report displays each partner's tax basis in the partnership. For details, look up **Partners' Capital Balances report** in the Advent Partner Help index.

Recording Income and Expenses

During a break period, a partnership can receive income from its investments (such as dividend or interest payments), and pay expenses (such as management fees). Rather than passing income and expenses through to the partners' capital accounts on the day it receives them, the partnership allocates them to the partners at the end of the break period, generally according to their capital percentages for that break period.

Example: A partnership has quarterly break periods. It allocates any income received or expenses paid between January 1 and March 31 to the partners on March 31, regardless of the actual date when the cash flows occur. The partners' capital accounts and percentages remain unchanged from January 1 to March 31. The partnership uses these capital percentages to allocate all of the income and expenses that occur between January 1 and March 31 because, no matter when the cash flow occurs, the partners' capital percentages are the same on that date.

In addition to actual income payments, partnerships use accrual basis accounting and record income (or offsets to income) from amortization, accretion, and accrued interest (as well as other income and expense accruals) each period. The following sections describe how to calculate these amounts.

Important: Partners must report amortization, accretion, and accrued interest from their partnership's investments as their partnership reports it, even if they do not amortize, accrete, or accrue interest on their own security holdings.

Note: For more information about how partnerships categorize and allocate income and expenses, see Chapter 4, Understanding Items of Profit and Loss.

Recording Market Discount Accretion

If a partnership purchases a bond at a market discount (that is, at a price below the bond's face value), the partnership can elect to adjust the cost basis of the bond upwards towards its par value until it sells the bond. This process is called *accretion*. The partnership records the amount the bond accretes (that is, the difference between its original and adjusted cost) as interest income, to the extent of accrued market discount (adjusted cost basis), with any excess income treated as capital gain.

Note: Taxpayers can elect to adjust the cost basis of municipal bonds purchased at a discount. Upon sale of the municipal bond, the market discount is treated as taxable interest income, not capital gain.

The amount by which the partnership adjusts the bond's cost basis at any time while the partnership holds the bond is shown in this formula.

$$\frac{\text{Number of days in period the partnership holds the bond}}{\text{Number of days from the purchase date of the bond to maturity}} \times \text{Market discount}$$

You can represent this formula as a line (called the *accretion line*) that begins at the bond's purchase date and original cost, and ends at the bond's maturity date and par value.

Example: The following diagram shows the accretion line of a coupon-bearing bond that matures on 1/1/2015. The partnership purchases the bond at 90 on 1/1/1997, then sells the bond on 1/1/2005 when the accretion line has reached 94.

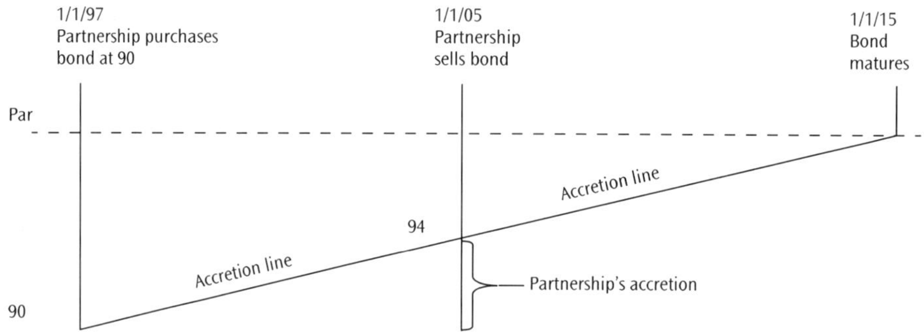

As of 1/1/2005, the bond has accreted from 90 to 94. The partnership records this difference as interest income, and uses 94 as the bond's cost basis for determining capital gain/loss from the sale.

Note: This formula represents "straight-line" accretion. The partnership can also use other accretion methods, such as "yield-to-maturity" (sometimes referred to as "scientific" or "constant yield").

Partnerships can record the interest income from a bond's accretion in one of two ways: deferred accretion or incremental accretion. In both cases, the partnership records the same amount and character of income and gain/loss, but the timing differs.

Deferred accretion The partnership records all of the bond's accretion in the period when it sells the bond, and allocates it to the partners according to their capital percentages in that period. This allows the partners to recognize the income later, which can be advantageous to partners who expect to be in a lower tax bracket when the partnership sells the bond.

> **Example:** On 2/1/1999, a partnership purchases a $10,000 bond that matures on 1/1/2005 (5,813 days to maturity) at 90 ($9,000, or a $1,000 discount). The partnership sells the bond on 8/1/1999 (182 days later) at 90.25 ($9,025), when it has accreted 182 / 5,813 × $1,000 = $31 of its discount.
>
> - The partnership records the bond's $31 of accretion as interest income.

- The partnership adjusts the bond's cost basis to \$9,000 + \$31 = \$9,031, and records \$9,025 – \$9,031 = \$6 of realized loss on the sale.

Incremental accretion The partnership records accretion incrementally each period, and allocates it to the partners according to their current capital percentages. This allows the partners to recognize the income over time, which can be advantageous to partners who expect to be in a higher tax bracket when the partnership sells the bond.

Example: On 2/1/1999, a partnership purchases a \$10,000 bond that matures on 1/1/2015 (5,813 days to maturity) at 90 (\$9,000, or a \$1,000 discount).

1. The break period when the partnership buys the bond ends 3/31/1999, 59 days after it purchases the bond. The partnership records 59 / 5,813 × \$1,000 = \$10 of accretion and allocates it to the partners in this period.
2. The next break period ends on 6/30/1999, 91 days after the end of the previous break period. The partnership records 91 / 5,813 × \$1,000 = \$16 of accretion and allocates it to the partners in this period.
3. The partnership sells the bond on 8/1/1999, 32 days after the end of the previous break period, at 90.25 (\$9,025). The partnership records:
   - 32 / 5,813 × \$1,000 = \$5 of accretion and allocates it to the partners in this period.
   - The difference between the sale price (\$9,025) and the bond's adjusted cost (\$9,000 + \$10 + \$16 + \$5 = \$9,031) as \$6 of realized loss, as in the previous example.

Recording Original Issue Discount Accretion

Bonds that are issued at a discount from their face value (original issue discount or OID bonds) have two accretion lines.

- *Original issue discount accretion*, as the bond accretes from its original issue discount to its face value at maturity.
- *Market discount accretion*, as the bond accretes the difference between its purchase price and its par value at the time you purchased it.

Example: A partnership purchases an OID bond with a maturity date of 1/1/2015 (5,813 days to maturity) and a maturity value of $10,000, on 2/1/1999, at 65 ($6,500), when the bond's par value is 67 ($6,700). This means that:

- The partnership purchased the bond at a $6,700 – $6,500 = $200 market discount.
- The bond must still accrete $10,000 – $6,700 = $3,300 of its original issue discount.

The break period ends on 3/31/1999, 59 days after the partnership purchased the bond. The partnership records:

- Market value accretion of 59 / 5813 × ($6,700 – $6,500) = $2.03.
- OID accretion of 59 / 5813 × ($10,000 – $6,700) = $33.49.

Unlike market discount accretion, original issue discount accretion cannot be deferred. You must record it incrementally each period.

Recording Amortization

If a partnership purchases a taxable bond at a premium (that is, at a price above the bond's face value), the partnership can elect to adjust the cost basis of the bond downward towards its par value until it sells the bond. This process is called *amortization*. The partnership records the amount the bond amortizes (that is, the difference between its original and adjusted cost) as negative interest income.

Important: The IRS does not allow you to adjust interest income for amortization on tax-free bonds, such as municipal bonds. You must adjust the cost basis of these bonds, however, for purposes of calculating your capital gain/loss when you sell them.

The amount by which the partnership adjusts the bond's cost basis at any time while the partnership holds the bond is shown in this formula. You can

$$\frac{\text{Number of days in period the partnership holds the bond}}{\text{Number of days from the purchase date of the bond to maturity}} \times \text{Market premium}$$

represent this formula as a line (called the *amortization line*) that begins at the bond's purchase date and original cost, and ends at the bond's maturity date and par value.

Example: The following diagram shows the amortization line of a coupon-bearing bond that matures on 1/1/2015. The partnership purchases the bond at 110 on 1/1/1997, then sells the bond on 1/1/2005 when the amortization line has reached 104.

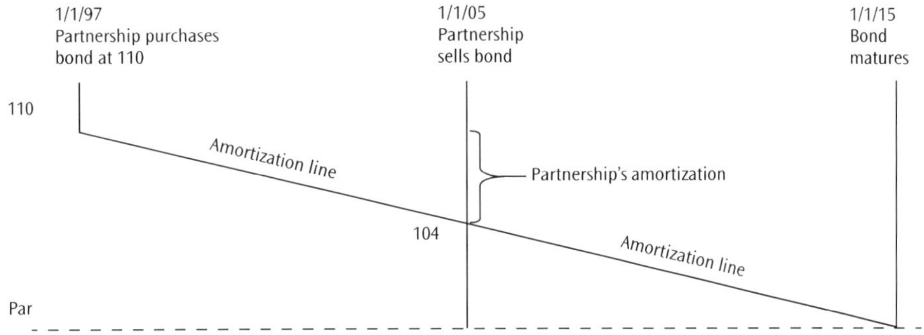

As of 1/1/2005, the bond has amortized from 110 to 104. The partnership records this difference as negative interest income, and uses 104 as the bond's cost basis for determining capital gain/loss from the sale.

Note: Partnerships must use the "yield-to-maturity" method (sometimes referred to as "scientific" or "constant yield") to amortize the premium. For demonstration purposes, however, this example uses "straight-line" amortization.

Because the partners' interests in the bond change with their capital percentages, the partnership must allocate the amortization incrementally each break period. When the partnership sells the bond, it subtracts the bond's adjusted cost basis from its sale price to determine the amount of gain/loss it recognizes.

Example: On 2/1/1999, a partnership purchases a $10,000 bond that matures on 1/1/2015 (5,813 days to maturity) at 110 ($11,000, or a $1,000 premium).

1. The break period when the partnership buys the bond ends on 3/31/1999, 59 days after it purchases the bond. The partnership records 59/5,813 × $1,000 = $10 of amortization and allocates it to the partners in this period as negative interest income.

2 The next break period ends on 6/30/1999, 91 days after the end of the previous break period. The partnership records 91/5,813 × $1,000 = $16 of amortization and allocates it to the partners in this period as negative interest income.

3 The partnership sells the bond on 8/1/1999, 32 days after the end of the previous break period, at 109.75 ($10,975). The partnership records:

- 32/5,813 × $1,000 = $5 of amortization, and allocates it to the partners in this period as negative interest income.
- The difference between the sale price ($10,975) and the adjusted cost ($11,000 – $10 – $16 – $5 = $10,969) as $6 of realized gain.

Recording Interest Accrual

If a partnership purchases or sells a bond that pays a coupon, partners' interests in the bond will change over the time that the bond's coupon accrues (unless the coupon payments coincide with the end of your break periods). The partnership must therefore allocate the interest that has accrued on the bond during the break period, as interest income. The amount of accrued interest that the partnership must allocate to the partners during each break period is shown in this formula.

$$\frac{\text{Number of days partnership held bond during break period}}{\text{Number of days in accrual period (from last coupon payment to next coupon payment)}} \times \text{Coupon payment amount}$$

Note: In the break period when the coupon payment actually occurs, the partnership only allocates the portion of the payment that has not yet accrued. If the coupon payment does not occur on the last day of the break period, the partnership also allocates the amount of the next coupon payment that accrues during the break period.

Example: On 2/1/1999, a partnership purchases a $10,000 bond with an 8% coupon that pays on January 1 and July 1 (182 days in the current coupon period, each coupon pays $400). The break period ends on 3/31/1999, 59 days after the partnership purchased the bond. The partnership must allocate 59/182 × $400 = $129.67 of accrued interest to the partners.

Recording Realized and Unrealized Gain/Loss

If a partnership sells a security during a break period, it receives a cash flow from the sale much like an income cash flow. The difference between the sale amount and the security's original cost or tax basis (or, for short positions, the proceeds of the short sale and the cost basis of the covering position) is the gain/loss the partnership realizes for tax purposes on the security.

If a partnership has held a security for more than one break period, however, partners' interests in the security may have changed as their capital percentages changed due to contributions, withdrawals, and assignments. For this reason, partnerships record and allocate the gain or loss represented by the change in the security's price from the beginning to the end of each break period. Because the partnership has not sold the security, this gain is called the *change in unrealized gain*, or simply *unrealized gain*.

By allocating unrealized gains to the partners, the partnership can track each partner's historical interest in the partnership's securities. When the partnership finally sells the security, it can allocate the security's realized gain according to the partners' historical interests in that gain, as required by the IRS's "substantial economic effect" rule, IRC Section 704(b)(2). Therefore, the partnership must do the following.

1 For each break period that the partnership holds the security, it calculates the change in unrealized gain (that is, the change in price from the end of the previous period to the end of the current period) for the securities it holds, and allocates it to the partners. If the partnership allocates gain using:

   - *Aggregate methodology,* the partnership adds the amount of unrealized gain allocated to each partner to that partner's aggregate account balance. This account represents the historical unrealized gains allocated to the partner.

   - *Tax lot layering methodology,* the partnership records the amount of unrealized gain from each security allocated to each partner every period. This creates *layers* of historical unrealized gains for each period that the partnership holds the security.

2 When the partnership sells the security, it allocates the realized gain as follows.

- *Aggregate methodology*: The partnership allocates the realized gain according to the partners' aggregate account balances (which represent their historical interest in the partnership's unrealized gain), or their current capital percentages, or both, depending on how the partnership's realized gains compare to its aggregate account balance.

- *Tax lot layering methodology*: The partnership calculates the gain realized in the current break period (that is, the difference between the price at the end of the previous period and the actual sale price), and allocates it according to the partners' current capital percentages. The partnership then allocates the remaining realized gain according to the partners' interests in the security's unrealized gain in historical break periods.

Note: Aggregate and tax lot layering are the *only* two methodologies approved by the IRS for allocating realized gains. The following chapters describe these methodologies in more detail.

For Information about	See
Aggregate allocation	Chapter 6, Allocating Aggregate Gains.
Tax lot layering allocation	Chapter 7, Allocating Layered Gains.

Interim and Final Periods In Advent Partner

ADVENT PARTNER

Because performance fees and other tax issues can affect the allocation of prior periods, Advent Partner distinguishes two kinds of break periods: interim and final.

- *Interim* periods can be modified for tax reallocation purposes.

  Example: A partnership has monthly break periods, but charges performance fees quarterly. Performance fees always reallocate the partners's appreciation since the last performance fee charge (in this case, on 12/31/1998). Therefore, if the partnership charges a performance fee at the end of period 3 (on 3/31/1999), it must reallocate periods 1

(1/1/1999 to 1/31/1999), 2 (2/1/1999 to 2/28/1999), and 3 (3/1/1999 to 3/31/1999).

❖ *Final* periods cannot be modified for tax reallocation purposes, regardless of whether the appreciation allocated in that period subjected the partner(s) to a performance fee charge. Generally, the last period of the fiscal year is a final period, so that reallocation cannot change the information the partners file on their Schedule K-1s for the year ending on the close of the final period.

Example: A partnership that charges a 20% performance incentive fee with a 5% hurdle rate allocates a partner positive appreciation in 1998, but not enough to subject the partner to a performance fee charge. The partnership does allocate the partner enough appreciation for a fee charge in 1999, however, and reallocates 20% of the partner's appreciation since the last performance fee charge on 12/31/1997. Because the partnership closed final on 12/31/1998, however, it must reallocate this amount only from the appreciation allocated in 1999. The section "Profit Since Last Charge vs. Current Year's Profit" on page 162 describes this situation in more detail.

For more information about interim and final periods in Advent Partner, look up **period: interim** and **period: final** in Advent Partner's Help index.

Understanding Items of Profit and Loss

Chapter 3 described how partnerships allocate each break period's income and expenses to the partners. This chapter describes in detail how to categorize income and expenses from the partnership's investment activities into groups called *allocation items*. It also describes some of the typical allocation items partnerships use, and tax and accounting issues associated with them.

In This Chapter

What Are Allocation Items?

Partnerships divide their income and expenses into categories, called *items of profit and loss* or *allocation items* (or simply *items*). The reasons for doing this are:

- **Schedule K-1s:** Partnerships enter different components of their income and expenses on different lines on Form 1065, Schedule K-1. Categorizing income and expenses into allocation items that match the K-1 lines is necessary for preparing the partnership's K-1s.

- **Non-*pro rata* allocation:** Partnerships allocate certain types of income or expenses non-*pro rata* (that is, not according to the partners' capital percentages), and require separate items to allocate them.

  Example: The partnership allocates some fees to all of the partners pro-rata, but allocates other fees (such as management fees) only to the limited partners.

  Note: For examples of non-*pro rata* allocations, see Chapter 5, Understanding Economic Allocations.

- **Reporting:** Partnerships categorize income and expenses on reports to the partners.

- **Calculating tax basis:** Partnerships can categorize items as taxable (including tax-free) or non-taxable to determine which item amounts to include when calculating a partner's tax basis in the partnership.

The following sections describe typical allocation items that partnerships use to categorize their profits and losses. This chapter divides these items into the following broad categories.

Category	What It Is	For Details, See
Realized gains/losses	Taxable (capital) gains from closing a security position.	"Realized Gain (Loss) Items" on page 70.
Unrealized gains/losses	Non-taxable gains due to a security's price change during a break period.	"Unrealized Gain (Loss) Items" on page 76.

Category	What It Is	For Details, See
Management fees	Fees charged to limited partners to fund the partnership's operations	"Management Fee Items" on page 77.
Income	Non-capital income and losses, such as from interest and dividends.	"Other Income and Expenses Items" on page 83.
Expenses	Other expenses charged to the partnership, such as operating expenses.	"Other Income and Expenses Items" on page 83.

ADVENT PARTNER

For information on defining allocation items in Advent Partner, look up the following topics in Advent Partner's Help index.

For Information on	Look Up This Topic
Assigning allocation methodologies to items	**items, creating.**
Assigning individual Axys income and expense transactions to specific allocation items	**mapping income and expenses.**
Grouping items together for different levels of reporting detail	**roll-up items, creating.**
Assigning allocation item amounts to Form 1065 and Schedule K-1 lines	**mapping items to Form 1065/ K-1 lines.**
Reporting partners' tax basis and capital accounts	**Partners' Capital Balances report, including items in tax basis.**
Categorizing interest income as state taxable or federally taxable	**taxability: state and federal.**

Realized Gain (Loss) Items

A partnership generates a realized gain transaction (also called "capital gains") when it closes a security position, that is, sells a security held long or covers a security sold short. Realized gains represent:

- *For a long position*, the amount by which the proceeds of the sale exceed the cost basis of the securities.
- *For a short position*, the proceeds from selling the security short, less the cost basis of the long position needed to cover the sale.

Conversely, the partnership realizes a loss when:

- *For a long position*, the cost basis of the security exceeds the sale proceeds.
- *For a short position*, the cost basis of the covering position exceeds the proceeds of the short sale.

Partners report their share of the partnership's realized gains in the following Schedule K-1 line items.

- For investor partnerships:
  - Line 4(d) Net short-term capital gain (loss)
  - Line 4(e), Net long-term capital gain (loss)
- For trader partnerships, line 7, Other income (loss).

(For details on trader and investor partnerships, see "Traders and Investors" on page 41.)

Because partnerships allocate realized gains non-*pro rata*, according to their chosen realized gain allocation methodology (aggregate or layering), they must have separate realized gain allocation items, corresponding to the Schedule K-1 items where they record realized gain. Partnerships may also need additional realized gain items, depending on other types of securities they trade.

Security	See
Hot issue securities	"Hot Issue Realized Gain (Loss) Items" on page 71.
Section 1256 contracts	"Section 1256 Realized Gain (Loss) Items" on page 71.
Non-U.S. dollar securities	"Realized FX Gain (Loss) Items" on page 73.

Hot Issue Realized Gain (Loss) Items

As described in the section "Allocating Hot Issue Gains" on page 96, partnerships with partners who are restricted from receiving "hot issue" gains must allocate those gains only to non-restricted partners. Because this allocation differs from the non-hot issue realized gain allocations, partnerships should use separate items for allocating short- and long-term realized gains from hot issue securities.

Section 1256 Realized Gain (Loss) Items

Section 1256 of the Internal Revenue Code requires that investment partnerships mark-to-market certain financial instruments at year end. (For accounting purposes, partnerships usually mark-to-market these transactions at the end of each break or reporting period.) For tax purposes, the partnership allocates the change in the security's market value to the partners as realized gain as if sold, 60% long-term and 40% short term, regardless of the actual holding period. These instruments include:

- Regulated futures contracts (defined in IRC Section 1256(g)(1)) that are:
  - Subject to a mark-to-market margin system.
  - Traded on or subject to the rules of a "qualified board of exchange."
- Foreign currency contracts (defined in IRC Section 1256(g)(2)) that:
  - Require delivery of, or the settlement of which depends on the value of, a foreign currency, upon which regulated futures contracts are traded. (These currencies currently include: Australian dollars, Brazilian real, Canadian dollars, Euros, French francs, German marks, Japanese yen, Mexican pesos, Swiss francs, and United Kingdom pounds.)

    - Are traded in the interbank market.
    - Are entered into at an "arm's length" price as determined by reference to the price in the interbank market.
- Non-equity options (that is, listed options that are not on equity or narrow-based equity indexes).
- Dealer equity options, that is, listed options (defined in IRC Section 1256(g)(4)) that are:
    - Equity-based options.
    - Purchased or sold by a dealer in the normal course of its dealing in options.
    - Listed on a qualified board or exchange on which the options dealer is registered.

To perform a tax allocation to mark these securities to market, the partnership must reclassify 60% of the security's change in unrealized gain (loss) for the break period as long-term realized gain (loss), and 40% as short-term realized gain (loss). Therefore, partnerships should use separate items for allocating short- and long-term realized gains, and (for economic allocation only) unrealized gains, from Section 1256 securities.

ADVENT PARTNER

Advent Partner automatically marks Section 1256 contracts to market at the end of each break period, and records the required allocation adjustments. For more information about how Advent Partner allocates gains from Section 1256 securities, look up **Section 1256 securities** in Advent Partner's Help index, and see the following topics.

If You Allocate Gains With	See
Aggregate methodology	"Allocating Aggregate Section 1256 Gains" on page 136.
Tax lot layering methodology	"Allocating Layered Section 1256 Gains" on page 150.

Realized FX Gain (Loss) Items

Partnerships report foreign exchange (FX) gains and losses from non-U.S. dollar positions as follows for tax purposes.

Gains From Non-U.S. Dollar	Reported on Schedule K-1 as
Securities	Capital gains/losses (lines 4(d) and 4(e))
Currency holdings and forward contracts	Ordinary income (line 7)

Partnerships therefore do not require separate capital gain or ordinary income items for Schedule K-1 reporting. A partnership may want to separate allocation items for FX gains and ordinary income, however, to separate FX gains from price gains on reports to the partners or for calculating performance.

About Section 988 and Section 1256 Overlap

Internal Revenue Code Section 988 requires that partnerships treat gains and losses from foreign currency movement as ordinary gains or losses. Certain foreign currency instruments, however, are covered by both Section 988 and Section 1256. A partnership can elect how to treat the gain from these securities as follows.

- Regulated futures contracts in a foreign currency: These securities are mark-to-market, 60% long-/40% short-term gain/loss, unless you elect to mark them to market as ordinary gain/loss.
- Foreign currency contracts: These securities are mark-to-market, ordinary gain/loss, unless you elect to mark them to market as 60% long-/40% short-term gain/loss.
- Non-equity options on foreign currencies: These securities are mark-to-market, 60% long-/40% short-term gain, unless you elect to mark them to market as ordinary gain/loss.

About Closing Methods

If a fund has multiple lots of the same security acquired at different costs, the order in which it sells the lots determines the amount of gain or loss realized on each specific sale transaction.

Current tax law states that, unless otherwise indicated, partnerships sell lots of securities using the first in, first out method (FIFO). A fund can also sell a specific lot (known as a "versus purchase" sale). For example, the high cost method sells lots from highest cost basis to lowest.

The following example shows the differences in gain realized depending on the sale method used.

Example: A partnership buys lots of XYZ stock as follows.

Date	Shares	Cost/ Share	Amount	June 30, 1998		
				Price	Value	Unrealized
1/2/91	5,000	$2	$10,000	$100	$500,000	$490,000
1/2/92	2,500	$5	$12,500	$100	$250,000	$237,500
1/2/93	1,000	$10	$10,000	$100	$100,000	$90,000
1/2/94	400	$20	$8,000	$100	$40,000	$32,000
1/2/95	500	$30	$15,000	$100	$50,000	$35,000
1/2/96	300	$50	$15,000	$100	$30,000	$15,000
1/2/97	300	$75	$22,500	$100	$30,000	$7,500
Total	**10,000**		**$93,000**		**$1,000,000**	**$907,000**

On 7/5/1998, the partnership sells 5,000 shares at $100 per share.

- If the partnership uses the FIFO method, it sells all of the 5,000 shares from the lot opened on 1/2/1991.

Date	Shares Sold	Cost of Shares	Sales Proceeds	Capital Gain
1/2/91	5,000	$10,000	$500,000	$490,000

- If the partnership uses the high-cost method, it starts by selling the lot with the highest cost basis, then the next highest, until it has sold all 5,000 shares.

Date	Shares Sold	Cost of Shares	Sales Proceeds	Capital Gain
1/2/97	300	$22,500	$30,000	$7,500
1/2/96	300	$15,000	$30,000	$15,000
1/2/95	500	$15,000	$50,000	$35,000
1/2/94	400	$8,000	$40,000	$32,000
1/2/93	1,000	$10,000	$100,000	$90,000
1/2/92	2,500	$12,500	$250,000	$237,500
Total	**5,000**	**$83,000**	**$500,000**	**$417,000**

The $73,000 difference in the capital gain amounts ($490,000 – $417,000) matches the difference in the cost basis of the securities sold ($83,000 – $10,000).

Note: For tax purposes, partnerships recognize sales of long positions on the trade date. Short positions, however, close when the partnership delivers the borrowed security, generally on the settlement date.

Example: A fund opens a short position in 1998, and covers it at a loss on 12/31/1998. The position settles on 1/6/1999 (the third business day after trade date). If the fund covers the short position by:

- Purchasing the borrowed security in the market, the position closes in 1999 if its settlement date falls in 1999.
- Acquiring the borrowed security, *and* settles the transaction on the same day (12/31/1998), the position closes in 1998.

Important: The method used to cover a short position affects when the partnership recognizes the gain or loss from the short sale, and is important for year-end tax planning.

Unrealized Gain (Loss) Items

Unrealized appreciation/depreciation (or unrealized gain/loss) of an investment the partnership holds is the difference between its cost (or adjusted cost) and its current market value or price. The unrealized gain or loss a fund records on its investments in a break period equals:

Unrealized gain (loss) at the end of the current period − Unrealized gain (loss) at the end of the pervious period

This amount is known as the change in unrealized appreciation or depreciation, or the change in unrealized gain. The following example shows this calculation.

Example: Schedule of Change in Unrealized Appreciation

❖ January 1, 1998

Market value of long positions		$3,200	
Cost of long securities		$3,000	
	Unrealized gain		$200
Market value of short positions		-$1,150	
Proceeds of securities sold short		-$1,250	
	Unrealized gain		$100
Total unrealized gain at 1/1/98			$300

❖ December 31, 1998

Market value of long positions		$5,500	
Cost of long securities		$4,000*	
	Unrealized gain		$1,500
Market value of short positions		-$1,200	
Proceeds of securities sold short		-$1,000*	
	Unrealized gain		-$200
Total unrealized gain at 12/31/98			$1,300
1998 change in unrealized gain			$1,000*

*This schedule agrees with "Trial Balance of Simple Fund at December 31, 1998" on page 36.

Partnerships should create separate allocation items for unrealized gains that are not taxed or reported on Schedule K-1s. In addition, as noted previously in the sections "Hot Issue Realized Gain (Loss) Items" on page 71, "Section 1256 Realized Gain (Loss) Items" on page 71, and Realized FX Gain (Loss) Items, partnerships should also use separate items for allocating unrealized gains from hot issue and Section 1256 securities, and FX gains and ordinary income.

Management Fee Items

Investment partnerships typically pay a management fee to a management company, usually owned by or related to the general partner, to fund the operation of the partnership, to pay for rent, salaries, supplies, and so forth. This fee is generally a percentage of each limited partner's capital, and generally ranges from .75% to 2% annually. The fee is often paid quarterly, at either the beginning or the end of the quarter. The limited partnership agreement should specify how the fund calculates and allocates the management fee.

Many partnerships do not charge management fees to the general partners or affiliated entities. In addition, many funds have agreements with certain limited partners to pay either a reduced fee or no fee.

Example: The following example shows a management fee calculation, along with a schedule showing how the partnership allocates the fee. In this example:

- The general partner does not charge a management fee to itself or to related entities (REs).
- All other limited partners pay at a rate of 1.5% (.375% quarterly).

The total balance of the non-RE limited partners' capital accounts is $17,000,000, for a total management fee for the quarter of $17,000,000 x .375% = $63,750. The following table shows each partner's management fee allocation for the quarter.

Partner (Status)	Beginning Capital		Management Fee		Percentage of Total Fee Paid by Partner
	Balance	Percent	Percent	Amount	
GP	$100,000	.55%	0%	$0	
LP1 (RE)	$1,000,000	5.52%	0%	$0	
LP2 (LP)	$10,000,000	55.25%	0.375%	$37,500	55.82%
LP3 (LP)	$2,000,000	11.05%	0.375%	$7,500	11.76%
LP4 (LP)	$5,000,000	27.62%	0.375%	$18,750	29.41%
Total	**$18,100,000**	**100%**	**0.352%**	**$63,750**	**100%**

Note: In this example, the allocation does *not* use the partners' capital percentages, but rather realigns the percentages of the partners participating in the allocation to 100%.

Management Fee Accrual

Some funds may allow management fee accrual (to smooth out the impact on performance) if the partnership's break periods (and corresponding cash flows) follow a different schedule than the management fee payment period. Two common fee accrual methods are:

- Bill Forward, which calculates fees based on beginning capital.

  Note: When billing forward, some partnership agreements require management fee to be allocated before other profit items are allocated. This will effectively reduce the amount of the profit and loss to each partner's capital account.

- Bill in Arrears, which calculates fees based on ending capital.

The following table summarizes the effects of cash flows and performance fees based on these two billing schedules.

	Bill Forward	Bill in Arrears
Contributions	The management fee amount *increases* in accordance with contribution amounts. Profits associated with cash flows *do not* affect management fees.	The management fee amount *decreases* in accordance with contribution amounts. Profits associated with cash flows *increase* management fees.
Assignments	The management fee amount *decreases* for the assignor and *increases* for the assignee.	The management fee amount *increases* for the assignor and *decreases* for the assignee.
Withdrawals	Withdrawals in excess of payment period profit *decrease* the management fee in accordance with withdrawn amounts.	The management fee amount *increases* in accordance with the withdrawn amount.
Performance Fees	Performance fees in excess of payment period profit *decrease* in accordance with payment period profit.	The management fee amount *increases* in accordance with the Performance Fee amount.

The following examples demonstrate these two billing schedules, and the affects of in contributions and withdrawals on each.

Forward Billing with In Flows and Out Flows: an Example

Partner A and Partner B belong to a partnership. The partnership follows a forward billing schedule and it accounts for contributions and withdrawals. The payment period is quarterly (January 1 through March 31), but the fees are being calculated on the 59th day remaining in the payment period (February 1).

Partner A and Partner B both start with a beginning capital of 10,000. Because they follow a forward billing schedule and are charged 1% of their beginning capital, their total quarterly management fee calculation is

(Beginning Capital × Annual Percentage Rate) × (Days in Payment Period / Days Per Year)

or, in this case, $(10000 \times .01) \times (90 / 365) = \$24.66$.

	Partner A	Partner B
Beginning Capital on 1/1	$10,000.00	$10,000.00
Quarterly Management Fee without cash flow	$24.66	$24.66
Appreciation between 1/1 and 1/31	$2,000.00	$2,000.00
Cash Flow on 2/1	Contribution: $4,000.00	Withdrawal: $4,000.00
Cash Flow eligible for Management Fee	$4,000.00	-$2,000.00
Fee/(Rebate) related to 2/1 cash flow	$6.48	-$3.24
Total Quarterly Management Fee	$31.14	$21.42

On February 1, Partner A makes a contribution of $4000 to the partnership. To calculate the management fee for that cash flow, the $4000 is multiplied by 1% for a yearly total of $40. On February 1, 59 days remain in the payment period, so 59 is divided by 365 to determine the percentage of the yearly management fee total that should apply on February 1. That figure is 16.2%. Thus, $40 \times .162 = 6.48$, so $6.48 is the fee that can be charged for the contribution on February 1.

Note: Because the partnership follows a forward billing schedule, the partner's appreciation of $2000 on January 31 is not eligible for management fee rebate.

On February 1, Partner B makes a withdrawal of $4000 from the partnership. Partner B's capital has appreciated by $2000 as of January 31, so the withdrawal comprises the $2000 of appreciation plus $2000 from the beginning capital.

The $2000 of appreciation during the payment period is ineligible for management fees this period, because the forward billing schedule is based on beginning capital. The remaining $2000 of the withdrawn $4000 comes from the partner's beginning capital, which had been charged upon at the beginning of the payment period. Therefore, for Partner B, the cash flow eligible for management fee is $2000.

Note: When billing forward and accounting for interim cash "outflows" (such as withdrawals, assignments, and performance fee payouts) the management fee rebate is calculated on only the outflow *in excess* of payment period profit.

So, $2000 is multiplied by the management fee schedule's annual percentage rate of 1% for a yearly total of $20. Because 59 days remain in the quarter, 59 is divided by 365 to determine the amount of the yearly total that should apply on February 1. That amount is 16.2%. 20 × .162 = 3.24, so on that date, the partner is eligible for a management fee rebate in the amount of $3.24.

Billing in Arrears with In Flows and Out Flows: an Example

Partner A and Partner B belong to a partnership. It follows a billing in arrears schedule and accounts for contributions and withdrawals. The payment period is quarterly (January 1 through March 31), and fees are being calculated on the final day of the payment period (March 31).

Partner A starts with a beginning capital of $10,000 and Partner B starts with a beginning capital of $18,000. After cash flows, each has an ending capital of $15,000. Because the partnership follows a billing in arrears schedule and charges 1% of the ending capital for management fees, their total quarterly management fee calculation before cash flows is:

(Ending Capital × Annual Percentage Rate) × (Days in Payment Period / Days Per Year)

or, in this case, (15000 × .01) × (90 / 365) = 36.99.

	Partner A	Partner B
Beginning Capital	$10,000	$18,000
Appreciation	$1,000	$1,000
Cash Flow on 2/1	Contribution: $4,000	Withdrawal: $4,000
Ending Capital on 3/31	$15,000	$15,000
Cash Flow eligible for Management Fee	$4,000	-$4,000
Quarterly Management Fee Calculation before Cash Flows	$36.99	$36.99
Impact of 2/1 cash flow on Management Fee	-$3.40	$3.40
Total Quarterly Management Fee on 3/31	$35.59	$40.39

On February 1, Partner A makes a contribution of $4000 to the partnership. To calculate the management fee for that cash flow, the $4000 is multiplied by 1% for a yearly total of $40. The contribution was made on February 1, after 31 days had passed in the payment period, and the formula *decreases* the management fee associated with the contribution for the amount of time during the payment period the contribution did not affect the partner's capital. Therefore, $40 \times 31 / 365 = 3.40$, and Partner A is eligible for a rebate of $3.40 on March 31. Partner A's total management fee for the payment period $35.59.

On February 1, Partner B makes a withdrawal of $4000 from the partnership. To calculate the management fee for that cash flow, the $4000 is multiplied by 1% for a yearly total of $40. The withdrawal was made on February 1, after 31 days had passed in the payment period, and the formula *increases* the management fee associated with the withdrawal for the amount of time during the payment period the withdrawal did not affect the partner's capital. Therefore, $40 \times 31 = 3.40$, and Partner B is eligible for a management fee charge of $3.40 on March 31. Partner B's total management fee for the payment period is $40.39.

ADV ENT PARTNER

Advent Partner's management fee module lets you specify management fee options; calculate, modify, and allocate management fees; and populate corresponding expense items within Advent Partner. You can choose to calculate fees on either a bill forward or a bill in arrears basis, and also select a payment period of annual, semi-annual, quarterly, monthly, or periodic.

For information on non-*pro rata* formulas Advent Partner can use to allocate management fees, see "Advent Partner's Uneven Methodologies" on page 100.

Other Income and Expenses Items

Other common investment-related income and expense items include:

Dividends

Partnerships report income from dividends on Schedule K-1 (Form 1065), as follows.

- Investor partnerships report dividend income on line 4(b), ordinary dividends.
- Trader partnerships report dividend income on line 1, Ordinary income (loss) from trade or business activities.

In addition, both trader and investor partnerships must report foreign dividend income on line 17(c), Total gross income from sources outside the United States.

(For details on trader and investor partnerships, see "Traders and Investors" on page 41.)

Partnerships should create separate items for dividends from domestic and foreign securities. This also allows partnerships to report foreign dividends net and gross of withholding taxes. Partnerships can also create separate allocation items for dividends that qualify for the dividends received deduction ("DRD"), and dividends from hot issue securities (if they have partners excluded from hot issue income).

Interest and Dividend Expenses

Partnerships can record the following items as expenses for tax purposes.

- Interest paid on short positions
- Dividends paid on short positions held longer than 45 days
- Margin interest incurred from opening a short positions

Note: An investor who holds a short position in a security must pay any dividend to the lender of the security.

Interest Income

Partnerships categorize interest income in a number of ways. Partnerships can create four items to record interest income according to the tax treatment of the interest, as shown in the table below.

Item	State Taxable	Federal Taxable	Example
Fully taxable interest income	Yes	Yes	Corporate bonds
State taxable interest income	Yes	No	Municipal bonds (depending on the state of the issuer and residency of the partner) State-issued bonds (for partners not residing in the state that issued the bonds)
Federal taxable interest income	No	Yes	U.S. Treasury notes and bonds
Tax free interest income	No	No	Municipal bonds (depending on the state of the issuer and residency of the partner) State-issued bonds (for partners residing in the state that issued the bonds)

Note: Partnerships generally include accrued interest in the appropriate interest income item. For details about recording accrued interest, see "Recording Interest Accrual" on page 62.

ADVENT PARTNER

Advent Partner automatically assigns interest income transactions imported from Axys to these items. It also categorizes interest from state-issued bonds allocated to each partner according to that partner's state of residency. For details, look up **income and expense tracking** in Advent Partner's Help index.

Organizational Expenses

Investment partnership organizational expenses generally include:

- Legal costs to write the private placement memorandum (PPM), limited partnership agreement (LPA), and related documents.
- Accounting consulting costs in connection with preparing the PPM and LPA.
- Document printing costs.
- Advertising the formation of the partnership in a legal publication.

The partnership itself usually pays organizational costs, although in some circumstances the general partner pays for all or part of the costs. The Internal Revenue Code provides that partnerships can elect to amortize organizational costs over a period of not less than 60 months. The partnership must make this election on the first tax return it files. If the partnership elects to amortize organizational costs for tax purposes, it generally does so for accounting purposes as well.

In 1998, the AICPA issued Statement of Position 98-5, Reporting on the Costs of Start-Up Activities. This SOP requires that "start-ups:"

- Expense organizational costs incurred after June 30, 1998 as incurred.
- Write off any unamortized start-up costs at the beginning of the fiscal year in which they first adopt the SOP.

Investment partnerships are exempt from the second provision. Partnerships should consult the appropriate professionals about adopting these provisions going forward from June 30, 1998. Partnerships must capitalize and amortize costs incurred prior to this date as fund assets.

The majority of organizational costs are usually related to legal fees. Organizational costs as billed by the partnership's attorneys, however, generally include syndication costs (costs incurred to sell limited partnership interests), which are *not* deductible for tax purposes. The partnership may want to refer to its attorneys for the allocation between organizational and syndication costs, and make an appropriate allocation between the two. For accounting purposes, the partnership treats syndication costs as it does organizational costs.

Other Expenses

Other expenses of an investment partnership include:

- Accounting, auditing, and legal fees, generally paid directly by the fund.
- Management, investment advisory, administrative, and overhead fees, paid either directly by the fund or to the general partner or a company controlled by the general partner.

Note: In New York City, a fee paid to a general partner operating in the form of a partnership or a limited liability company may result in the imposition of New York City unincorporated business tax (UBT). A recent amendment to the UBT law provides for segregating trading income (which is not subject to UBT under certain conditions) from fee income (which is subject to UBT). New York City general partners should have the fee paid to a separate entity (such as a management company), in order to segregate the fee from the trading income. Partnerships should consult an appropriate tax professional when structuring this entity.

- Some partnerships do not pay investment advisory and administrative fees. The general partner absorbs such expenses.
- If the partnership is on the accrual basis, and pays fees to any related entity (such as a partner or a management company controlled by a partner) that is on the cash basis, the partnership must pay those fees before year end. This allows the partners who are charged to deduct the expense. Fees paid to general partners that are considered guaranteed payments are deductible in the year to which they are related.

Accretion

Section 1276 of the IRC specifies that partnerships treat accretion (accrued market discount) as ordinary income. To assign accretion to an allocation item, partnerships should either:

- Include accretion in an ordinary income item, such as interest income, or
- Create a separate accretion income item, but include this item as ordinary income on their Schedule K-1s.

For details about recording accretion, see "Recording Market Discount Accretion" on page 57.

Amortization

Section 171(e) of the IRC specifies that amortization of bond premiums be treated as an offset to interest income, rather than an expense item. To assign amortization to an allocation item, partnerships should either:

- Include amortization in the appropriate interest income item, or
- Create a separate amortization income item with a negative amount, but include this item as an adjustment to ordinary income on their Schedule K-1s.

For details about recording amortization, see "Recording Amortization" on page 60.

Note: For municipal bonds, partnerships calculate realized gains based on the bond's adjusted cost (original cost – amortization), but the partnership does not reduce its interest income for amortization.

Foreign Taxes

Partnerships should separately allocate taxes paid on investments in foreign securities, such as withholding taxes, for Schedule K-1 (Form 1065), line 17e.

Investment, Trade, and Business Expenses

IRC Section 67 limits the deduction for miscellaneous itemized deductions, to the aggregate of such deductions exceeding 2% of adjusted gross income. The Tax Reform Act of 1986 added Section 67(b) to the IRC, however, which excludes interest expenses (defined in IRC Section 163) from the definition of miscellaneous itemized deductions under IRC Section 67, and therefore from the 2% rule.

IRC Section 67(b) does not exclude trade or business expenses (Section 162), or expenses for production of income, from the 2% floor on miscellaneous itemized deductions.

- *Investor partnerships*: The miscellaneous itemized deductions of investor partnerships are subject to the 2% floor, and should be so highlighted to the partners on their Schedule K-1s. (These items are reported on Schedule K-1, line 10, Deductions related to portfolio income.)
- *Trader partnerships*: The trade or business expenses (defined in Section 162) of trader partnerships are deductible from adjusted gross income, because trade or business expenses are not included in the definition of miscellaneous itemized deductions. These expenses are not subject to the 2% rule, and are reported as ordinary expense on line 1 of Schedule K-1.

Depending on whether the partnership is classified as a trader or an investor partnership, it may need to provide more detailed information about its various investment, trade, and business expenses for the limited partners' Schedule K-1s. To provide this detail, the partnership must allocate each type of expense separately. (For details on trader and investor partnerships, see "Traders and Investors" on page 41.)

Understanding Economic Allocations

Chapter 4 described how partnerships must allocate each period's profits, losses, and expenses to the partners. This chapter describes in detail the economic allocation of these items, in particular:

- ✔ The difference between economic and tax allocation
- ✔ How to exclude partners from allocations of hot issue gains
- ✔ How to allocate income from "side pocket" investments
- ✔ The non-*pro rata* (or "uneven") methodologies that Advent Partner can use to allocate items.

In This Chapter

What Are Economic Allocations?

At the end of each fiscal year (or break period if partners have contributed or withdrawn capital on an interim date), the partnership tentatively allocates its net economic (also called "book") income (with certain exceptions noted later) to the partners *pro rata* according to their capital percentages during the period.

Example: The following table shows an economic allocation schedule for 1998 for a partnership with quarterly break periods.

Period	Economic Income
1/1/98 to 3/31/98	$50
4/1/98 to 6/30/98	$20
7/1/98 to 9/30/98	-$40
10/1/98 to 12/31/98	$40
Total	**$70**

Each of the following tables show the partners':

- Previous ending capital balances.
- Beginning capital changes: contributions, positive; withdrawals negative.
- Beginning capital balances and percentages (updated for beginning capital changes).
- Allocations of economic profit/loss for the quarter.
- Ending capital balances.

❖ Year-to-date (YTD) allocations of economic profit/loss.

1 First Quarter

	1/1/98 Capital Balance	1/1/98 Capital Percent	1st Quarter Profit/Loss Allocations	3/31/98 Capital Balance	YTD Profit/ Loss
GP	$10	10%	$5	$15	$5
LP1	$40	40%	$20	$60	$20
LP2	$50	50%	$25	$75	$25
Total	**$100**	**100%**	**$50**	**$150**	**$50**

2 Second Quarter

	3/31/98 Capital Balance	4/1/98 Capital Changes	4/1/98 Capital Balance	4/1/98 Capital Percent	2nd Quarter Profit/Loss Allocations	6/30/98 Capital Balance	YTD Profit/ Loss
GP	$15		$15	8%	$2	$17	$7
LP1	$60	$20	$80	44%	$9	$89	$29
LP2	$75		$75	42%	$8	$83	$33
LP3		$10	$10	6%	$1	$11	$1
Total	**$150**	**$30**	**$180**	**100%**	**$20**	**$200**	**$70**

3 Third Quarter

	6/30/98 Capital Balance	7/1/98 Capital Changes	7/1/98 Capital Balance	7/1/98 Capital Percent	3rd Quarter Profit/Loss Allocations	9/30/98 Capital Balance	YTD Profit/ Loss
GP	$17		$17	8%	-$3	$14	$4
LP1	$89		$89	42%	-$17	$72	$12
LP2	$83	-$25	$58	28%	-$11	$47	$22
LP3	$11		$11	5%	-$2	$9	-$1
LP4		$35	$35	17%	-$7	$28	-$7
Total	**$200**	**$10**	**$210**	**100%**	**-$40**	**$170**	**$30**

4 Fourth Quarter

	9/30/98 Capital Balance	10/1/98 Capital Changes	10/1/98 Capital Balance	10/1/98 Capital Percent	4th quarter Profit/Loss Allocations	12/31/98 Capital Balance	YTD Profit/ Loss
GP	$14		$14	7%	$3	$17	$7
LP1	$72		$72	36%	$14	$86	$26
LP2	$47		$47	23.5%	$9	$56	$31
LP3	$9	$30	$39	19.5%	$8	$47	$7
LP4	$28		$28	14%	$6	$34	-$1
Total	**$170**	**$30**	**$200**	**100%**	**$40**	**$240**	**$70**

The previous example illustrates a simple economic allocation, in which the partnership allocates all of its net profit or loss to the partners according to their capital percentages in the current period. A partnership can, however, have items that it does not allocate *pro rata*.

- If the partnership holds "hot issue" securities, and any of the partners are excluded from hot issue income, the partnership must allocate hot issue income only to non-excluded partners. For details, see "Allocating Hot Issue Gains" on page 96.
- If the partnership has any "side pocket" investments in which only some of the partners participate, it must allocate income from those investments only to the partners who participate in them. For details, see "Allocating Side Pocket Investments" on page 98.

ADVENT PARTNER

- Partnerships can also specify other allocation items, such as management fees, from which it excludes some partners, or which it allocates to the partners non-*pro rata*. The section "Advent Partner's Uneven Methodologies" on page 100 describes the formulas you can use in Advent Partner to allocate non-*pro rata* allocation items (called *uneven* items).

How Do Tax and Economic Allocations Differ?

Tax allocations differ from economic allocations in the following ways.

- For tax purposes, partnerships allocate realized gains according to the historical unrealized gains already allocated to the partners. Economic allocations use partners' capital percentages in the current period.
- Partnerships that charge a performance incentive fee do so by adjusting the partners' allocation percentages to shift (or *reallocate*) appreciation from the limited partners to the general partner.
- Certain IRC provisions, such as for wash sales, require different allocation for tax purposes than would normally be done in an economic allocation.

The following sections describe these differences in detail, and point you towards more information about specific aspects of tax allocation.

Realized Gain Allocations

Generally, partnerships allocate items such as dividends, interest income and expense, management fees, and other ordinary income items using the tax percentages of the period in which they occur. The tax allocation for capital (gain) transactions, however, is complicated because for tax purposes, only realized gains and losses are reported as taxable, but unrealized gains (and losses) are not taxed currently. Because the partnership has already allocated unrealized appreciation and depreciation of securities in its portfolio in previous periods to the partners' capital accounts through the economic allocation, it must use an allocation method for realized transactions that fairly allocates the realized gain to the partners who have previously been credited or charged for the related unrealized appreciation or depreciation.

In general, IRC Section 704 and its related regulations provide that the limited partnership agreement governs allocations of tax items, or, if the allocation provided for does not have substantial economic effect, the partners' beneficial interests govern the allocations. Treasury Regulation Section 1.704-3(e)(3) identifies the aggregate and tax lot layering methods as "approved" methods.

Partnerships must consider the following factors when selecting their gain allocation methodology.

- *Aggregate method* may be more appropriate for funds that:
  - Actively trade securities.
  - Have a high rate of portfolio turnover.
  - Do not hold many positions long-term.
- *Layering method* may be more appropriate for funds that:
  - Hold securities long-term.
  - Have a low rate of portfolio turnover.

The following chapters discuss these two gain allocation methodologies.

For More Information About	See
Aggregate methodology	Chapter 6, Allocating Aggregate Gains.
Tax lot layering methodology	Chapter 7, Allocating Layered Gains.

Performance Incentive Reallocations

General partners usually receive compensation based on the partnership's performance. This compensation most commonly takes the form of a *performance incentive reallocation* (also called a "performance fee"). This reallocation shifts a portion of the limited partners' appreciation to the general partner. For details, see Chapter 8, Reallocating Performance Incentives.

Partnerships allocate taxable items to partners using the same capital percentages they used in the economic allocation (sometimes called *economic percentages*), adjusted according to the reallocation formula. This adjusted capital percentage is known as the *tax percentage*. Partnerships perform their tax allocations using tax percentages.

Example: A limited partner has a capital percentage of 10%, and receives 10% of the partnership's net economic income in the economic allocation. The partnership agreement, however, specifies a 20% performance fee, that is, if the partnership meets its appreciation goals, 20% of the limited partner's appreciation is reallocated to the general partner. The limited partner's tax percentage is 10% – (10% × 20%) = 8%.

For more information about tax percentages and performance fees, see Chapter 8, Reallocating Performance Incentives.

Tax Adjustment Allocations

The Internal Revenue Code requires taxpayers to adjust how they recognize gains and losses from certain securities or positions for tax purposes. This can involve:

- Recognizing certain unrealized gains as realized.
- Deferring recognition of certain realized losses.
- Reclassifying certain long-term gains or losses as short-term, or short-term as long-term.

For more information about these allocations, see the following sections.

Tax Adjustment	See
Section 1091 wash sales	"Understanding Wash Sales" on page 223.
Section 1092 straddles	"Understanding Straddles" on page 2291.
Section 1233 short sales	"Understanding Short Sales" on page 231.
Section 1256 contracts	*Aggregate allocation*: "Allocating Aggregate Section 1256 Gains" on page 136. *Layering allocation*: "Allocating Layered Section 1256 Gains" on page 150.
Section 1259 constructive sales	"Understanding Constructive Sales" on page 233.

The remaining sections in this chapter describe non-*pro rata* economic allocations.

Allocating Hot Issue Gains

The National Association of Securities Dealers, Inc. (NASD) has defined "hot issue" securities as securities (such as initial public offerings) that are part of a public distribution, but trade at a premium in the secondary market immediately after the distribution has begun. Members of the NASD may not sell such securities to an account in which any of the following have an interest.

- A member of the NASD
- A person affiliated with the NASD
- Certain persons related to a member of the NASD
- Security underwriters and brokers
- Registered investment advisers and unregistered investment managers
- Other persons as defined by NASD rules

The NASD refers to these persons and affiliates as "restricted." When a partnership has restricted partners, it can purchase hot issue securities provided that:

- The selling and clearing brokers set up a special account for the purchase of hot issues, with the profit in that account specially allocated to the partners who are not restricted.
- The fund's counsel advises the broker that no restricted persons have a beneficial interest in the special account.
- The general partner confirms to the fund's accountant that all hot issues have been purchased in the special account.
- The accountant confirms to the general partner that the partnership has allocated profits solely to partners who are not restricted.

Important: Although the NASD rules bar restricted persons such as the general partner from receiving *any* gains from hot issue securities, they *can* receive gains reallocated as performance fees. Limited partnership agreements can exclude restricted partners from economic allocations of hot issue gains, but allow them to receive hot issue gains in their performance fee reallocations. The limited partnership agreement may specify how restricted partners receive hot issue gain tax reallocations. For details, see "Hot Issue Gains" on page 176.

Example: The following is an economic allocation schedule with hot issues. The general partner and LP3 are restricted and cannot receive hot issue income.

	Beginning Capital		**Allocation Percentages**		**Income Allocations**		**Total Income**	**Actual Return**
	Non-hot Issue	**Hot Issue**	**Non-hot Issue**	**Hot Issue**	**Non-hot Issue**	**Hot Issue**		
GP	$100		4%		$16		$16	15%
LP1	$500	$500	19%	33%	$76	$33	$109	22%
LP2	$600	$600	23%	40%	$92	$40	$132	22%
LP3	$1,000		39%		$156		$156	16%
LP4	$400	$400	15%	27%	$60	$27	$87	22%
Total	**$2,600**	**$1,500**	**100%**	**100%**	**$400**	**$100**	**$500**	**19%**

For details on how Advent Partner handles hot issue gains, see the following sections.

For Information on How Advent Partner	See
Allocates hot issue gains with aggregate methodology	"Allocating Aggregate Hot Issue Gains" on page 138.
Allocates hot issue gains with tax lot layering methodology	"Allocating Layered Hot Issue Gains" on page 152.
Identifies hot issue securities	**hot issues, defining** in Advent Partner's Help index.
Identifies restricted partners	**hot issues, excluding partners from gains on** in Advent Partner's Help index.

Allocating Side Pocket Investments

Many investment partnership managers invest in securities that are not readily marketable, such as private securities of public companies or securities of non-public companies. Because such securities are illiquid, it may be difficult to determine the value of these investments each break period.

To avoid having to value these investments to allocate their unrealized gains, some partnerships segregate these investments in a "side pocket" and value them at cost, not recognizing or allocating any gain or loss on them until the partnership liquidates them. Partners cannot withdraw capital from a side pocket investment until the partnership liquidates it.

Note: Funds can mark a side pocket investment to market for valuation purposes, but generally do not allow withdrawals, or allocate profits or fees, from the investment until it becomes more liquid.

Note: Partnerships can also use side pocket investments for investments from which certain partners want to exclude themselves, such as purchases of "sin stocks."

The following steps describe the life of a side pocket investment.

1 When the partnership decides to segregate an investment in a side pocket, it creates a side pocket account, separate from the fund's other marketable investments. The partners contribute capital, or the partnership allocates capital, to the side pocket (called *designated capital*) as follows.

- *For an illiquid investment,* the only participants in the investment are partners in the fund when it makes the investment, or when it moves the investment to the side pocket. Partners designate capital to the investment proportionate to their capital accounts in the fund as a whole.

- *For elective investments,* each partner determines how much capital it contributes to the investment.

Designated capital stays in the side pocket investment (and in the partnership) until the partnership closes the investment. The partnership does not count this capital as part of the partners' capital accounts for calculating the partners' capital percentages in non-side pocket investments. The side pocket is, in effect, a separate partnership within the partnership.

2 The partnership uses the capital contributed by each partner to the side pocket, and the total amount of capital contributed to the investment, to calculate each partner's capital percentage (also called a *designated percentage*) in the side pocket investment.

3 The partnership makes the investment. The partnership must separately record the income, expenses, and gain related to this investment, as described in the section "What Are Allocation Items?" on page 68.

4 The partnership uses the contributing partners' designated percentages to allocate profits and losses from the investment.

Example: The following example shows economic allocation schedules including a side pocket investment.

1 A partnership starts on 1/1/1997 with one general partner (GP) and two limited partners (LP1 and LP2). The partnership purchases an illiquid investment at a cost of $50. The partnership still holds this investment at year-end.

	1/1/97 Capital		Designated Capital	12/31/97		
	Balance	Percent		Allocation	Ending Capital	Non-side Pocket Capital
GP	$100	10%	$5	$25	$125	$120
LP1	$400	40%	$20	$100	$500	$480
LP2	$500	50%	$25	$125	$625	$600
Total	**$1,000**	**100%**	**$50**	**$250**	**$1,250**	**$1,200**

Note: The partnership does not mark the side pocket investment to market, so it does not record unrealized gains for the investment.

2 Limited Partner 3 joins the partnership on 1/1/1998. Later that year, the partnership closes the side pocket investment, and realizes a $200 gain. (The total proceeds is $250.)

	1/1/98	Non-side Pocket			Side Pocket			12/31/98 Total		
	Beginning Capital	Capital Balance	Capital Percentage	Allocation	Designated Balance	Designated Percentage	Allocation	Allocation	Return	Ending Capital
GP	$125	$120	8%	$25	$5	10%	$20	$45	36%	$170
LP1	$500	$480	33%	$99	$20	40%	$80	$179	36%	$679
LP2	$625	$600	42%	$124	$25	50%	$100	$224	36%	$849
LP3	$250	$250	17%	$52	-		-	$52	21%	$302
Total	**$1,500**	**$1,450**	**100%**	**$300**	**$50**	**100%**	**$200**	**$500**	**33%**	**$2,000**

ADVENT PARTNER

For information about setting up side pocket investments in Advent Partner, look up **side pocket allocations, defining** in Advent Partner's Help index.

Advent Partner's Uneven Methodologies

ADVENT PARTNER

Limited partnership agreements can stipulate that the partnership allocates certain items (such as management fees) non-*pro rata*, but still according to a set formula. Advent Partner refers to such allocations as *uneven allocations*, and the formulas as *uneven* methodologies.

In general, Advent Partner's uneven methodologies still allocate the item according to partners' capital percentages, but can:

- Exclude certain partners from the allocation.
- Allocate a percentage (called the *uneven amount*) of the item to specific partners (called *uneven partners*) before or after allocating the remainder to the (non-excluded) partners according to their ownership percentages.
- Specify which uneven partners also *participate* in the remainder, that is:
  - *For off-the-top allocations,* the partners who "participate" *receive* an evenly allocated portion of the remainder of the item, after the uneven allocations have taken place.

- *For off-the-bottom allocations,* the partnership *reduces* the even allocations to partners who "participate," then reallocates these amounts to the uneven partner(s).

The following topics describe the three uneven methodologies that Advent Partner supports. For details, look up **uneven allocation** in Advent Partner's Help index.

- "Allocating With Off-the-Top Realigned Methodology" on page 101.
- "Allocating With Off-the-Top Literal Methodology" on page 103.
- "Allocating With Off-the-Bottom Methodology" on page 105.

Allocating With Off-the-Top Realigned Methodology

Off-the-top realigned uneven allocation methodology:

1. Allocates the uneven amount(s) (uneven percent × item amount) to the uneven partner(s).
2. Subtracts the uneven amount(s) from the original item amount to arrive at the remainder to be distributed to the remaining partners (and any uneven partners who also participate in the remainder).
3. Realigns the remaining and participating uneven partners' economic percentages to 100%.
4. Allocates the remainder of the item.

Tip: You can exclude a partner from an item (for example, a general partner who does not receive dividends from hot issue securities) by:

- Allocating the partner a 0% uneven percentage.

  and

- Having the partner not participate in the remainder.

Example: A partnership has five partners. In allocating hot issue dividends:

- Partners A and B each receive 10% off the top, and participate in the remainder.
- Partner C receives 10% off the top, but does not participate in the remainder.
- Partner D receives no off-the-top allocation, but participates in the remainder.
- Partner E, the general partner, is excluded from hot issue dividends.

Partner	Capital balance	Capital percentage	Off-the-Top Percentage	Participate in Remainder?
A	$3,000	12%	10%	yes
B	$7,500	30%	10%	yes
C	$2,000	8%	10%	no
D	$2,500	10%	0%	yes
E	$10,000	40%	0%	no
Total	**$25,000**	**100%**		

Off-the-top methodology allocates a $100 dividend as follows.

1. Allocate A, B, and C each $10 (10% off the top) of the dividend.
2. Calculate that $70 of the dividend remains.
3. Take the economic percentages of the partners who participate in the remainder (A: 12%; B: 30%; D: 10%; for a total of 52%), and realign them to 100%.
   - Partner A: 12% / 52% = 23.08%
   - Partner B: 30% / 52% = 57.69%
   - Partner D: 10% / 52% = 19.23%
4. Allocate the remaining $70 according to the realigned percentages.
   - Partner A: 23.08% × $70 = $16.16

- Partner B: 57.69% × $70 = $40.38
- Partner D: 19.23% × $70 = $13.46

The following table shows the final results of the off-the-top realigned allocation.

Partner	Uneven Allocation	Participation in Remainder	Total
A	$10	$16.16	$26.16
B	$10	$40.38	$50.38
C	$10	$0	$10
D	$0	$13.46	$13.46
E	$0	$0	$0
Total	**$30**	**$70**	**$100**

Allocating With Off-the-Top Literal Methodology

Off-the-top literal uneven allocation methodology:

1. Allocates the uneven amount(s) (uneven percent × item amount) to the uneven partner(s).
2. Subtracts the uneven amount(s) from the original item amount to arrive at the remainder to be distributed to the remaining partners (and any uneven partners who also participate in the remainder).
3. Allocates the remainder of the item to the remaining partners and participating uneven partners according to their beginning economic percentages.

   Note: If any uneven partners do not participate in the remainder of the item, Advent Partner will not allocate the full item amount.

Tip: You can exclude a partner from an item (for example, a general partner who does not receive hot issue dividends) by allocating the partner a 0% uneven percentage and not having the partner participate in the remainder.

Example: A partnership has five partners. In allocating hot issue dividends:

- Partners A and B each receives 10% off the top, and participates in the remainder.
- Partner C receives 10% off the top, but does not participates in the remainder.
- Partner D receives no off the top, but participates in the remainder.
- Partner E, the general partner, is excluded from hot issue dividends.

Partner	Capital Balance	Capital Percentage	Off-the-Top Percentage	Participate in Remainder?
A	$3,000	12%	10%	yes
B	$7,500	30%	10%	yes
C	$2,000	8%	10%	no
D	$2,500	10%	0%	yes
E	$10,000	40%	0%	no
Total	**$25,000**	**100%**		

Off-the-top literal uneven methodology allocates a $100 dividend as follows.

1. Allocate A, B, and C each $10 (10% off the top) of the dividend.
2. Calculate that $70 of the dividend remains.
3. Allocate the remaining $70 to the partners who participate in the remainder according to their economic percentages.
   - Partner A: 12% × $70 = $8.40

- Partner B: 30% × $70 = $21.00
- Partner D: 10% × $70 = $7.00

Note: In this example, because Partner C receives an off-the-top allocation but does not participate in the remainder, Advent Partner does not allocate the entire $100.

Partner	Off-the-Top	Remainder	Total
A	$10.00	$8.40	$18.40
B	$10.00	$21.00	$31.00
C	$10.00		$10.00
D		$7.00	$7.00
E			$0
		Total	**$66.40**

Allocating With Off-the-Bottom Methodology

Off-the-bottom uneven allocation methodology:

1. Evenly allocates the item amount to all partners according to their economic percentages.

   Note: You cannot exclude any partners from this allocation.

2. Calculates the total uneven amount as the item amount × the sum of the uneven percentages.
3. Realigns the remaining (and participating uneven) partners' economic percentages to 100%.
4. Reduces the allocations to the remaining and participating uneven partners by their realigned percentage of the total uneven amount.
5. Distributes the uneven amounts to the uneven partners, according to their uneven percentages.

Example: A partnership has five partners. In allocating dividends:

- Partners A and B each receive 10% off the bottom, and participate in the remainder.
- Partner C receives 10% off the bottom, but does not participate in the remainder.
- Partner D receives no off-the-bottom percentage, but participates in the remainder.
- Partner E, the general partner, receives no off-the-bottom percentage and does not participate in the remainder.

Partner	Capital Balance	Capital Percentage	Off-the-Bottom Percentage	Participate in Remainder?
A	$3,000	12%	10%	yes
B	$7,500	30%	10%	yes
C	$2,000	8%	10%	no
D	$2,500	10%	0%	yes
E	$10,000	40%	0%	no
Total	**$25,000**	**100%**		

Advent Partner would allocate a $100 dividend as follows.

1. Evenly allocate the $100 to all partners, according to their economic percentages (A: $12; B: $30; C: $8; D: $10; E, $40).
2. Calculate that $30 of the dividend must be unevenly allocated (three 10% uneven allocations).
3. Take the economic percentages of the partners who participate in the remainder (A: 12%; B: 30%; D: 10%; for a total of 52%), and realign them to 100%.
   - Partner A: 12% / 52% = 23.08%
   - Partner B: 30% / 52% = 57.69%
   - Partner D: 10% / 52% = 19.23%

4 Reduce the remaining and participating uneven partners' original even allocations by their realigned percentages of the $30 uneven allocation.

Partner	Even Allocation (from Step 1)	Uneven Reduction	Remainder
A	$12.00	23.08% × $30.00 = $6.92	$12.00 – $6.92 = $5.08
B	$30.00	57.69% × $30.00 = $17.31	$30.00 – $17.31 = $12.69
C	$8.00	none	$8.00
D	$10.00	19.23% × $30.00 = $5.77	$10.00 – $5.77 = $4.23
E	$40.00	none	$40.00

5 Allocate the uneven amounts to the uneven partners.

Partner	Remainder from Uneven Reduction (from Step 4)	Uneven Allocation	Final Allocation
A	$5.08	10% × $100 = $10	$5.08 + $10.00 = $15.08
B	$12.69	10% × $100 = $10	$12.69 + $10.00 = $22.69
C	$8.00	10% × $100 = $10	$8.00 + $10.00 = $18.00
D	$4.23	none	$4.23
E	$40.00	none	$40.00
Total	**$70**	**$30**	**$100**

Allocating Aggregate Gains

Chapter 5 explained how partnerships allocate each period's unrealized gains and losses on their securities to the partners, so that the partnership can allocate realized gains according to the partners' historical interests in the partnership's investments. This chapter explains the aggregate methodology, one of the methodologies approved by the IRS for allocating realized gains. It includes:

✔ How to allocate realized gains using aggregate methodologies.

✔ How withdrawals and assignments affect aggregate accounts.

✔ How to allocate gains from Section 1256 securities.

✔ How to allocate gains from hot issue securities.

✔ How the "ceiling rule" affects aggregate allocation.

In This Chapter

Understanding Aggregate Methodologies

Aggregate gain allocation methodologies assume that a partner purchases an undivided share of an investment partnership's assets. The partnership maintains an *aggregate account* (also called an "unrealized memo account," "memo account," or "revaluation account") for each partner, where it records the aggregate (net) amount of each partner's share of the fund's unrealized gains or losses (appreciation or depreciation). This allows the partnership to track each partner's historical interest in the partnership's unrealized appreciation without maintaining information on a security-by-security basis.

As the partnership realizes its prior periods' unrealized gains, it allocates those realized gains according to the partners' historical interests in the partnership's unrealized appreciation, as represented by their aggregate account balances.

The partnership allocates aggregate realized gains or losses to each partner according to the partner's *aggregate percentage* (the partner's aggregate balance as a portion of the partnership's total aggregate balance), or its tax percentage (economic percentages adjusted for performance reallocations), or both, depending on how the partnership's realized gains or losses compare to the partners' aggregate account balances. For details, see "Understanding Aggregate Assumptions" on page 112.

Note: The amount of unrealized gain in a partner's capital and aggregate accounts changes when:

- The partner is allocated realized gains.
- Any partner withdraws capital in excess of its tax basis (unrealized gains) from the partnership. For details, see "How Total Withdrawals Affect Aggregate Accounts" on page 133.
- The partner assigns a portion of its interest in the partnership to (or receives an assignment from) another partner. For details, see "How Assignments Affect Aggregate Accounts" on page 136.

Several different aggregate methodologies are available. This chapter describes three popular methodologies, two of which are available in Advent Partner.

PARTNER

Advent Partner's Aggregate Methodologies

Advent Partner supports two methodologies for implementing aggregate allocation: Aggregate with Book Gains, Full Netting; and Aggregate Full Netting.

The essential difference between these methodologies is that:

- Aggregate with Book Gains, Full Netting adds the current period's book gains (realized gains + change in unrealized gains) to the partners' aggregate accounts *after* the current period's realized gains are allocated.
- Aggregate, Full Netting adds the current period's book gains *before* the current period's realized gains are allocated.

Aggregate with Book Gains, Full Netting:

1. The partnership allocates the current period's *book gains* (realized gains + change in unrealized gains) to each partner's aggregate account according to its tax percentages.
2. The partnership allocates realized gain according to the updated (called *interim*) aggregate balances.
3. The partnership subtracts the partners' tax allocations of realized gain from their aggregate account balances.

For details, see "Aggregate With Book Gains, Full Netting" on page 121.

Aggregate, Full Netting:

1. The partnership allocates the current period's realized gain according to the partners' aggregate account balances at the beginning of the period.
2. The partnership adds each partner's tax allocation of the change in unrealized gains during the period to the partner's aggregate account.

For details, see "Aggregate, Full Netting" on page 128.

Calculating the Change in Unrealized Gains

In addition to allocating realized gains, aggregate methodologies also allocate the change in the partnership's unrealized gains each period. To calculate the change in unrealized gains, the partnership subtracts the previous period's total unrealized gain from the current period's total unrealized gain. The result also includes any unrealized gains that "leave" the partnership when it closes a position and realizes the gain.

Example: In period 1, a partnership buys 1,000 shares of a security at $100 (total market value of $100,000). At the end of the period 1, the security's price is $110, for an unrealized gain of ($110 price – $100 cost) × 1,000 shares = $10,000.

In period 2, the partnership sells 100 shares of the security at $111. At the end of period 2, the security's price is $109, for an unrealized gain of ($109 price – $100 cost) × 900 shares = $8,100. The partnership allocates the *change* in unrealized gain to the partners: $8,100 (period 2) – $10,000 (period 1) = -$1,900.

Notice that the change in unrealized gain in period 2 comprises:

Unrealized gain (from period 1) associated with 100 shares sold, no longer held by the partnership (($110 period 1 price – $100 cost) × 100 shares)	-$1,000
Change in unrealized gain for remaining shares ($109 period 2 price – $110 period 1 price) × 900 shares	-$900
Total	**-$1,900**

Understanding Aggregate Assumptions

Aggregate methodologies allocate realized gains to the partners according to their *aggregate percentages* (that is, their aggregate account balances divided by the partnership's overall aggregate balance), unless:

- The realized gains (losses) exceed the partners' aggregate positive (negative) account balances.

- The partnership realizes a loss when the partners have positive aggregate account balances, or a gain when the partners have negative aggregate account balances.

- Some partners have positive aggregate account balances, and others have zero or negative balances.

In these cases, the partnership allocates realized gains according to the partners' current tax percentages, or a combination of their tax and aggregate percentages. These conditions that the partnership meets to determine how it allocates realized gain are called "aggregate assumptions," or simply "assumptions".

The following table summarizes the conditions the partnership meets for each assumption, and how aggregate methodologies allocate realized gains under that assumption.

Note: All aggregate assumptions (1 through 4) apply identically regardless of aggregate methodology (Aggregate with Book Gains, Full Netting or Aggregate, Full Netting).

ASSUMPTION 1

IF	AND	THEN
All Partners Have	**The Partnership's Aggregate Beginning Account Balance is**	
Positive beginning or interim account balances	Equal to or exceeds the partnership's net realized gain,	Realized gain or loss is allocated to each partner based on the partner's proportionate share of the partnership's beginning account balance.
Negative beginning or interim account balances	Equal to or exceeds the partnership's net realized loss,	

ASSUMPTION 2

IF	AND	THEN
All partners have	**The Partnership's Aggregate Beginning Account Balance is**	
Positive beginning or interim account balances	Less than the partnership's net realized gain,	Realized gain or loss is first allocated to each partner based on the partner's proportionate share of the partnership's beginning account balance, with any excess allocated in accordance with the partner's current economic percentage.
Negative beginning or interim account balances	Less than the partnership's net realized loss,	

ASSUMPTION 3

IF	AND	THEN
All Partners Have	**The Partnership Realizes a Net**	
Positive beginning or interim account balances	Loss	Realized gain or loss is allocated in accordance with the partners' current economic percentages.
Negative beginning or interim account balances	Gain	

	IF	AND	Then
	Some Partners Have	The Partnership Realizes a Net	
ASSUMPTION 4	Positive beginning or interim account balances, and some partners have negative beginning or interim account balances	Gain	Net realized gain is first allocated to those partners with positive beginning account balances in accordance with the partners' beginning account balances. Any excess gain is allocated in accordance with the partners' current economic percentages.
		Loss	Net realized loss is first allocated to those partners with negative beginning account balances in accordance with the partners' beginning account balances. Any excess loss is allocated in accordance with the partners' current economic percentages.

The following sections show examples of allocation using each of the aggregate assumptions.

Assumption 1

Allocate according to Assumption 1:

If

- ❖ All of the partners have *positive* aggregate account balances.

and

- ❖ The partnership realizes a net *gain* less than or equal to the partnership's total aggregate account balance.

Or

- All of the partners have *negative* aggregate account balances.

and

- The partnership realizes a net *loss* less than or equal to the partnership's total aggregate account balance.

To allocate according to Assumption 1, allocate all of the realized gain (*loss*) according to the partners' aggregate account percentages.

Example: A partnership has three partners, with aggregate account balances A: $80; B: $70; and C: $50. The partnership records $40 in realized gain. Because all of the partners' aggregate account balances are positive, and the realized gain is less than the total of the partners' aggregate account balances, the partnership allocates the realized gain according to Assumption 1 as follows.

Partner	Aggregate Balance	Aggregate Percent	Realized Gain
A	$80	40%	$40 × .40 = $16
B	$70	35%	$40 × .35 = $14
C	$50	25%	$40 × .25 = $10
Total	**$200**	**100%**	**$40**

Assumption 2

Allocate according to Assumption 2:

If

- All of the partners have *positive* aggregate account balances.

and

- The partnership realizes a net *gain* greater than the partnership's total aggregate account balance.

Or

- All of the partners have *negative* aggregate account balances.

and

- The partnership realizes a net *loss* greater than the partnership's total aggregate account balance.

To allocate according to Assumption 2:

1 Allocate each partner an amount of realized gain (loss) equal to that partner's aggregate account balance.

2 Allocate the remaining realized gain (loss) according to the partners' economic percentages.

Example: A partnership has three partners, with:

- Aggregate account balances A: $80; B: $70; C: $50.
- Tax percentages A: 35%; B: 35%; C: 30%.

The partnership records $240 in realized gain. Because all of the partners' aggregate account balances are positive, and the realized gain exceeds the total of the partners' aggregate account balances, the partnership allocates the realized gain according to Assumption 2 as follows.

Partner	Aggregate Balance	Tax Percent	Realized Gain
A	$80	35%	$80 + (.35 × $40) = $94
B	$70	35%	$70 + (.35 × $40) = $84
C	$50	30%	$50 + (.30 × $40) = $62
Total	**$200**	**100%**	**$240**

Assumption 3

Allocate according to Assumption 3:

If
❖ All of the partners have *positive* aggregate account balances. *and* ❖ The partnership realizes a net *loss*.
Or
❖ All of the partners have *negative* aggregate account balances. *and* ❖ The partnership realizes a net *gain*.

To allocate according to Assumption 3, allocate the realized loss (*gain*) according to the partners' tax percentages.

Example: A partnership has three partners, with:

- ❖ Aggregate account balances A: $80; B: $70; C: $50.
- ❖ Tax percentages A: 35%; B: 35%; C: 30%.

The partnership records $40 in realized losses. Because all of the partners' aggregate account balances are positive, the partnership allocates the realized loss according to Assumption 3 as follows.

Partner	Aggregate Balance	Tax Percent	Realized Loss
A	$80	35%	.35 × -$40 = -$14
B	$70	35%	.35 × -$40 = -$14
C	$50	30%	.30 × -$40 = -$12
Total	**$200**	**100%**	**-$40**

Assumption 4

Allocate according to Assumption 4:

If	And
❖ Some of the partners have positive account balances.	❖ Others have negative or zero balances.

To allocate according to Assumption 4 if the partnership realizes a *gain:*

1. Allocate realized gain first to the partners with positive aggregate account balances, according to their aggregate percentages, realigned to 100%.
2. Allocate any remaining realized gain to all of the partners according to their tax percentages, regardless of whether they have negative or zero aggregate account balances.

To allocate according to Assumption 4 if the partnership realizes a *loss:*

1. Allocate realized loss first to the partners with negative aggregate account balances, according to their aggregate percentages, realigned to 100%.
2. Allocate any remaining realized loss to all of the partners according to their tax percentages, regardless of whether they have positive or zero aggregate account balances.

Example: A partnership has four partners, with:

- ❖ Aggregate account balances A: $80; B: $70; C: $50; D: -$10.
- ❖ Tax percentages A: 20%; B: 35%; C: 30%; D: 15%.

The partnership records $240 in realized gain. Because some of the partners' aggregate account balances are positive, others are negative, the partnership allocates the realized gain according to Assumption 4 as follows.

Allocation 1 – According to Aggregate Percentages

Partner	Aggregate Balance	Realigned Aggregate Percent	Tax Percent	Realized Gain
A	$80	$80 / $200 = 40%	20%	$80
B	$70	$70 / $200 = 35%	35%	$70
C	$50	$50 / $200 = 25%	30%	$50
D (Excluded)	-$10	--	15%	--
Total	**$190**	**100%**	**100%**	**$200**

Allocation 2 – According to Tax Percentages

Partner	Tax Percent	Realized Gain
A	20%	.20 × $40 = $8
B	35%	.35 × $40 = $14
C	30%	.30 × $40 = $12
D	15%	.15 × $40 = $6
Total	**100%**	**$40**

Total Allocations – Allocation 1 + Allocation 2

Partner	Aggregate Balance	Realigned Aggregate Percent	Tax Percent	Realized Gain
A	$80	$80 / $200 = 40%	20%	$80 + (.20 × $40) = $88
B	$70	$70 / $200 = 35%	35%	$70 + (.35 × $40) = $84
C	$50	$50 / $200 = 25%	30%	$50 + (.30 × $40) = $62
D	-$10	--	15%	.15 × $40 = $6
Total	**$190**	**100%**	**100%**	**$240**

Aggregate With Book Gains, Full Netting

If a partnership uses aggregate with book gains, full netting methodology, it allocates realized and unrealized gains each period as follows.

1 Calculate each partner's book gain as:

$$\left(\text{Partnership realized gain} + \text{Partnership change in unrealized gain}\right) \times \text{Partner beginning capital percentage}$$

Note: For information on calculating the change in unrealized gains, see "Calculating the Change in Unrealized Gains" on page 112.

2 Add each partner's book gain (along with the partner's allocations of non-gain items) to the partner's capital account to determine the partner's ending capital balance.

3 Reallocate the appropriate amount of the limited partner's book gains to the general partner(s) *if:*

- The limited partner is subject to a performance fee charge this period.

  and

- The partner's ending capital balance exceeds its target capital.

For details, see Chapter 8, Reallocating Performance Incentives.

4 Add each partner's adjusted book gain to the partner's beginning aggregate account balance for the period to calculate the partner's interim aggregate account balance and interim aggregate percentage.

5 Allocate realized gain according to the partners' interim aggregate and tax percentages, as dictated by the aggregate assumption the partnership meets this period. For details, see "Understanding Aggregate Assumptions" on page 112.

6 Allocate the difference between the partner's adjusted book gains, and the partner's allocation of realized gain, as unrealized gain.

7 Subtract each partner's tax allocation of realized gain from the partner's interim aggregate account balance to calculate the partner's ending aggregate account balance.

Aggregate with Book Gains, Full Netting: An Example

The following example shows a partnership's tax allocations for four periods. The partnership begins with one limited partner (A), who contributes $1,000, and one general partner (B), who contributes $3,000. The partnership reallocates 20% of the limited partners' appreciation to the general partner as a performance incentive each period.

Period 1

In the first period, the partnership records $20 of realized gain + $500 *change* in unrealized gain = $520 book gain.

Because all of the partners' interim aggregate account balances are positive, and the amount of gain the partnership realizes ($20) is less than the partnership's total interim aggregate balance ($520), the partnership uses Assumption 1 to perform its tax allocation.

According to Assumption 1, the partnership allocates the realized gain according to the partners' tax or interim aggregate percentages (Partner A: 20%; Partner B: 80%).

The following table shows the results of the period 1 tax allocation on the partners' capital and aggregate accounts.

Period 1 Allocation	Partner A	Partner B	Partnership
Beginning capital	$1,000	$3,000	$4,000
Capital percentage	.25	.75	
Beginning aggregate balance	$0	$0	$0
Tax percentage*	.20	.80	
Adjusted book gain	$104	$416	$520
Interim aggregate balance	$104	$416	$520
Interim aggregate percent	.20	.80	
Realized gain	$4	$16	$20
Unrealized gain	$100	$400	$500
Ending capital	$1,104	$3,416	$4,520
Ending aggregate balance	$100	$400	$500

*For limited partners, Tax percentage = Economic percentage × (1 – Payout percentage). Partnerships must infer general partners' tax percentages from the limited partners' percentages. For details, see "Calculating Tax Percentages and Carve-Outs" on page 169.

Period 2

In the second period, a third partner (C) joins the partnership with a contribution of $1,000. The partnership records $300 of realized gain + $0 *change* in unrealized gain = $300 book gain.

Because all of the partners' interim aggregate account balances are positive, and the amount of gain the partnership realizes ($300) is less than the partnership's total interim aggregate balance ($800), the partnership performs its tax allocation using Assumption 1.

According to Assumption 1, the partnership allocates the realized gain according to the partners' aggregate percentages (Partner A: 19%; Partner B: 76%; Partner C: 5%).

The following table shows the results of the period 2 tax allocation

Period 2 Allocation	Partner A	Partner B	Partner C	Partnership
Beginning capital	$1,104	$3,416	$1,000	$5,520
Capital percentage	.20	.62	.18	
Beginning aggregate balance	$100	$400	$0	$500
Tax percentage	.16	.70	.14	
Adjusted book gain	$48	$210	$42	$300
Interim aggregate balance	$148	$610	$42	$800
Interim aggregate percent	.19	.76	.05	
Realized gain	$57	$228	$15	$300
Unrealized gain	-$9	-$18	$27	$0
Ending capital	$1,152	$3,626	$1,042	$5,820
Ending aggregate balance	$91	$382	$27	$500

Important: In a tax allocation according to straight tax percentages, Partner C would have received 14% × $300 = $42 of realized gain. Because Partner C just joined the partnership, however, its aggregate percentage differs from its tax percentage, leading to a difference between its realized gain based on straight tax percentages, and its realized gain based on aggregate percentages. As a result:

- The difference between Partner C's straight tax percentage and aggregate allocations of realized gain ($42 – $15 = $27) appears as unrealized gain in the tax allocation, even though the partnership did not record any unrealized gain this period.
- The difference between Partner A and Partner B's adjusted book gains and tax allocations of realized gain appears as negative unrealized gain.

The total unrealized gain in the tax allocation is zero, however.

Period 3

In the third period, the partnership records $600 of realized gain + $100 *change* in unrealized gain = $700 book gain.

Because all of the partners' interim aggregate account balances are positive, and the amount of gain the partnership realizes ($600) is less than the partnership's total interim aggregate balance ($1,200), the partnership performs its tax allocation using Assumption 1.

According to Assumption 1, the partnership allocates the realized gain according to the partners' aggregate percentages (Partner A: 17%; Partner B: 73%; Partner C: 10%).

The following table shows the results of the period 3 tax allocation.

Period 3 Allocation	Partner A	Partner B	Partner C	Partnership
Beginning capital	$1,152	$3,626	$1,042	$5,820
Capital percentage	.20	.62	.18	
Beginning aggregate balance	$91	$382	$27	$500
Tax percentage	.16	.70	14	
Adjusted book gain	$112	$490	$98	$700
Interim aggregate balance	$203	$872	$125	$1,200
Interim aggregate percent	.17	.73	.10	
Realized gain	$102	$438	$60	$600
Unrealized gain	$10	$52	$38	$100
Ending capital	$1,264	$4,116	$1,140	$6,520
Ending aggregate balance	$101	$434	$65	$600

Period 4

At the beginning of the fourth period, Partner A contributes $500 to the partnership. The partnership records -$200 of realized loss + $100 *change* in unrealized gain = -$100 book loss.

Because all of the partners' aggregate account balances are positive, and the partnership realized a net loss, the partnership performs its tax allocation using Assumption 3.

According to Assumption 3, the partnership allocates the realized gain according to the partners' tax percentages (Partner A: 20%; Partner B: 67%; Partner C: 13%).

The following table shows the results of the period 4 tax allocation.

Period 4 Allocation	Partner A	Partner B	Partner C	Partnership
Beginning capital	$1,764	$4,116	$1,140	$7,020
Capital percentage	.25	.59	.16	
Beginning aggregate balance	$101	$434	$65	$600
Tax percentage	.20	.67	.13	
Adjusted book gain	-$20	-$67	-$13	-$100
Interim aggregate balance	$81	$367	$52	$500
Realized gain	-$40	-$134	-$26	-$200
Unrealized gain	$20	$67	$13	$100
Ending capital	$1,744	$4,049	$1,127	$6,920
Ending aggregate balance	$121	$501	$78	$700

Separating Long- and Short-Term Realized Gains

The previous examples of allocating gains showed all realized gains together in a single allocation item. As described in the section "Realized Gain (Loss) Items" on page 70, however, for U.S. tax purposes, partnerships must have separate allocation items for short- and long-term realized capital gains.

The partnership can aggregate long- and short-term capital gains in order to calculate book gains (and adjusted book gains) for economic allocations. In the tax allocation, the partnership allocates long- and short-term realized gains according to aggregate or tax percentages, or both, as dictated by the assumption the partnership meets that period. The partnership can then determine the percentage of the aggregate gains that each partner receives, and apply that percentage to determine each partner's allocation of short-term and long-term realized gains.

Example: A partnership has three partners, with aggregate account balances and tax percentages as follows.

Partner	Aggregate Balance	Tax Percentage
A	$200	29%
B	$200	29%
C	$300	42%
Total	**$700**	**100%**

The partnership records net $1,000 of realized gain, comprising -$200 of short-term loss, and $1,200 of long-term gain.

Because the realized gain exceeds the partnership's total aggregate balance, the partnership uses Assumption 2 to allocate the realized gain.

According to Assumption 2, the partnership allocates realized gain up to the partnership's total aggregate account balance ($700) according to the partners' aggregate balances, and then allocates the remainder ($300) according to their tax percentages. The partnership allocates this gain as follows.

Partner	Net Realized Gain for			Percentage of Aggregate Gains	Short-term Gain Allocation	Long-term Gain Allocation
	Aggregate Balance	Tax Percent	Total			
A	$200	.29 × $300 = $87	$287	28.7%	.287 × -$200 = -$57	.287 × -$1,200 = -$344
B	$200	.29 × $300 = $87	$287	28.7%	.287 × -$200 = -$57	.287 × -$1,200 = -$344
C	$300	.42 × $300 = $126	$426	42.6%	.426 × -$200 = -$86	.426 × -$1,200 = -$512
Total	**$700**	**$300**	**$1,000**		**-$200**	**$1,200**

ADV ENT PARTNER

Advent Partner uses the following items to allocate aggregate gains.

Advent Partner Item Name	Item Code
Short-Term Realized Gain	RGSTNHIA
Long-Term Realized Gain	RGLTNHIA
Unrealized Gain	UGNHIA

Aggregate, Full Netting

If a partnership uses aggregate, full netting methodology, it allocates realized and unrealized gains each period as follows.

1 Calculate each partner's book gain as:

$$\left(\text{Partnership realized gain} + \text{Partnership change in unrealized gain}\right) \times \text{Partner beginning capital percentage}$$

Note: For information on calculating the change in unrealized gains, see "Calculating the Change in Unrealized Gains" on page 112.

2 Add each partner's book gain (along with the partner's allocations of non-gain items) to the partner's capital account to determine the partner's ending capital balance.

3 Reallocate the appropriate amount of the limited partner's book gains to the general partner(s) *if:*

- The limited partner is subject to a performance fee charge this period.

  and

- The partner's ending capital balance exceeds its target capital.

For details, see Chapter 8, Reallocating Performance Incentives.

4 Allocate realized gain according to the partners' aggregate and tax percentages, as dictated by the aggregate assumption the partnership meets this period. For details, see "Understanding Aggregate Assumptions" on page 112.

5 Allocate the difference between the partner's adjusted book gains, and the partner's allocation of realized gain, as unrealized gain.

6 Add the partner's allocation of unrealized gain to the partner's beginning aggregate account balance to find the partner's ending aggregate account balance.

Aggregate, Full Netting: An Example

The following example shows a partnership's tax allocations for four periods. The partnership begins with one limited partner (A), who contributes $1,000, and one general partner (B), who contributes $3,000. The partnership reallocates 20% of the limited partner's appreciation to the general partner as a performance incentive each period.

Period 1

In period 1, the partnership records $20 of realized gain + $500 *change* in unrealized gain = $520 book gain.

Because one or more partners' aggregate account balances is zero, the partnership allocates according to Assumption 4.

According to Assumption 4, because neither of the partners has a positive aggregate account balance, the partnership allocates the realized gain according to the partners' tax percentages (capital percentages adjusted for performance fees) (Partner A: 20%; Partner B: 80%).

The following table shows the results of the period 1 tax allocation on the partners' capital and aggregate accounts.

Period 1 Allocation	Partner A	Partner B	Partnership
Beginning capital	$1,000	$3,000	$4,000
Capital percentage	.25	.75	
Beginning aggregate balance	$0	$0	$0
Tax percentage*	.20	.80	
Adjusted book gain	$104	$416	$520
Realized gain	$4	$16	$20
Unrealized gain	$100	$400	$500
Ending capital	$1,104	$3,416	$4,520
Ending aggregate balance	$100	$400	$500

*For limited partners, Tax percentage = Capital percentage × (1 – Payout percentage). Partnerships must infer general partners' tax percentages from the limited partners' percentages. For details, see "Calculating Tax Percentages and Carve-Outs" on page 169.

Period 2

In period 2, a third partner (C) joins the partnership with a contribution of $1,000. The partnership records $300 realized gain + $0 *change* in unrealized gain = $300 book gain.

Because one of the partners' (C) aggregate account balances is zero, the partnership performs its tax allocation using Assumption 4.

According to Assumption 4, the partnership allocates the realized gain to the partners with positive aggregate balances (A and B), according to their (realigned) aggregate percentages (Partner A: 20%; Partner B: 80%).

Because the partnership's total aggregate balance exceeds the realized gain, no gain remains to be allocated according to tax percentages.

The following table shows the results of the period 2 tax allocation.

Period 2 Allocation	Partner A	Partner B	Partner C	Partnership
Beginning capital	$1,104	$3,416	$1,000	$5,520
Capital percentage	.20	.62	.18	
Beginning aggregate balance	$100	$400	$0	$500
Aggregate percentage	.20	.80	.00	
Tax percentage	.16	.70	.14	
Adjusted book gains	$48	$210	$42	$300
Realized gain	$60	$240	$0	$300
Unrealized gain	-$12	-$30	$42	$0
Ending capital	$1,152	$3,626	$1,042	$5,820
Ending aggregate balance	$88	$370	$42	$500

Important: In a tax allocation according to straight tax percentages, Partner C would have received 14% × $300 = $42 of realized gain. Because Partner C has an aggregate account balance of zero, however, it receives no realized gain in the tax allocation. Instead:

- Partner C's book gain appears as unrealized gain in the tax allocation, even though the partnership did not record any unrealized gain this period.
- The difference between Partner A's and Partner B's adjusted book gains and tax allocations of realized gain appears as negative unrealized gain.

The total unrealized gain in the tax allocation is zero, however.

Period 3

In period 3, the partnership records $600 of realized gain + $100 *change* in unrealized gain = $700 book gain.

Because all of the partners' aggregate account balances are positive, and the realized gain ($600) exceeds the partnership's total aggregate balance ($500), the partnership uses Assumption 2 to perform its tax allocation.

According to Assumption 2, the partnership allocates realized gain up to the partnership's total aggregate account balance ($500) according to the partners' aggregate balances, then allocates the remainder ($100) according to their tax percentages (Partner A: 16%; Partner B: 70%; Partner C: 14%).

The following table shows the results of the period 3 tax allocation.

Period 3 Allocation	Partner A	Partner B	Partner C	Partnership
Beginning capital	$1,152	$3,626	$1,042	$5,820
Capital percentage	.20	.62	.17	
Beginning aggregate balance	$88	$370	$42	$500
Aggregate percentage	.18	.74	.08	
Tax percentage	.16	.70	.14	
Adjusted book gain	$112	$490	$98	$700
Realized gain for:				
aggregate balance	$88	$370	$42	$500
tax percentage	$16	$70	$14	$100
Total realized gain	$104	$440	$56	$600
Unrealized gain	$8	$50	$42	$100
Ending capital	$1,264	$4116	$1,140	$6,520
Ending aggregate balance	$96	$420	$84	$600

Period 4

At the beginning of period 4, Partner A contributes $500 to the partnership. The partnership records -$200 realized loss + $100 *change* in unrealized gain = -$100 book loss.

Because all of the partners' aggregate account balances are positive, and the partnership realized a net loss, the partnership uses Assumption 3 to perform its tax allocation.

According to Assumption 3, the partnership allocates the realized loss according to partners' tax percentages (Partner A: 20%; Partner B: 67%; Partner C: 13%).

The following table shows the results of the period 4 tax allocation.

Period 4 Allocation	Partner A	Partner B	Partner C	Partnership
Beginning capital	$1,764	$4,116	$1,140	$7,020
Capital percentage	.25	.59	.16	
Beginning aggregate balance	$96	$420	$84	$600
Aggregate percentage	.16	.70	.14	
Tax percentage	.20	.67	.13	
Adjusted book gain	-$20	-$67	-$13	-$100
Realized gain	-$40	-$134	-$26	-$200
Unrealized gain	$20	$67	$13	$100
Ending capital	$1,744	$4,049	$1,127	$6,920
Ending aggregate balance	$116	$487	$97	$700

Aggregate with Partial Netting

If a partnership uses aggregate, partial netting methodology, it segregates realized gains from realized losses, tracks separate memo account balances for each, and allocates each separately according to aggregate assumptions.

How Capital Changes Affect Aggregate Accounts

Aggregate accounts represent the historical unrealized gains in partners' capital accounts. The following sections describe how partners' reductions of their capital accounts through withdrawals and assignments affect their aggregate accounts.

How Total Withdrawals Affect Aggregate Accounts

When a partner makes a total cash withdrawal (that is, leaves the partnership, and does not receive its interest in the form of distributed securities), the partnership distributes the partner's aggregate account balance to the remaining partners, according to their current capital percentages, realigned to 100%. This increases the remaining partners' shares of unrealized gains, which in turn increases the taxable realized gains allocated to the partners when the partnership sells securities.

Example: A partnership has three partners with capital balances and percentages, and aggregate account balances, as follows.

Partner	Capital Account		Aggregate Account Balance
	Balance	Percentage	
A	$10,000	50%	$1,000
B	$5,000	25%	$500
C	$5,000	25%	$500

Partner C completely withdraws from the partnership, and is paid in cash. The partnership distributes Partner C's aggregate account balance to partners A and B as follows.

Partner	Original Capital Percent	Realigned Capital Percentage	Original Aggregate Balance	Distribution of Partner C's Aggregate Balance	New Aggregate Balance
A	50%	50% / 75% = 67%	$1,000	67% × $500 = $335	$1,335
B	25%	25% / 75% = 33%	$500	33% × $500 = $165	$665
Total	**75%**	**100%**	**$1,500**	**$500**	**$2,000**

Distributing Partner C's aggregate account balance does not affect the remaining partners' capital balances or percentages; it only assigns them more historical unrealized gains.

How Withdrawals In Excess of Tax Basis Affect Aggregate Accounts

Generally, in aggregate partnerships, a partner's tax basis is its capital balance minus its memo account balance. If a partner withdraws capital in excess of its tax basis, both the withdrawing partner and the remaining partners are ultimately taxed on the withdrawn unrealized gain. If the partnership liquidates securities to pay out the withdrawing partner in cash, or when it ultimately sells the securities in which the withdrawing partner had a historical interest, those taxable gains are allocated to the partners. Therefore, the partner's withdrawal effectively increases the tax burden on the remaining partners. Chapter 10, Understanding Distributions and Redemptions, describes the ways that partnerships can minimize this effect, as defined in their partnership agreement.

ADVENT PARTNER

How Advent Partner Handles Withdrawals in Excess of Tax Basis

If a partner withdraws capital in excess of its tax basis, both the withdrawing partner and the remaining partners are ultimately taxed on the withdrawn unrealized gain. Advent Partner offers three strategies that can counteract this effect.

- **Enable 754 Election for the Partnership.** This allows the partnership to adjust the tax basis of security positions by allocating realized gain based on non-realigned percentages, and putting the amount that would have been allocated to the withdrawn partner into a non-taxable item that is an Item J(c) reconciling item.
- **Direct Realized Gains to the Partner.** This allows the partnership to allocate realized gains to the withdrawing partner in place of unrealized gains that the partner would otherwise have withdrawn. The unrealized gain is then allocated based on current ownership percentages.
- **Deliver Out Appreciated Securities to the Partner.** This allows the partner to withdraw with securities rather than cash. Since the securities leave the partnership, the remaining partners will not be taxed on realized gain when they are sold, but rather when they either withdraw in excess of tax basis or when the partnership liquidates, whichever comes first.

How Partial Withdrawals Affect Aggregate Accounts

When a partner makes a partial cash withdrawal, the partnership can choose to distribute the partner's aggregate account balance to the remaining partners, according to their current capital percentages, realigned to whatever percentage was withdrawn. Some partnerships do not distribute aggregate account balances on partial withdrawals.

How Assignments Affect Aggregate Accounts

When one partner assigns a portion of its interest in the partnership to another partner, the assignment includes a proportionate amount of the unrealized gains in the assigning partner's capital account.

Example: Partner A has a capital account balance of $1,000, of which $600 is unrealized gains. Partner A assigns 5% ($50) of its capital to Partner B. This capital assignment must include .05 × $600 = $30 of unrealized gains.

If the partnership uses an aggregate methodology to allocate gains, the assignment also includes a proportionate amount of the assigning partner's aggregate account balance.

Example: Partner A has a capital account balance of $1,000, and an aggregate account balance of $600. Partner A assigns 5% of its interest in the partnership to partner B. This assignment comprises: .05 × $1,000 = $50 of Partner A's capital account balance; and .05 × $600 = $30 of Partner A's aggregate account balance.

Allocating Aggregate Section 1256 Gains

For tax purposes, partnerships mark-to-market Section 1256 contracts each period, and allocate the gain as if realized. Because partnerships never allocate any unrealized gain for Section 1256 contracts, these securities do not affect aggregate account balances. Partnerships allocate the gains from Section 1256 contracts according to partners' current tax percentages.

ADV ENT PARTNER

How Advent Partner Allocates Section 1256 Gains

When Advent Partner performs a tax allocation of gains from Section 1256 contracts the partnership *holds*, it allocates three tax adjustments.

- An adjustment to "reverse out" the economic allocation of unrealized gain from Section 1256 contracts.
- An adjustment to assign 60% of the contract's gain as 60% long-term realized gain.

- An adjustment to assign 40% of the contract's gain as short-term realized gain.

When the partnership *sells* the contract, Advent Partner allocates:

- All of the contract's realized gain (60% long-term, 40% short-term).
- A negative adjustment to realized gain for the amount of unrealized gain allocated in previous periods as realized gain (60% long-term, 40% short-term).

This effectively allocates only the contract's gain in the period the partnership sells it (the current period).

Advent Partner uses the following items to allocate Section 1256 gains.

Advent Partner Item Name	Item Code
Short-Term Realized Gain (1256 contracts)	RGST56A
Long-Term Realized Gain (1256 contracts)	RGLT56A
Unrealized Gain (1256 contracts) (*economic allocation only*)	UG56A

Example: A partnership has two partners, A and B, with equal interests.

1 At the end of period 1, the partnership records $100 of unrealized gain from Section 1256 securities, and allocates it as follows.

Section 1256 Gains	Partner A	Partner B	Total
Unrealized gain	$50	$50	$100
Unrealized gain adjustment	-$50	-$50	-$100
Short-term realized gain	$20	$20	$40
Long-term realized gain	$30	$30	$60

2 In period 2, the partnership records $200 of realized gain from Section 1256 securities, and allocates it as follows.

Section 1256 Gains	Partner A	Partner B	Total
Short-term realized gain	$40	$40	$80
Short-term realized gain adjustment (for period 1 short-term realized gain)	-$20	-$20	-$40
Net short-term realized gain	$20	$20	$40
Long-term realized gain	$60	$60	$120
Long-term realized gain adjustment (for period 1 long-term realized gain)	-$30	-$30	-$60
Net long-term realized gain	$30	$30	$60

Notice that the net realized gain allocated in period 2 ($40 short-term + $60 long-term = $100) matches the change in gain in period 2 ($200 period 2 realized gain – $100 period 1 unrealized gain).

Allocating Aggregate Hot Issue Gains

If a partnership uses an aggregate methodology to allocate capital gains, it must use the same methodology to allocate hot issue gains. (For more information about hot issues, see "Allocating Hot Issue Gains" on page 96.) To do this, it must set up separate hot issue aggregate accounts for each partner. The partnership follows the aggregate assumptions to allocate hot issue realized gains, using the non-restricted partners':

- Hot issue aggregate percentages.
- Tax percentages, realigned to 100%.

The partnership records unrealized hot issue gains from the tax allocation only in the non-restricted partners' hot issue aggregate accounts.

When a partner withdraws from the partnership, the partnership redistributes the partner's hot issue aggregate account balance only to the remaining partners who participate in hot issue gains, according to their hot issue tax percentages (realigned to 100%). For details, see "How Total Withdrawals Affect Aggregate Accounts" on page 133.

Note: General partners who are "restricted" from hot issue gains, but receive performance fee reallocations from limited partners' hot issue gains, must also have hot issue aggregate accounts so that the partnership can calculate their tax allocations of realized gain. The partnership:

1. Uses the non-restricted limited partners' realigned capital percentages to calculate their hot issue book gains.
2. Reduces the limited partners' hot issue book gains by the performance fee (if applicable).
3. Uses this amount as the general partner's hot issue book gain.
4. Uses the partners' hot issue aggregate accounts and realigned tax percentages in the assumptions to allocate realized gains.

For details, see "Hot Issue Gains" on page 176.

If the partnership agreement excludes a restricted general partner from a performance fee on hot issue gains, the partnership simply uses the non-restricted partners' realigned capital percentages to determine their hot issue book gains. The partnership also uses their hot issue aggregate and realigned capital (rather than tax) percentages in the assumptions to allocate realized gains.

How Advent Partner Allocates Hot Issue Gains

ADV ENT PARTNER

Advent Partner uses the following items to allocate hot issue gains.

Advent Partner Item Name	Item Code
Short-Term Realized Gain (Hot Issue)	RGSTHIA
Long-Term Realized Gain (Hot Issue)	RGLTHIA
Unrealized Gain (Hot Issue)	UGHIA

Example: A partnership has three partners: A (the general partner), B, and C (the limited partners). General Partner A is excluded from hot issue gains, but receives a 20% performance reallocation from all items (including hot issue gains) each period. The partnership uses the aggregate with book gains, full netting methodology.

In period 1, the partnership records $100 realized hot issue gain + $500 *change* in unrealized hot issue gain = $600 hot issue book gain.

1 The partnership allocates the $600 of hot issue book gain to the limited partners, according to their economic percentages, realigned to 100%.

Allocation	Partner A	Partner B	Partner C	Partnership
Beginning capital	$1,200	$3,500	$1,000	$5,700
Capital percentage	21%	61%	18%	
Beginning hot issue aggregate balance	$100	$200	$100	$400
Realigned capital percentage *(excluding General Partner A)*	00%	77%	23%	
Hot issue book gain	Excluded	$462	$138	$600

2 The partnership allocates 20% of each limited partner's book gain as a performance fee to General Partner A, and calculates the partners' interim aggregate account balances.

Allocation	Partner A	Partner B	Partner C	Partnership
Beginning capital	$1,200	$3,500	$1,000	$5,700
Capital percentage	21%	61%	18%	
Beginning hot issue aggregate balance	$100	$200	$100	$400
Realigned capital percentage *(excluding General Partner A)*	00%	77%	23%	
Hot issue book gain	Excluded	$462	$138	$600
Adjusted hot issue book gain *(including General Partner A's 20% performance fee)*	$120	$370	$110	$600

3 The partnership calculates the partners' interim aggregate account balances and percentages.

Allocation	Partner A	Partner B	Partner C	Partnership
Beginning capital	$1,200	$3,500	$1,000	$5,700
Capital percentage	21%	61%	18%	
Beginning hot issue aggregate balance	$100	$200	$100	$400
Adj. hot issue book gain	$120	$370	$110	$600
Interim hot issue aggregate balance	$220	$570	$210	$1,000
Interim hot issue aggregate percentage	22%	57%	21%	

4 Because all of the partners' hot issue interim aggregate account balances are positive, and the total aggregate balance exceeds the amount of realized gain, the partnership allocates using Assumption 1. According to assumption 1, the partnership uses the partners' aggregate percentages to allocate the realized gain.

The following table shows the results of the tax allocation.

Allocation	Partner A	Partner B	Partner C	Partnership
Beginning capital	$1,200	$3,500	$1,000	$5,700
Capital percentage	.21	.61	.18	
Beginning hot issue aggregate balance	$100	$200	$100	$400
Adj. hot issue book gain	$120	$370	$110	$600
Interim hot issue aggregate balance	$220	$570	$210	$1,000
Interim hot issue aggregate percentage	22%	57%	21%	
Realized hot issue gain	$22	$57	$21	$100
Unrealized hot issue gain	$98	$313	$89	$500
Ending hot issue aggregate balance	$198	$513	$189	$900
Ending capital	$1,320	$3,870	$1,110	$6,300

Ceiling Rule: Aggregate Allocation

According to Treasury Regulation Section 1.704-3(b)(1), a partnership cannot allocate gain or loss on a property to the partners that exceeds the gain or loss recognized on that property by the partnership overall. (This rule is referred to as the "ceiling rule.") Aggregate allocation can theoretically produce violations of the ceiling rule, but it is unlikely because:

- Aggregate allocation takes into account the partnership's appreciation or depreciation as a whole, rather than the appreciation or depreciation of individual properties.
- If a partner joins a partnership in a period when the partnership records a loss (the most common situation that creates a ceiling rule violation), aggregate methodologies allocate the difference between the partner's book and tax gains as *unrealized*, rather than realized, gain. For examples, see the :
  - Aggregate, Full Netting example, "Period 2" on page 130.
  - Aggregate With Book Gains, Full Netting example, "Period 2" on page 123.

7 Allocating Layered Gains

Chapter 5 described how partnerships allocate each period's unrealized gains and losses on their securities to the partners, so that the partnership can allocate realized gains according to the partners' historical interests in the partnership's investments. This chapter describes one of the methodologies approved by the IRS for allocating realized gains, tax lot layering, including:

- ✔ How to allocate realized gains using tax lot layering methodology.
- ✔ How capital withdrawals and assignments affect layered unrealized gains.
- ✔ How to allocate gains from Section 1256.
- ✔ How to allocate gains from hot issue securities.
- ✔ How the "ceiling rule" affects layering allocation.

In This Chapter

Understanding Tax Lot Layering

The tax lot layering (or "tracking") methodology assumes that each partner purchases a *pro rata* share of each security position owned by the partnership at the time when the partner joins the partnership. During each subsequent period that the partnership holds the security, and that partner remains in the partnership, the partnership tracks the change in each security's market value (appreciation or depreciation). This creates historical *layers* of unrealized gain for each security in the partnership's portfolio, one layer for each period that the partnership holds the security.

In addition to tracking the change in the security's market value each period, the partnership also tracks each partner's tax percentage during each period. When the partnership closes (sells or covers) the position, the partnership allocates the realized gain or loss to the partners according to their historical tax percentages in each layer of the security's unrealized gain.

Tax Lot Layering: An Example

A partnership with two partners buys 100 shares of a security at $10. The partners each begin with a 50% interest in the partnership.

1 In the first period, the security's price rises $2 to $12, for an unrealized gain of $2 / share × 100 shares = $200. The partnership allocates the unrealized gain in this first layer as follows.

Partner	Gain Layer	Period 1 Change in Unrealized Gain
A	1	$100
B	1	$100
	Total	**$200**

2 In the second period, a third partner (C) joins the partnership, changing the partners' capital percentages to: A: 33%; B: 33%; C: 34%. The security's price rises $1 to $13, for an unrealized gain of $1 / share × 100 shares = $100. The partnership allocates this unrealized gain in the second layer as follows.

Partner	Gain Layer	Period 1 Change in Unrealized Gain	Period 2 Change in Unrealized Gain	Total Layers
A	1	$100		$100
	2		$33	$33
B	1	$100		$100
	2		$33	$33
C	1			
	2		$34	$34
Total		**$200**	**$100**	**$300**

3 In the third period, the partnership sells the security for $13/share, for a realized (capital) gain of ($13 price – $10 cost) × 100 shares = $300. The partnership allocates this gain as follows.

Partner	Gain Layer	Period 1 Change in Unrealized Gain	Period 2 Change in Unrealized Gain	Period 3 Realized Gain
A	1	$100		$100
	2		$33	$33
			Partner A Total	$133
B	1	$100		$100
	2		$33	33
			Partner B Total	$133
C	1			
	2		$34	$34
			Partner C Total	$34
Total		**$200**	**$100**	**$300**

Notice that the partnership:

1 Allocates the first layer of gain (($12 period 1 price – $10 cost) × 100 shares = $200 gain) to partners A and B according to their historical tax percentages in period 1 (50% each).

2 Allocates the second layer ($13 period 2 price – $12 period 1 price × 100 shares = $100 gain) to the partners according to their historical tax percentages in period 2 (33% to partners A and B, 34% to Partner C).

3 Totals the partners' layers of gain (including the current layer) to determine how to allocate the $300 realized gain ($13 proceeds – $10 cost × 100 shares = $300 realized gain).

If the partnership had allocated the realized gain according to the partnership's current tax percentages in the period when it sold the security, their allocations would have been: A: $100; B: $100; C: $100.

ADVENT PARTNER

Advent Partner allocates each period's layers of unrealized gains to the partners. When the partnership closes a security position, it must "reverse out" these unrealized gains by allocating each partner a negative amount of unrealized gain equal to the total of their historical layers of unrealized gain in that position, excluding the current layer.

Example: In the prior example, Advent Partner would have allocated $133 of unrealized gain to Partner A's capital account ($100 in period 1, and $33 in period 2). When the partnership sold the security in period 3, it would have allocated $133 of unrealized loss to Partner A, to "reverse out" this unrealized gain, at the same time that it allocated the partner $133 of realized gain.

Separating Long- and Short-Term Realized Gains

The previous example of allocating gains shows realized gain as a single allocation item. As described in the section "Realized Gain (Loss) Items" on page 70, for U.S. tax purposes, partnerships must have separate allocation items for short- and long-term realized capital gains.

Because layering methodology tracks gains by security tax lot, the partnership can assign each realized gain transaction to long- and short-term gain allocation items as appropriate for its holding period.

ADV ENT PARTNER

Advent Partner uses the following items to allocate layered gains.

Advent Partner Item Name	Item Code
Short-Term Realized Gain	RGSTNHIL
Long-Term Realized Gain	RGLTNHIL
Unrealized Gain	UGNHIL

How Capital Changes Affect Layered Gains

The following sections describe how partners' reductions of their capital accounts through withdrawals and assignments affect their shares of historical gain layers.

How Withdrawals Affect Layered Gains

If a partner withdraws completely from the partnership, its final withdrawal includes its share of the unrealized gain in securities the partnership holds. When the partnership sells the securities, however, the realized gains include both the remaining partners' interests and the interest of the partner who left the partnership.

In order to allocate the realized gain that would have been allocated to the withdrawn partner, the partnership must distribute the withdrawn partner's share of the historical layers of unrealized gain to the remaining partners, according to their tax percentages in each period. It does this by:

1. *Realigning* the remaining partners' tax percentages to 100% for each period that the withdrawn partner was in the partnership.
2. *Allocating* the historical layers in each period according to the realigned percentages (when it closes a position that it held while the withdrawn partner was in the partnership).

Example: A partnership has three partners with the following tax percentages.

Partner	Period 1	Period 2
A	25%	33%
B	35%	33%
C	40%	34%

Partner C withdraws at the end of period 2. The partnership realigns the remaining partners' tax percentages as follows.

Partner	Period 1	Period 2
A	25% / 60% = 42%	33% / 66% = 50%
B	35% / 60% = 58%	33% / 66% = 50%

When the partnership closes any security positions it held during periods 1 or 2, it allocates the layers of gain for those periods to partners A and B according to their realigned percentages.

Important: The withdrawing partner is generally taxed on withdrawal in excess of its tax basis as capital gains. If the partnership liquidates securities to pay out the withdrawing partner in cash, or when it ultimately sells the securities in which the withdrawing partner had a historical interest, those taxable gains are allocated to the partners. Therefore, the partner's withdrawal effectively increases the tax burden on the remaining partners. Chapter 10, Understanding Distributions and Redemptions, describes several ways that partnerships can minimize this effect, as defined in their partnership agreement.

How Assignments of Interest Affect Layered Gains

When one partner assigns a portion of its interest in a partnership to another partner, the assigned capital must include a proportionate amount of the unrealized gains in the assigning partner's capital account. To do this, the partnership can update both partners' historical tax percentages in each period to reflect the assignment. When the partnership allocates realized gains according to the historical layers of unrealized gains, the unrealized gains will reflect the assignment.

Example: A partnership has three partners with equal interests in the partnership. Partner A has a capital account balance of $1,000, of which $60 is unrealized gains in security XYZ.

Partner	Layer	Period 1 Change in Unrealized Gain	Period 2 Change in Unrealized Gain	Total Layers
A	1	$40		$40
	2		$20	$20
B	1	$40		$40
	2		$20	$20
C	1	$40		$40
	2		$20	$20
Total		**$120**	**$100**	**$400**

At the end of period 2, Partner A assigns 5% ($50) of its capital to Partner B. This capital assignment must include 5% × $60 = $3 of unrealized gains in security XYZ. The partnership changes Partner A's and Partner B's historical percentages in the partnership in periods 1 and 2 to reflect the assignment as follows.

Partner	Tax Percentage Before Assignment	Assignment (as a Percentage of Partnership Interest)	Tax Percentage after Assignment
A	33.3%	33.3% × 5% = 1.65%	33.3% – 1.65% = 31.65%
B	33.3%		33.3% + 1.65% = 34.95%
C	33.3%		

The partners' new layers in security XYZ are:

Partner	Layer	Period 1 Change in Unrealized Gain	Period 2 Change in Unrealized Gain	Total Layers
A	1	$38		$38
	2		$19	$19
B	1	$42		$42
	2		$21	$21
C	1	$40		$40
	2		$20	$20
Total		**$120**	**$100**	**$400**

Notice that the $60 – $57 = $3 change in Partner A's unrealized gain matches the 5% assignment of Partner A's $60 of unrealized gains in the security.

Allocating Layered Section 1256 Gains

For tax purposes, partnerships mark-to-market Section 1256 contracts each period, and allocate the gain as if realized. Because partnerships do not allocate any unrealized gain for Section 1256 contracts in the tax allocation, these securities do not have layers of unrealized gain. Partnerships allocate the gains from Section 1256 contracts according to partners' current tax percentages.

ADVENT PARTNER

How Advent Partner Allocates Section 1256 Gains

When Advent Partner performs a tax allocation of gains from Section 1256 securities the partnership *holds*, it allocates three tax adjustments.

- An adjustment to "reverse out" the economic allocation of unrealized gain from Section 1256 contracts.
- An adjustment to assign 60% of the contract's gain as long-term realized gain.
- An adjustment to assign 40% of the contract's gain as short-term realized gain.

When the partnership *sells* the contract, Advent Partner allocates:

- ❖ All of the contract's realized gain (60% long-term, 40% short-term).
- ❖ A negative adjustment to realized gain for the amount of unrealized gain allocated in previous periods as realized gain (60% long-term, 40% short-term).

This effectively allocates only the contract's gain in the period when the partnership sells it (the current period).

Advent Partner uses the following items to allocate Section 1256 gains.

Advent Partner Item Name	Item Code
Short-Term Realized Gain (1256 contracts)	RGST56L
Long-Term Realized Gain (1256 contracts)	RGLT56L
Unrealized Gain (1256 contracts) (*economic allocation only*)	UG56L

Example: A partnership has three partners with tax percentages: LP1: 25%; LP2: 25%; GP: 50%.

1 At the end of period 1, the partnership records $200 of unrealized gain from Section 1256 contracts, and allocates it as follows.

Section 1256 Gains	LP1	LP2	GP	Total
Unrealized gain	$50	$50	$100	$200
Unrealized gain adjustment	-$50	-$50	-$100	-$200
Short-term realized gain	$20	$20	$40	$80
Long-term realized gain	$30	$30	$60	$120

2 In period 2, the partnership records $300 of realized gain from Section 1256 contracts, and allocates it as follows.

Section 1256 Gains	LP1	LP2	GP	Total
Short-term realized gain	$30	$30	$60	$120
Short-term realized gain adjustment (for period 1 short-term realized gain)	-$20	-$20	-$40	-$80
Net short-term realized gain	$10	$10	$20	$40
Long-term realized gain	$45	$45	$90	$180
Long-term realized gain adjustment (for period 1 short-term realized gain)	-$30	-$30	-$60	-$120
Net long-term realized gain	$15	$15	$30	$60

Notice that the net realized gain allocated in period 2 ($40 short-term + $60 long-term = $100) matches the change in gain in period 2 ($300 period 2 realized gain – $200 period 1 unrealized gain).

Allocating Layered Hot Issue Gains

If the partnership uses the tax lot layering methodology to allocate gains, it uses the tax percentages of the partners who participate in hot issue securities, realigned to 100%, to calculate each layer of each hot issue security's gain.

Tip: If the partnership agreement also excludes the general partner from a performance fee on hot issue gains, the partnership's tax allocation of hot issue gains uses the participating partners' realigned capital (rather than tax) percentages.

ADV ENT PARTNER

How Advent Partner Allocates Layered Hot Issue Gains

Advent Partner uses the following items to allocate hot issue gains.

Advent Partner Item Name	Item Code
Short-Term Realized Gain (Hot Issues)	RGSTHIL
Long-Term Realized Gain (Hot Issues)	RGLTHIL
Unrealized Gain (Hot Issues)	UGHIL

Example: A partnership has three partners with the following tax percentages.

Partner	Period 1	Period 2
Limited1	25%	33%
Limited2	35%	33%
General	40%	34%

The general partner does not participate in hot issue gains, but receives a 20% performance fee from all items (including hot issue gains). The partnership realigns the limited partners' tax percentages as follows.

Partner	Period 1	Period 2
Limited1	25% / 60% = 42%	33% / 66% = 50%
LImited2	35% / 60% = 58%	33% / 66% = 50%

In period 1, the partnership purchases 100 shares of a hot issue security at $10/share. The security's price is $12 at the end of period 1 ($200 change in unrealized gain), and $13 at the end of period 2 ($100 change in unrealized gain), at which point the partnership sells the security ($300 of realized gain). The partnership allocates the realized gain as follows

Partner	Layer	Period 1 Unrealized Gain	Period 1 Adjusted Unrealized Gain	Period 2 Unrealized Gain	Period 2 Adjusted Unrealized Gain	Realized Gain
Limited1	1	$84	$67			$67
			(20% perf. fee = $17)			
	2			$50	$40	$40
					(20% Perf. fee = $10)	
					Limited1 Total	$107
Limited2	1	$116	$93			$93
			(20% perf. fee = $23)			
	2			$50	$40	$40
					(20% Perf. fee = $10)	
					Limited2 Total	$133
General (Perf. Fee Only)	1	Excluded	$17 + $23 = $40			$40
	2			Excluded	$10 + $10 = $20	$20
					General Total	$60
Total		**$200**	**$200**	**$100**	**$100**	**$300**

Ceiling Rule: Tax Lot Layering Allocation

According to Treasury Regulation Section 1.704-3(b)(1), a partnership cannot allocate gain or loss on a property to the partners that exceeds the gain recognized on that property by the partnership overall. (This rule is referred to as the "ceiling rule.") Layering allocation can produce violations of the ceiling rule, most commonly when some partners receive economic losses, and others receive economic gains.

Important: Partnerships that use tax lot layering are more likely to violate the ceiling rule, because they allocate on a security-by-security basis, rather than allocating the partnership's net appreciation. An opinion on this issue, however, is that if at least one security in the partnership's portfolio exceeds the net gain or loss to be allocated to a given partner, such an allocation does not violate the ceiling rule. Partnerships should consult the appropriate professionals concerning this issue.

Example: A partnership has 2 partners, A and B, with equal economic percentages.

1 The partnership buys 100 shares of a security at $10/share. At the end of the first period, the security's price has risen to $30, for an unrealized gain of ($30/share closing price – $10/share original cost) × 100 shares = $2,000.

		Period 1
Partner	**Layer**	**UGain**
A	1	$1,000
B	1	$1,000
Total for layer		**$2,000**

2 At the beginning of the second period, Partner C joins the partnership. All three partners have equal economic percentages. The security's price drops to $12, at which point the partnership sells it. The realized loss in period 2 is ($12/share sale price – $30/share previous closing price) × 100 shares = $1,800.

Partner	Layer	Period 1 UGain	Period 2 RGain
A	1	$1,000	$1,000
	2		-$600
		Partner A Total	$400
B	1	$1,000	$1,000
	2		-$600
		Partner B Total	$400
C	2		-$600
Total for layer		**$2,000**	**$200**

The partnership records a total of $200 of realized gain, but allocates Partner C $600 of realized loss. Because Partner C received more loss than the partnership as a whole, this allocation violates the ceiling rule.

Reallocating/ Charging Performance Fees

General partners of investment partnerships generally receive compensation based upon the partnership's performance, called a performance incentive reallocation or performance fee. This chapter describes:

- ✔ When partnerships can charge performance fees.
- ✔ How partnerships define their appreciation goals.
- ✔ How to calculate partners' reallocation amounts.
- ✔ How to include performance fees in the tax allocation.
- ✔ Special considerations for performance fees in offshore funds.

In This Chapter

Understanding Performance Incentive Reallocations

General partners of investment partnerships generally receive compensation based upon the partnership's performance. If the partnership's performance meets the provisions for incentive compensation in the limited partnership agreement, the partnership "reallocates" to the general partner a portion of the appreciation allocated to the limited partners.

As described in previous chapters, the performance incentive reallocation (often called a "performance fee") is not a separate allocation. Instead, it is embedded in the tax allocation. The partnership decreases the capital percentages of the limited partners subject to the reallocation, and increases the general partner's capital percentage, to "reallocate" the limited partners' appreciation to the general partner. The adjusted percentages used in the tax allocation are called *tax percentages*.

Partnerships usually perform their performance incentive reallocation at the end of the fiscal year. If a limited partner withdraws capital at an interim date, however, the partnership generally charges the withdrawing partner at that time, based on its net appreciation on the date of its withdrawal.

Partnerships generally include a performance reallocation structure in their partnership agreement. The sections in this chapter describe how to set up and implement performance fees as follows.

For information about	See
When partnerships can charge performance fees	"Selecting Reallocation Dates" on page 159.
How partnerships define their appreciation goals	"Calculating Target Capital" on page 163.
How to calculate partners' reallocation amounts	"Calculating Tax Percentages and Carve-Outs" on page 169.
How to perform the tax reallocation	"Reallocating Profit Items" on page 173.

Note: Although most partnerships structure their incentive compensation as a reallocation, some structure it as a fee payment.

Benefits of reallocation-structured incentive compensation	Drawbacks of fee-structured incentive compensation
❖ Reallocated appreciation not included in the limited partner's income in the year when it is charged. ❖ No specific payment must be made for the fee to be deductible.	❖ Limited deductibility for the limited partners.
❖ Reallocated appreciation retains its tax character (short-term, long-term, ordinary, or non-taxable (unrealized).	❖ General partner taxed on the fee as ordinary income.
	❖ Drain on the partnership's cash to pay the fee.

Note: Except where noted, this chapter assumes that partnerships apply a single performance fee structure to all of the limited partners, and that a single general partner receives the performance reallocation. Partnerships can, however, apply different structures to each partner, have several general partners, or can allocate a portion of the performance fee to selected limited partners (called "special limited partners"), as defined in their partnership agreement.

Selecting Reallocation Dates

The first step in structuring a partnership's performance incentive reallocation is to determine when to charge the fee. The partnership should consider the following factors.

✔ How frequently during the year the partnership performs the reallocation.

✔ Whether the partnership determines reallocation dates based on the partnership's fiscal year, or the date the partner entered the partnership.

ADVENT PARTNER

Advent Partner can also estimate fees for break periods when the partnership does not charge a fee, in order to provide more accurate tax estimates to the limited partners. For more information, see "Estimating Performance Fees" on page 162.

Frequency

In order to prepare its Schedule K-1s, a partnership must perform a final allocation for tax purposes at the end of its fiscal year (typically 12/31). Once the partnership closes the period ending the fiscal year, it cannot reallocate appreciation later to charge a performance fee. Therefore, most partnerships charge their performance fee as part of the allocation for the last period of their fiscal year.

Limited partnership agreements can also specify other performance incentive reallocation dates, such as quarterly, monthly, or at every break period. Because performance fees are part of an allocation of appreciation, however, the charge date will correspond with a break period, even if no other capital changes occur on that date, because charging the fee changes the partners' interests in the partnership.

Twelve Month Rule

The partnership agreement can specify different performance fee charge dates for each partner, based on its entry date into the partnership. Previously, the Investment Adviser's Act of 1940 permitted registered investment advisers (RIAs) to charge performance incentives only over periods not less than twelve months (the "Twelve Month" rule). The Act has been amended, however, so that a partner can be charged at any time if certain criteria are met, but some funds choose not to charge partners for their first twelve months.

Important: The Twelve Month rule may still apply to partnerships created before the Act was amended because of provisions in the partnership agreement. Partnerships should consult the appropriate professionals to determine their status.

Charging Performance Fees For Assignments

When a partner assigns a portion of its interest in the partnership to another partner, the partnership can choose to charge the assigning partner a performance fee, even if the partner is not scheduled to be charged a fee that period. This ensures that:

- ❖ The general partner receives all of the fee due for the appreciation allocated to the assigning partner, before it reduces that partner's capital account.
- ❖ The assigning partner, rather than the receiving partner, is charged on the assigned appreciation.

The performance fee charge takes place before the assignment takes effect. If the partner makes the assignment at the:

- ❖ *Beginning of the period*, the partnership reallocates the periods from the last performance charge to the period before the current period.
- ❖ *End of the period*, the partnership reallocates the periods from the last performance charge through the current period.

Charging Performance Fees For Withdrawals

When a partner withdraws a portion of its capital from its capital account, the partnership can choose to charge the withdrawing partner a performance fee, even if the partner is not scheduled to be charged a fee that period. This ensures that the general partner receives all of the fee due for the appreciation allocated to the withdrawing partner, before it reduces that partner's capital account.

The performance fee charge takes place before the withdrawal takes effect. If the partner makes the withdrawal at the:

- ❖ *Beginning of the period*, the partnership reallocates the periods from the last performance charge to the period before the current period.
- ❖ *End of the period*, the partnership reallocates the periods from the last performance charge through the current period.

Estimating Performance Fees

When a partnership charges a performance fee, it reallocates appreciation from the limited partners' capital accounts to the general partner's account. Partnerships can also estimate performance fees on dates when they do not charge the partners, for example, if a partner requests information for filing estimated tax returns.

To estimate partners' performance fees, Advent Partner calculates two capital balances for the partner each period that it estimates the fee.

- **Economic capital balance:** The partner's capital balance according to economic allocations. This balance is not adjusted for performance fees, layering or aggregate allocation of realized gains, or other tax issues.
- **Tax capital balance:** The partner's capital balance adjusted for estimated performance fees, layering or aggregate allocation of realized gains, and other tax issues.

After the partner is actually charged a fee, its economic and tax capital balances match.

Profit Since Last Charge vs. Current Year's Profit

Partnerships charge performance fees on a partner's net appreciation since the last performance fee charge. However, partnerships cannot reallocate appreciation from one year into the subsequent year.

If the partnership does not charge a partner during the last period of the fiscal year (because the partner did not meet its target capital; for details, see "Calculating Target Capital" on page 163), the next time the partnership charges the partner, it does so based on the appreciation allocated to the partner since the last performance fee charge, including appreciation from the prior year. However, the partnership can only reallocate the performance fee from the current year's appreciation. The reallocation amount, as a percentage of the current year's appreciation, may be higher or lower than the partner's payout percentage defined in the partnership agreement.

Example: A partner joins a partnership on 4/1/1998. The partnership charges a 20% performance fee after partners have been in the partnership for twelve months. The partnership's fiscal year ends on 12/31, but the new partner is not subject to a performance fee until 3/31/1999. (For details, see "Calculating Tax Percentages and Carve-Outs" on page 169.) The partner earns appreciation, and pays a performance fee, as follows.

Appreciation			Performance Fee (3/31/99)	
4/1/98 to 12/31/98	1/1/99 to 3/31/99	Total	Payout Percentage	Fee Amount
$50	$50	$100	× 20% =	$20

The partnership, however, must reallocate the $20 performance fee out of 1999's appreciation of $50. Therefore, the performance fee charged on 3/31/1999 is $20 / $50 = 40% of the appreciation out of which the partnership reallocates the performance fee.

Calculating Target Capital

A partner's *target capital* is the amount that the partner's capital account balance must exceed, after the period's capital changes, for the partner to be subject to a performance fee. A partner's target capital calculation is affected by the following factors in the partnership's performance fee structure.

- ✔ The partner's hurdle rate (also called a "benchmark").
- ✔ Whether the partnership applies a highwater mark (also called a "loss carryforward" provision) to the partner's capital account.
- ✔ The partner's capital changes.

The following sections describe how each of these factors affects target capital calculations.

- ❖ "Applying Hurdle Rates" on page 164
- ❖ "Applying Highwater Marks" on page 165
- ❖ "Applying Highwater Marks and Hurdle Rates" on page 167

- "How Contributions Affect Highwater Marks" on page 167
- "How Withdrawals Affect Highwater Marks" on page 167
- "How Assignments Affect Highwater Marks" on page 168

Note: If a partnership applies neither a hurdle rate nor a highwater mark, the partner is subject to a performance fee whenever it earns positive appreciation. Therefore, the partner's target capital equals the partner's beginning economic capital balance, adjusted for any beginning capital changes in the period.

> **Example:** A partner has a capital balance of $1,000. If the partnership applies neither a hurdle rate nor a highwater mark, and the partner does not make any capital changes, the amount of the partner's capital balance over $1,000 on the next charge date is subject to a performance fee charge.

Applying Hurdle Rates

A *hurdle rate* (also called a "benchmark") is the amount of appreciation a partner must earn, as a percentage of the partner's capital account balance, for the partner to be subject to a performance fee. The partner's target capital is its beginning capital balance, adjusted for capital changes during the year, plus the hurdle rate amount.

$$(\text{Beginning capital balance} \pm \text{Beginning capital changes}) \times \left(1 + \text{Hurdle rate}\right)$$

Example: A partnership applies a 5% annual hurdle rate. If a partner begins the year with a $1,000 capital balance, the partner's target capital is $1,050.

Some partnership agreements state that the hurdle rate applied each year is "mutually exclusive" of any other year. Other partnership agreements require the hurdle rate to compound each year.

Example: A partnership charges a performance fee with a 5% annual hurdle rate. If a partner begins the year with a $1,000 capital balance, the partner's target capital is $1,050. The partner ends the year with a capital balance of $900.

- ❖ If the partnership compounds the hurdle rate, the partner's target capital for the next year is $1,050 + 5% = $1,102.50.

  Note: If the partnership does not apply a highwater mark, the partner's target capital is $900 + 5% = $945.

- ❖ If the partnership uses mutually exclusive hurdle rates, the partner's target capital remains at $1,050.

If the partnership charges performance fees more than once per year, use the following formula to calculate a partner's target capital on each date when the partnership can charge the partner a fee.

$$\left(\begin{matrix}\text{Capital balance} \\ \text{after last charge}\end{matrix} \pm \begin{matrix}\text{Capital changes} \\ \text{since last charge}\end{matrix}\right) \times \left(1 + \left(\begin{matrix}\text{Hurdle} \\ \text{rate}\end{matrix} \times \frac{\text{Days since last charge}}{\text{Days in year}}\right)\right)$$

Applying Highwater Marks

If a partnership applies a *highwater mark* (also called a "loss carryforward" provision) to the partner's performance fee, it must compensate for all prior losses allocated to the partner before it can charge a performance fee. The partner's target capital is its capital account balance after the last performance fee charge, adjusted for the partner's capital changes since the last performance fee charge.

With a highwater mark, the partnership charges the performance fee only on the net appreciation since the last charge. Therefore, only the amount of appreciation above the highwater mark is subject to the performance fee.

Example: A partnership charges a 20% performance fee with a highwater mark with no hurdle rate. (For details about payout percentages, see "Calculating Tax Percentages and Carve-Outs" on page 169.) A partner begins with a capital balance of $1,000.

1. On the first charge date, the partner earns $15 of appreciation, so the partnership charges the partner a performance fee of $15 × 20% = $3. The partner's new capital balance and highwater mark are $1,012.
2. To be subject to a performance fee on the second charge date, the partner's capital balance must exceed $1,012. The partnership allocates the partner

a $10 loss. The partner's new capital balance is $1,002, but the partner's highwater mark remains at $1,012.

3 To be subject to a performance fee on the third charge date, again, the partner's capital balance must exceed the partner's highwater mark of $1,012. The partner earns $15 of appreciation, which raises the partner's capital balance to $1,017. The partnership charges a performance fee on the partner's net appreciation, ($1,017 – $1,012) × 20% = $1. The partner's new capital balance and highwater mark are $1,016.

A partnership without a highwater mark charges the performance fee on the appreciation since the partner's last charge date. A partner can be charged a loss on one charge date and, in the next charge period, be credited appreciation that is positive (or above the hurdle rate), but less than the amount of the previous loss. In this case, the partnership can charge the partner even though the partner's capital balance is lower than it was the last time the partnership charged the partner.

Example: A partner has a capital balance of $1,000. In the first performance fee period, the partnership allocates the partner a $100 loss. In the second performance fee period, the partnership allocates the partner $50 of profit. Without a highwater mark, the partnership can charge the partner a performance fee, even though the partner remains below its original capital balance.

Important: Because a partner's contributions, assignments, and withdrawals affect its capital balance, they also affect its highwater mark. In addition, withdrawals and assignments also decrease the amount of capital that the partnership has available to invest to make up the partner's losses. For more information about how capital changes affect partners' highwater marks, see the following sections.

Capital change	See
Contribution	"How Contributions Affect Highwater Marks" on page 167.
Withdrawals	"How Withdrawals Affect Highwater Marks" on page 167.
Assignments	"How Assignments Affect Highwater Marks" on page 168.

Applying Highwater Marks and Hurdle Rates

If a partnership applies a highwater mark *and* a hurdle rate to its performance fee calculation, partners only pay the fee when their capital balances exceed their previous highest capital account balance, plus the hurdle rate.

If the partnership charges performance fees more than once per year, it must calculate a partner's target capital on each date the partnership can charge the partner a fee. Use the following formula to calculate target capital with both a hurdle rate and a highwater mark.

$$\left(\text{Current highwater mark} + \text{Contributions since last charge}\right) \times \left(1 + \left(\text{Hurdle rate} \times \frac{\text{Days since last charge}}{\text{Days in year}}\right)\right)$$

How Contributions Affect Highwater Marks

Because a partner's contributions and received assignments increase its capital balance, they also raise the partner's highwater mark.

Example: A partner has a capital balance of $1,000, and a highwater mark (and target capital) of $1,100. At the beginning of the period (before appreciation), the partner contributes $100. The partner's new highwater mark is $1,100 + $100 = $1,200.

How Withdrawals Affect Highwater Marks

If your partnership applies a highwater mark for performance fees, and a partner withdraws capital while its account is "under water" (that is, below the highwater mark), this reduces the amount of capital the partnership can invest to bring the partner's capital account back above the highwater mark. Therefore, partnerships should specify that a partner's withdrawals have a proportionate effect upon that partner's highwater mark and target capital as follows.

$$\text{Highwater mark adjustment amount} = \text{Withdrawal amount} \times \frac{\text{Target capital on last charge date} + \text{Contributions since last charge date}}{\text{Beginning capital in withdrawal period} + \text{Appreciation before withdrawal}}$$

That is, the withdrawals' effect on the highwater mark is proportionate to the difference between the partner's target capital and its current capital balance.

The timing of the withdrawal determines when the adjustment takes affect. If the withdrawal takes place:

- *Before* the allocation, it affects the partner's highwater mark and target capital in the *current* period.
- *After* the allocation, it affects the partner's highwater mark and target capital in the *following* period.

Example: A partner has a capital balance of $1,000, and a highwater mark (and target capital) of $1,100. At the beginning of the period (before appreciation), the partner withdraws $100. The partner's highwater mark adjustment is $100 × $1,100 / $1,000 = $110. The partner's new highwater mark is $1,100 – $110 = $990.

How Assignments Affect Highwater Marks

If a partner assigns a portion of its interest to another partner, the partnership treats the assignment amount the same as a withdrawal for the purposes of calculating the assigning partner's highwater mark adjustment. For details, see "How Withdrawals Affect Highwater Marks" on page 167.

For the partner receiving the assignment, the partnership treats the amount of assigned capital the same as a contribution, that is, the partnership simply adds the amount to the partner's current highwater mark.

The timing of the assignment determines when the adjustment takes affect. If the assignment takes place:

- *Before* the allocation, it affects the partner's highwater mark and target capital in the *current* period.
- *After* the allocation, it affects the partner's highwater mark and target capital in the *following* period.

Clawback Provisions

In addition to performance fee hurdle rates and highwater marks that set a level of performance for the partnership, a partnership agreement can also contain a clawback provision. Clawback provisions refund all or part of the performance fee to the limited partners if the partnership's profits fall below a certain level.

Calculating Tax Percentages and Carve-Outs

After the partnership has determined when to charge performance fees, and what appreciation goal the partnership must meet for the partners to be subject to the fee, it must determine the amount of the fee. Because the performance fee charge is actually a reallocation, the partnership determines the fee amount by calculating a new allocation percentage for each partner. Because the performance reallocation determines the final amount of appreciation allocated to each partner, and is used to allocate taxable income, this new allocation percentage is often called the *tax percentage*.

The description of the partnership's performance fee structure in its limited partnership agreement should include:

- ✔ The percentage of the limited partner's appreciation (called the *payout percentage*) that the partnership reallocates to the general partner if, after the partnership performs its economic allocation, the limited partner's economic capital balance exceeds its target capital.
- ✔ *If the partnership applies a hurdle rate,* whether the partnership reallocates a percentage of the partner's:

- ❖ Total appreciation since the last performance fee charge.
- ❖ Appreciation above its target capital (also called "profit above the hurdle").

✔ *If the partnership has more than one general partner*, or if any limited partners also receive a portion of the fee, an agreement should be in place that defines the percentage of the fee (called the *carve-out*) that each special partner receives.

Calculating Limited Partners' Tax Percentages

Partnerships use the limited partners' payout percentages to calculate their tax percentages, which they then use to perform the tax allocations of each item of profit and loss. If the partnership charges a performance fee:

- ❖ **On all profit**, the partnership uses the following formula to calculate a limited partner's tax percentage.

  $$\text{Economic percentage} \times (1 - \text{Payout percentage})$$

  Example: A partnership charges a 20% performance fee. A limited partner with an economic percentage of 10%, would have a tax percentage of 10% × (1 – 0.2) = 8%.

- ❖ **Only on profit above target capital**, the partnership uses the following formula to calculate a limited partner's tax percentage.

  $$\left(\begin{matrix}\text{Economic}\\\text{percentage}\end{matrix} \times \left(1 - \begin{matrix}\text{Payout}\\\text{percentage}\end{matrix}\right)\right)$$

  $$+ \left(\begin{matrix}\text{Payout}\\\text{percentage}\end{matrix} \times \frac{\begin{matrix}\text{Capital balance}\\\text{after last charge}\end{matrix} \times \begin{matrix}\text{Hurdle}\\\text{rate}\end{matrix} \times \dfrac{\text{Days since last charge}}{\text{Days in year}}}{\text{Partnership appreciation since last charge}} \right)$$

  Note: Partnerships may find it easier to calculate the partners' reallocation amounts, rather than their tax percentages. For details, see "Reallocating Profit Above Target Capital" on page 171.

Example: A partnership with a 5% hurdle rate charges a 20% performance fee. A partner begins the year with $1,000, which is 10% of the partnership's capital. The partnership earns $600 of appreciation. The partner's tax percentage for the year would be:

$$(0.10 \times (1 - 0.2)) + \left(0.2 \times \frac{1000 \times 0.05 \times 365/365}{600}\right) = 9.67\%$$

After the partnership has determined the limited partners' tax percentages for the period, it can:

- Reallocate the performance fees on non-gain items from the limited partners to the general partner. For details, see "Allocating Non-Gain Items" on page 173.
- Allocate realized and unrealized gains using its chosen gains allocation methodology.
  - For aggregate methodology, see "Allocating Gains with Aggregate Methodologies" on page 174.
  - For tax lot layering methodology, see "Allocating Gains with Tax Lot Layering" on page 175.

Reallocating Profit Above Target Capital

If the partnership charges its performance fee on profit above target capital, it can use the following method to calculate partners' tax percentages.

1. Find the difference between the partner's ending economic balance and target capital.
2. Multiply the difference by the payout percentage to determine the performance fee charge.
3. Subtract the charge amount from the partner's net economic allocation.
4. Divide the difference by the partnership's total income to determine the partner's tax percentage.

Example: A partnership with a 10% hurdle rate charges a 10% performance fee on profit above target capital. The partnership records $400 appreciation for the period. A partner with 50% of the fund's capital has:

Beginning economic balance	$1,000
Target capital	$1,100
Economic appreciation (50% × $400)	$200
Ending economic balance	$1,200
Appreciation above target capital	$100

The partner is subject to a 10% × $100 profit above target capital = $10 performance fee charge. The partner's tax percentage is ($200 profit – $10 performance fee) / $400 total partnership profit = 47.5%.

Calculating General Partners' Tax Percentages

Calculating a general partner's tax percentage can be complicated if:

- Only some limited partners are subject to a fee on the charge date.
- The partnership charges limited partners at different payout percentages.
- The partnership uses different hurdle rates to calculate limited partners' target capital.
- The partnership charges on appreciation above target capital.

In these cases, the partnership can use the following formula *after* the reallocation to calculate a general partner's tax percentage.

$$\frac{\text{Total tax allocation amount}}{\text{Partnership appreciation since last charge}}$$

Assigning Carve-Outs

If the partnership has more than one general partner, each general partner receives a share of the performance fee. The partnership must specify, in its agreement or private placement memorandum, the percentages, or *carve-outs,* of the performance fee that it uses to distribute the performance incentive reallocation to the general partners.

Example: A partnership has three general partners. General Partner A receives 50% of the performance fee. General partners B and C each receive 25% of the performance fee.

For details on using carve-outs to reallocate performance fees, see the sections about specific item type reallocations in "Reallocating Profit Items" on page 173.

Reallocating Profit Items

The partnership performs its tax allocation after it:

1. Calculates the limited partners' target capital.
2. Performs an economic allocation.
3. Determines which limited partners are subject to a performance fee charge.
4. Calculates the limited partners' (and, where applicable or possible, the general partner's) tax percentages.

The tax allocation allocates income and expenses net of performance incentive fees to the partners.

Allocating Non-Gain Items

Partnerships allocate non-gain items according to the partners' current tax percentages, because only the partners' interests in the partnership on the specific date of the cash flow (as opposed to their historical interests in the partnership) affect their share of that income or loss.

Note: If the partnership cannot calculate a partner's tax percentage (for example, if it charges on profit above target capital), follow the procedure described in the section "Reallocating Profit Above Target Capital" on page 171.

ADV ENT PARTNER

Advent Partner embeds performance reallocations in each item allocation.

Advent Partner automatically determines which limited partners are subject to a performance fee when you run the tax allocation, and suggests a fee amount, based on their performance reallocation structures. You can modify this fee amount, choose not to charge the partner, or choose to estimate, rather than charge, the fee. For details, look up **tax allocation: running** in Advent Partner's Help index. (For information about estimating fees, see "Estimating Performance Fees" on page 162.)

Allocating Gains with Aggregate Methodologies

1 Partnerships allocate the period's book gains (realized gains + change in unrealized gains) in the same manner as non-gain items, that is, according to partners' tax percentages in the current period.

2 *If the partnership uses the aggregate with book gains, full netting methodology*, it adds each partner's tax allocation of book gains to its beginning aggregate account balance to determine the partner's interim aggregate account balance.

3 The partnership determines which aggregate assumption applies to the period, depending on:

- Whether the partnership is allocating a gain or loss.

  and

- How the amount of the gain or loss compares to the partners' aggregate account balances.

The assumptions determine whether the partnership allocates the period's realized gains according to aggregate percentages, tax percentages, or both. For details, see "Understanding Aggregate Assumptions" on page 112.

4 The partnership subtracts each partner's allocation of realized gain from its tax allocation of book gain, to find the partner's tax allocation of unrealized gain.

5 The partnership updates each partner's aggregate account balance by:

- *For aggregate, full netting*: Adding the partner's tax allocation of unrealized gain to the aggregate account balance.
- *For aggregate with book gains, full netting*: Subtracting the partner's tax allocation of realized gain from the aggregate account balance.

For examples of allocating gains with aggregate methodologies, see Chapter 6, Allocating Aggregate Gains.

Allocating Gains with Tax Lot Layering

When a partnership performs a tax allocation, it applies the performance fee to the unrealized gain in the current period for its open security positions. When the partnership closes a position and allocates the realized gains according to the historical layers, the performance fee is already embedded in that allocation. The partnership only needs to apply the partners' current tax percentages to the current layer of realized gains (that is, the difference between the last period's closing price and the sale price).

In effect, layering partnerships allocate gain items in the same manner as non-gain items. That is, the partnership allocates the gain in the current period (the current period's *change* in unrealized gain, and the current period's layer of realized gain) according to current tax percentages. The allocation of a security's *total* realized gain, however, reflects the tax percentages and gains in each period that the partnership held the security.

For an example of allocating gains with tax lot layering methodology, see Chapter 7, Allocating Layered Gains.

Section 1256 Gains

Because partnerships do not use historical percentages to allocate realized gains, they allocate Section 1256 realized gain items according to partners' current tax percentages, like non-gain items.

ADV ENT PARTNER

For more information about how Advent Partner allocates Section 1256 gains, see the following sections.

Methodology	See
Aggregate	"Allocating Aggregate Section 1256 Gains" on page 136.
Tax lot layering	"Allocating Layered Section 1256 Gains" on page 150.

Hot Issue Gains

If the partnership trades hot issue securities, its limited partnership agreement must specify whether or not general partners who are excluded from hot issues can receive hot issue gains in their performance fee reallocations. Consult legal counsel before making this decision.

Example: A partnership has one limited and one general partner with equal economic and tax percentages. The general partner is excluded from hot issue gains. The partnership charges a 20% performance fee.

The partnership earns $100 in hot issue gains, all of which it allocates to the limited partner. When the partnership performs the tax allocation, however, it either:

- Reallocates $20 of that gain as a performance fee to the general partner, or
- Excludes the hot issue gains from the performance fee, in which case it reallocates no hot issue gains to the general partner. The tax allocation matches the economic allocation.

  Important: If the partnership excludes hot issue gain items from tax reallocation, the general partner's performance fees will not reflect the performance fee percentage of the partnership's net profits.

ADV ENT PARTNER

For details on how Advent Partner allocates hot issue gains, see the following sections.

For	See
Economic allocation	"Allocating Hot Issue Gains" on page 80.
Aggregate allocation	"Allocating Aggregate Section 1256 Gains" on page 136.
Tax lot layering	"Allocating Layered Section 1256 Gains" on page 150.

Excluding Items From Performance Fees

Partnerships can exclude the general partner from the economic allocation of an item, such as a management fee. The performance fee reallocation, however, will allocate a portion of that item to the general partner.

Example: A partnership with one limited partner charges a 20% performance fee. In the current period, the partnership allocates a -$100 management fee, and $200 in interest income, to the limited partner. The limited partner's net profit is $100, so the performance reallocation should be $100 × 20% = $20. If the partnership reallocates:

- *Both items*, the general partner receives -$100 × 20% = -$20 of the management fee, and $200 × 20% = $40 of the interest income, for a total performance fee of $20. This matches the expected performance fee reallocation ($20), but the general partner *appears* to have paid a portion (-$20) of the management fee, from which it is excluded.

- *Only reallocates the $40 of interest income*, the general partner receives a $40 performance fee, which is $40 / $100 = 40% of the limited partner's net income for the period. The general partner does not appear to have paid a portion of the management fee, but the general partner's performance fee does not match the expected reallocation.

Performance Fees in Offshore Funds

This section addresses performance fee calculations and considerations pertinent to offshore funds.

Tip: Offshore funds use different terminology than U.S. investment partnerships. Before reading this section, you may want to review the list of terms in "Offshore Funds" on page 11. You can also consult the glossary on page 257.

Offshore funds calculate and charge performance fees differently from U.S. limited partnerships. Typically, an offshore fund is set up as a corporation.

Therefore, it charges performance fees at the "company" or "fund" level, and applies the fee among all the shareholders as an expense based on units held. This method, however, can result in unfair charges to shareholders that were not in the fund for the entire performance fee period or for those that have carryforward losses. This imbalance occurs because the strategy of allocating performance fee based on shares held fails to account for three important factors:

- The timing of each shareholder's entry into the fund.
- Changes in the fund's net asset value (NAV).
- Carryforward losses.

To ensure fair distribution of performance fees, the fund can make adjustments. The process of making these adjustments is generically called "equalization." The following example demonstrates the performance fee inequities that result when an offshore fund does not apply equalization.

Offshore Fund with No Equalization : An Example

Let's examine a newly formed offshore fund. It starts with one shareholder, A, who joins in period 1. Shareholders B and C join in periods 2 and 3, respectively. This fund's offering document states that:

- New subscriptions purchase shares of the fund at the previous period's ending NAV/share.
- The fund's performance fee is 20% of all profit and loss, and is calculated using highwater marks.
- Performance fee will be calculated for the fund as a whole, then allocated back to shareholders based upon shares owned.

Note: For simplicity, this example shows a single class of investors and does not account for hurdle rates.

Shareholder A enters the fund in period 1 with a subscription of $100,000, purchases 1,000 units at a NAV/share of $100, and owns 100% of the fund. The fund earns $400,000 profit during period 1, so Shareholder A's period 1 profit is $400,000. For the period, Shareholder A accrues a performance fee of $400,000 × .20 = -$80,000.

Period 1

Beginning NAV/Share: $100 Ending NAV/Share: $420

Share-holder	Subscrip.	Beg Cap	Units Purch.	Units Held	Cap %	Period 1 P&L	FY P&L	End Cap Before Accrued Perf. Fee	Accrued Perf. Fee	End Cap After Accrued Perf. Fee
A	$100,000	$100,000	1,000	1,000	100%	$400,000	$400,000	$500,000	*-$80,000	$420,000
B	--	--	--	--	--	--	--	--	--	--
C	--	--	--	--	--	--	--	--	--	--
Fund Total	**$100,000**	**$100,000**	**0**	**1,000**	**100%**	**$400,000**	**$400,000**	**$500,000**	**-$80,000**	**$420,000**

*Shareholder A's 1,000 units comprise 100% of the fund for period 1, so it accrues 100% of the performance fee.

Shareholder B enters the fund in period 2 with a subscription of $420,000, purchases 1,000 units at a NAV/share of $420 (the previous period's ending NAV/share), and owns 50% of the fund (to Shareholder A's 50%). The fund has a loss of -$500,000 during period 2, so Shareholder B has a loss of -$250,000. Shareholder A also has a loss of -$250,000 for the period, reducing its fiscal year profit to $150,000. Because the fund's year-to-date profit and loss is negative (-$100,000), at the end of period 2, it reverses the -$80,000 accrued performance fee from period 1 to $80,000, and allocates that amount to each shareholder according to its percentage of shares held: Shareholder A accrues $40,000 and Shareholder B accrues $40,000

Period 2

Beginning NAV/Share: $420 Ending NAV/Share: $210

Share-holder	Subscrip.	Beg Cap	Units Purch.	Units Held	Cap %	Period 2 P&L	FY P&L	End Cap Before Accrued Perf. Fee	YTD Accrued Perf. Fee	End Cap After Accrued Perf. Fee
A	$0	$420,000	0	1,000	50%	-$250,000	$150,000	$170,000	$40,000	$210,000
B	$420,000	$420,000	1,000	1,000	50%	-$250,000	-$250,000	$170,000	$40,000	$210,000
C	--	--	--	--	--	--	--	--	--	--
Fund Total	**$420,000**	**$840,000**	**1,000**	**2,000**	**100%**	**-$500,000**	**-$100,000**	**$340,000**	**$80,000**	**$420,000**

Shareholder C enters the fund in period 3 with a subscription of $210,000, purchases 1,000 units at a NAV/share of $210 (the previous period's ending NAV/share), and owns 33% of the fund (to Shareholder A's 33% and Shareholder B's 33%). The fund earns $600,000 profit during period 3, so Shareholder C has a profit of $200,000. Shareholders A and B also earn $200,000 each. Shareholder A's fiscal year profit is now $350,000; Shareholder B's fiscal year loss is -$50,000; and shareholder C's fiscal year profit is $200,000.

Because the end of period 3 is also the fiscal year end, the fund charges performance fee. The fund's year-to-date profit and loss is positive, so it calculates performance fee at the fund level, and charges performance fee to each shareholder based on units held (3,000 divided equally among all shareholders). It multiplies the fund's fiscal year profit of $500,000 by 20% and applies a portion of that amount to each shareholder. In this case: $500,000 × .20 = $100,000 × .33 = $33,333.

Notice that when no method of equalization is applied to performance fee calculations, all shareholders end up paying the same fee, regardless of when they entered the fund and of how much profit each made. Shareholder B, who had a loss for the fiscal year, pays the same amount as Shareholders A and C. Further, Shareholders A and C pay the same amount, even though they have different amounts of fiscal year profit and loss.

Period 3

Beginning NAV/Share: $210 | Ending NAV/Share: $376.667

Shareholder	Subscrip.	Beg Cap	Units Purch.	Units Held	Cap %	Period 3 P&L	FY P&L	End Cap Before Accrued Perf. Fee	Charged Perf. Fee	End Cap After Accrued Perf. Fee
A	$0	$210,000	0	1,000	33%	$200,000	$350,000	$410,000	-$33,333	$376,667
B	$0	$210,000	0	1,000	33%	$200,000	-$50,000	$410,000	-$33,333	$376,667
C	$210,000	$210,000	1,000	1,000	33%	$200,000	$200,000	$410,000	-$33,333	$376,667
Fund Total	**$210,000**	**$630,000**	**1,000**	**3,000**	**100%**	**$600,000**	**$500,000**	**1,230,000**	**-$100,000**	**1,130,000**

Equalization

There are a number of different equalization methods a fund can use. These include, but are not limited to, performance fee deposits, multiseries shares, and average performance fee. There may be variations on each method, depending on the fund's offering document.

The goal of each method is to more fairly administer the performance fee so that it is based on the profit each shareholder/subscription earns, à la U.S. partnership accounting.

This discussion focuses on the multiseries shares method, because it most closely resembles U.S. partnership accounting and is one of the easiest methods for investors to understand.

Multiseries Shares Method

Using multiseries shares is equivalent to tracking each shareholder's subscription separately. To use this method, a fund issues a new series of shares whenever there is a new subscription. Multiseries shares applies the following principles and procedures.

- At inception, the fund creates a "main" (or "base") series of shares and issues them to subscribing shareholders.
- When there are new subscriptions to the fund, the fund creates a new series of shares to issue to the subscribing shareholders. (All shareholders entering the fund at the same time receive shares from the same series.) These series are tracked separately from previously issued series and each maintains its own NAV, GNAV, and HNAV.
- At year end, each shareholder's profit from its series of shares is calculated on a highwater mark basis.
- Only shares that had profit during the year are charged a fee.
- At the end of the performance fee period, all shares that are charged a performance fee or whose NAV *is not* below their highwater mark are converted or "rolled into" the main series of shares.
- Shares whose NAV *is* below their highwater mark carry forward in their original series until they are charged a performance fee; then they are rolled into the main series.
- Generally, both the series that is converting and the base series are charged performance fee at the same time.

The multiseries shares method offers a number of advantages:

- It bases performance fees on profit earned on a particular subscription.
- It is similar in concept and intention to U.S. partnership accounting, and much simpler than most other equalization methods.
- It is easier than other methods for offshore funds to administer and for shareholders to understand.

The disadvantages of the multiseries shares method include:

- It can create a large number of series of shares, each with a different NAV/share. (For example, if a fund has a number of subscriptions during a year when the market is down, all series that have losses will be carried forward into the following year.)

- The fund must manage a number of highwater marks and charge fees accordingly.
- It can be confusing for investors who own shares of several series. (For example, shareholders who want to redeem shares must decide which series to redeem them from.)
- The NAV cannot be published (and is not necessarily meaningful) if the fund has large numbers of series not converted to the base series.

Multiseries Shares Method: An Example

Now, let's apply the multiseries shares method of equalization to the same offshore fund with the same three shareholders, and examine the difference. This fund's offering document states that:

- New subscriptions purchase shares of the fund at the previous period's ending GNAV. (Compare NAV in the "no equalization method" example on page 178.)
- The fund's performance fee is 20% of all profit and loss, and is calculated using highwater marks.
- Performance fee is accrued each period, and charged at year end.

The key point to note in this example is that performance fees are calculated for each shareholder/subscription according to the performance of its capital account, resulting in a more equitable allocation of performance fees.

This example shows activity for three periods, and period 3 ends at year end.

Shareholder A joins the fund in period 1 with a subscription of $100,000, and purchases 1,000 units of Series 0 (the base series) at a NAV/share of $100. The fund earns $400,000 profit during period 1, so Shareholder A's period 1 profit is $400,000. Series 0's GNAV exceeds its HNAV ($100/share), so Shareholder A accrues performance fee: $400,000 × .20 = -$80,000. Series 0's ending NAV is $420/share.

Period 1

Beginning GNAV/Share: $100 | Ending GNAV/Share: $500

Series	Share-holder	Sub-scrip.	Beg Cap	Cap %	Period P&L	FY P&L	End Cap Before Accrued Perf. Fee	YTD Accrued Perf. Fee	End Cap After Accrued Perf. Fee
0 (base)	A	$100,000	$100,000	100%	$400,000	$400,000	$500,000	-$80,000	$420,000
1	B	--	--	--	--	--	--	--	--
2	C	--	--	--	--	--	--	--	--
Fund Total		**$100,000**	**$100,000**	**100%**	**$400,000**	**$400,000**	**$500,000**	**-$80,000**	**$420,000**

Period 1

Series	Share-holder	Units Purch.	Units Held	HNAV/ Share	GNAV/ Share	YTD Accrued Perf. Fee	End NAV/ Share
0 (base)	A	1,000	1,000	$100	$500	-$80,000	$420
1	B	--	--	--	--	--	--
2	C	--	--	--	--	--	--

Shareholder B joins the fund in period 2 and the fund creates a new series of shares: Series 1. Shareholder B makes a subscription of $500,000 to purchase 1,000 shares of Series 1 at $500/share (the fund's ending GNAV/share from period 1). The fund has a loss of -$500,000 during period 2, so Shareholder A's period 2 loss is -$250,000 and Shareholder B's loss is -$250,000.

Series 0's GNAV ($250/share) exceeds its HNAV ($100/share), so it accrues performance fee for period 2. Series 1's GNAV ($250/share), however, is less than its HNAV ($500/share), so it does not accrue performance fee for the period. Series 0's ending NAV is $220/share. Series 1's ending NAV is $250/share.

Period 2

Beginning GNAV/Share: $500 Ending GNAV/Share: $250

Series	Shareholder	Subscrip.	Beg Cap	Cap %	Period P&L	FY P&L	End Cap Before Accrued Perf. Fee	YTD Accrued Perf. Fee	End Cap After Accrued Perf. Fee
0 (base)	A	$0	$500,000	50%	-$250,000	$150,000	$250,000	$30,000	$220,000
1	B	$500,000	$500,000	50%	-$250,000	-$250,000	$250,000	$0	$250,000
2	C	--	--	--	--	--	--	--	--
Fund Total		**$500,000**	**$1,000,000**	**100%**	**-$500,000**	**-$100,000**	**$500,000**	**$30,000**	**$470,000**

Period 2

Series	Shareholder	Units Purch.	Units Held	HNAV/ Share	GNAV/ Share	YTD Accrued Perf. Fee	End NAV/ Share
0 (base)	A	0	1,000	$100	$250	$30,000	$220
1	B	1,000	1,000	$500	$250	$0	$250
2	C	--	--	--	--	--	--

Shareholder C joins the fund in period 3 and the fund creates another new series of shares: Series 2. Shareholder C makes a subscription of $250,000 to purchase 1,000 shares of Series 1 at $250/share (the fund's ending GNAV/share from period 2).

The fund has a profit of $600,000 during period 3, so Shareholder A's period 3 profit is $200,000; Shareholder B's profit is $200,000; and Shareholder C's profit is $200,000.

Period 3

Beginning GNAV/Share: $250 Ending GNAV/Share: $500

Series	Share-holder	Sub-scrip.	Beg Cap	Cap %	Period P&L	FY P&L	End Cap Before Perf. Fee	Charged Perf. Fee	End Cap After Perf. Fee
0 (base)	A	$0	$250,000	33%	$200,000	$350,000	$450,000	-$70,000	$380,000
1	B	$0	$250,000	33%	$200,000	-$50,000	$450,000	$0	$450,000
2	C	$250,000	$250,000	33%	$200,000	$200,000	$450,000	-$40,000	$410,000
Fund Total		**$250,000**	**$750,000**	**100%**	**$600,000**	**$500,000**	**$1,350,000**	**-$110,000**	**1,240,000**

Because the end of period 3 is also the fiscal year end, the fund charges performance fee. With the equalization method, performance fee is calculated at the shareholder/subscription level. Shareholder A pays a fee of -$70,000, which is 20% of the $350,000 fiscal year profit from its Series 0 shares. Shareholder C pays a fee of -$40,000, which is 20% of the $200,000 fiscal year profit from its Series 2 shares. Notice that Shareholders A and C are charged different fees because they had differing profits from the shares in their series; Shareholder B is charged no fee, because it had a loss from its Series 1 shares.

Because Shareholder C's Series 2 shares have been charged a fee, they are converted to (rolled into) Series 0 shares. To convert the shares, Shareholder C's ending capital of $410,000 is divided by Series 0's ending NAV/share: $410,000 / $380 = 1,078.947, so Shareholder C is given 1,078.947 shares of Series 0. Series 0 now has a total 2,078.947 shares purchased (Shareholder C's conversion of 1078.947 plus the original purchase of 1,000 shares made by Shareholder A); and Series 2 has 0 shares purchased.

Series Conversion

	Fund		Series 0 (base)		Series 1		Series 2	
	NAV	Units Held	NAV	Units Purch.	NAV	Units Purch.	NAV	Units Purch.
Period 1		1,000						
Shareholder A			$100,000	1,000				
Profit/Loss	$400,000		$400,000					
End Cap Before Acc. Perf. Fee	$500,000		$500,000					
YTD Accrued Perf. Fee	-$80,000		-$80,000					
End Cap After Acc. Perf. Fee	$420,000		$420,000					
Period 2		2,000						
Shareholder B					$500,000	1,000		
Beg Cap	$1,000,000		$500,000		$500,000			
Profit/Loss	-$500,000		-$250,000		-$250,000			
End Cap Before Acc. Perf. Fee	$500,000		$250,000		$250,000			
YTD Accrued Perf. Fee	$30,000		$30,000		$0			
End Cap After Acc. Perf. Fee	$470,000		$220,000		$250,000			

Series Conversion

	Fund		Series 0 (base)		Series 1		Series 2	
	NAV	Units Held	NAV	Units Purch.	NAV	Units Purch.	NAV	Units Purch.
Period 3		3,000						
Shareholder C							$250,000	1,000
Beg Cap	$750,000		$250,000		$250,000		$250,000	
Profit/Loss	$600,000		$200,000		$200,000		$200,000	
End Cap Before Acc. Perf. Fee	$1,350,000		$450,000		$450,000		$450,000	
YTD Accrued Perf. Fee			-$70,000		$0		-$40,000	
End Cap After Acc. Perf. Fee			$380,000*		$450,000		$410,000*	
Year End								
Profit	$500,000		$350,000		-$50,000		$200,000	
End Cap Before Chgd. Perf. Fee	$1,350,000		$450,000		$450,000		$450,000	
Perf. Fee	-$110,000		-$70,000		$0		-$40,000	
NAV Before Conv.	$1,240,000		$380,000		$450,000		$410,000	
NAV/Share Bef. Conv.			$380†		$450		$410	
Shares Converted to Series 0			$410,000	1078.947			-$410,000†	-1,000
Period 4 Opening Balance	$1,240,000	3,000	$790,000*	2078.947†	$450,000	1,000	$0	0
Period 4 Opening NAV/Share			$380		$450			

*$380,000 + $410,000 = $790,000 adjusted NAV for Series 0.

†$410,000 / $380 =1078.947 shares converted + 1,000 original shares = 2078.947 total Series 0 shares after conversion.

Contributing Securities

Partnerships can accept contributions of appreciated securities to the partnership as capital, in lieu of or in addition to cash contributions. This chapter describes the issues associated with such contributions.

In This Chapter

Accepting Contributed Securities

Internal Revenue Code Section 721 allows investment partnerships to accept contributions of appreciated securities to the partnership as capital, in lieu of or in addition to cash contributions. If certain criteria (described in the section "When Are Built-In Gains Taxable?" on page 191) are met, the accepting of contributed securities (also called "in-kind contributions") can be deemed non-taxable. In such circumstances, that partnership must:

- ✔ Record the price the contributing partner originally paid for the security (called the security's *original cost*).
- ✔ Record the security's fair market value at the time the partner contributes it (called the security's *contributed cost*).
- ✔ Allocate the security's "built-in" gains (the difference between its original cost and contributed cost) separately to the contributing partner when the partnership sells the security.
- ✔ *For contributed fixed-income securities,* account for the security's "built-in" amortization, accretion, and accrued interest.

Partnerships should specify in their partnership agreements whether they accept contributed securities.

Important: Accepting contributed securities requires that the partnership maintain original and contributed cost information for specific security tax lots. Partnerships that use an aggregate gain allocation methodology normally do not maintain this information, as they aggregate all of their positions' gains and losses. In order for an aggregate partnership to accept contributed securities, the partnership must maintain original and contributed cost information for the contributed tax lots, and use this information to allocate built-in gains to the contributing partner when the partnership sells the security.

ADVENT PARTNER

If you interface Advent Partner with Axys, Advent Partner automatically maintains original and contributed cost information for all of the partnership's tax lots, even if the partnership uses aggregate gains allocation. Advent Partner can therefore track and allocate built-in gains from contributed securities to the contributing partners. For details, look up **contributed securities: aggregate gains** in Advent Partner's Help index.

Understanding Built-In Gains

A contributed security typically has some unrealized gain (loss) at the time the partner contributes it. This is the difference between the security's *original cost* (what the partner paid for it) and its market value at the time the partner contributes it (called its *contributed cost*). This unrealized gain (loss) is said to be "built-into" the security at the time the partnership receives it. IRC Section 704(c) specifies that, when the partnership sells the security, it must allocate this portion of the realized gain only to the contributing partner.

When Are Built-In Gains Taxable?

Internal Revenue Code Section 721 provides that neither the partnership nor any of its partners recognizes a gain or loss upon the contribution of property to the partnership in exchange for an interest in the partnership. The partnership's tax basis and holding period for the contributed property are the same as the contributing partner's.

IRC Section 721, however, provides an exemption to the general non-recognition rule if the partnership would be treated as an investment company if it were incorporated, as described in IRC Section 351. The code provides for the tax-free transfer of property to an investment company if, after the contribution, more than 80% of the value of the investment company's assets consist of money, stocks, evidences of indebtedness, derivative instruments, foreign currencies, interests in precious metals, and other similar assets.

The intent of the law is to prevent taxpayers from achieving tax-free diversification of their investments. Treasury regulations state that diversification ordinarily results if two or more persons transfer non-identical assets in the exchange. Therefore, even if a partnership qualifies for an exemption under IRC Section 721, it must still recognize gain if the transfer results in diversification of its interests. The regulation, however, does include exemptions for:

- Transfers of identical assets.
- Nominal disparities in contributed assets.

Treasury regulations also provide a "safe harbor" test for diversification, so that, if the contributed portfolio is already diversified, the contribution does not violate the diversification test. An already diversified portfolio must have:

- No more than 25% of its value comprising the stock and securities of any one issuer.
- No more than 50% of its value comprising the stock and securities of five or fewer issuers.

In general, when the partnership sells (or distributes to another partner) a contributed security, it must allocate to the contributing partner taxable gain to the extent of the built in appreciation in the securities on the date of their contribution. For this reason, contributors of appreciated portfolios do not necessarily achieve tax-free diversification over a lengthy deferral period.

If the partner must recognize gain on the contribution, the partnership assumes the security's fair market value as its tax basis.

For more information, see Treasury Regulations Section 1.351-1(c), and IRC Sections 351, 368, and 721(b), or consult your tax advisors.

What Is the Holding Period For Contributed Securities?

If the partner contributes the security to the partnership without realizing gain (a tax-free contribution), the holding periods for the partner's built-in gain and for the partnership's gains (for when it ultimately sells the security) begin when the contributing partner first purchased the security.

If the partner realizes gain from the contribution of the security (a taxable contribution), the partner's holding period for the gain on the security ends when the partner contributes the security. The partnership's holding period begins when the partner contributes the security to the partnership.

Can Built-In Gains Violate the "Ceiling Rule"?

When a partnership sells a contributed security, it calculates the gain or loss based on the security's original cost, that is, the price at which the contributing partner purchased it. The partnership allocates the built-in gain to the contributing partner first, then any remaining gain to all of the partners according to the partnership's chosen gain allocation methodology.

If the partnership sells the security below its contributed cost, however, allocating the built-in gain to the contributing partner leaves a loss for the partnership as a whole. This violates the ceiling rule, because the partnership must allocate losses to all of the partners (except the contributing partner), even though the partnership itself did not realize a net loss on the sale of the security.

Important: An opinion on this issue holds that, if at least one security's gain/loss in the partnership's portfolio exceeds the net gain/loss to be allocated to a given partner, such an allocation does not violate the ceiling rule. Partnerships should consult the appropriate professionals concerning this issue.

For more information about the ceiling rule, see the following sections.

Methodology	See
Aggregate	"Ceiling Rule: Aggregate Allocation" on page 142.
Tax lot layering	"Ceiling Rule: Tax Lot Layering Allocation" on page 154.

Example: On 1/1/1999, an investor purchases 100 shares of a security at $20. On 2/1/1999, the investor contributes the security to the partnership at a price of $22, for a contributed cost of 100 shares × $22/share = $2200. The security has 100 shares × $2 gain/share = $200 of built-in unrealized gain.

The partnership records $2,200 in the partner's capital account. When the partnership sells the security:

If the Proceeds are	The Partnership Allocates
Greater than original cost + built-in unrealized gain	❖ The built-in gain to the contributing partner. ❖ Gains above the built-in gain to all the partners in the partnership, according to the partnership's chosen gain allocation methodology. **Example:** The partnership sells the security at $23 per share. It allocates $200 of the gain to the contributing partner, and $100 to all of the partners in the partnership.
Equal to original cost + built-in unrealized gain	The built-in gain to the contributing partner. **Example:** The partnership sells the security at $22 per share. It allocates the entire $200 gain to the contributing partner.
Less than original cost + built-in unrealized gain	The built-in gain to the contributing partner, and the difference between the built-in gain and the actual gain (or loss) as a loss to all of the partners in the partnership. **Example:** The partnership sells the security at $21 per share. It allocates the $200 of gain to the contributing partner, and a $100 loss to all of the partners in the partnership. **Caution!** This allocation violates some interpretations of the ceiling rule. An alternative would be to allocate all of the security's actual gain (or loss) (not its built-in gain) to the contributing partner, and no gain or loss to the partnership. **Example:** The partnership sells the security at $21 per share. It allocates the $100 of gain to the contributing partner.

If the Proceeds are	The Partnership Allocates
Less than original cost	The built-in gain to the contributing partner, and the difference between the built-in gain and the actual loss as a loss to all of the partners in the partnership. **Example:** The partnership sells the security at $19 per share. It allocates the $200 of gain to the contributing partner, and a $300 loss to all of the partners in the partnership. **Caution!** This allocation violates some interpretations of the ceiling rule. An alternative would be to allocate all of the security's actual loss to the partnership. **Example:** The partnership sells the security at $19 per share. It allocates the $100 of loss to the contributing partner.

Contributing Fixed-Income Securities

Partnerships that invest in fixed-income securities normally allocate the securities' amortization, accretion, and accrued interest to the partners as income (or offsets to income) each period. If a partnership accepts contributions of fixed-income securities, in the period when the partner contributes the security, the partnership must account for the amortization or accretion of the security to date, and interest accrued on the security as of its contribution date.

Understanding Built-In Amortization and Accretion

Partnerships have two options for how to amortize or accrete a bond after it has been contributed.

- *Partnership only*: Once the partner contributes the bond to a partnership, the partner's amortization or accretion ends. The bond's adjusted cost basis at the time of contribution is its contributed cost. The partner's built-in gain is the difference between the bond's adjusted cost and its market value at contribution.

- *Partnership and partner*: The partnership calculates amortization or accretion for the bond for both the partner *and* the partnership. The partnership allocates amortization or accretion from the:
  - Contributing partner's original cost only to the contributing partner. The partnership continues to adjust the partner's cost basis.
  - Partnership's contributed cost (the security's market value at contribution) to either the contributing partner, or all of the partners. (Partnerships should consult the appropriate professionals in making this decision.)

  The contributing partner's built-in gain is the difference between the partner's and the partnership's adjusted cost bases when the partnership closes the position. This reduces the partner's built-in gain over time, as both of these values approach par.

In all cases:

- The amount of the partner's capital contribution is the market value of the bond at the time the partner contributed it.
- If the market value of the bond at the time it is contributed is:
  - *Higher than the bond's par value,* the partnership can amortize the premium paid on the bond.
  - *Lower than the bond's par value,* the partnership can accrete the discount received on the bond.

The following sections provide examples of both of the methods of amortizing and accreting contributed securities.

If the Partnership	See
Ends the partner's amortization or accretion at contribution	"Partner's Amortization/Accretion Ends at Contribution: An Example" on page 197.
Continues the partner's amortization or accretion after contribution	"Partner's Amortization/Accretion Continues After Contribution: An Example" on page 198.

Partner's Amortization/Accretion Ends at Contribution: An Example

On 1/1/1997, a partner purchases a $10,000 bond that matures on 1/1/2015 (6,574 days to maturity) at 90 ($9,000, a $1,000 discount).

1 On 1/1/1999 (5,844 days to maturity), the partner contributes the bond to the partnership. The bond's fair market value at the time of contribution is 105 ($10,500), for a $500 premium.

- The partner has recorded (730 days from purchase to contribution/6,574 days from purchase to maturity) × $1000 discount = $111 of accretion, so the partner's adjusted cost for the bond is $9,000 + $111 = $9,111.
- The contributing partner's built-in gain is $10,500 (the bond's market value) – $9,111 (the partner's adjusted cost basis) = $1,389.

2 On 1/1/2005 (3,652 days to maturity), the partnership sells the bond at 110 ($11,000).

- The partnership has recorded (2,192 days from contribution to sale/5,844 days from contribution to maturity) × $500 premium = $188 of amortization for the partnership, and allocated it to the partners. Therefore, the partnership's adjusted cost for the bond is $10,500 – $188 = $10,312.
- The partnership's realized gain is $11,000 (the proceeds from the sale) – $10,312 (the partnership's adjusted cost basis) = $688.
- The contributing partner's built-in gain (from step 1) is $1,389. Because the built-in gain exceeds the partnership's realized gain of $688, allocating it to the contributing partner would require allocating a $701 loss to all of the partners in the partnership, which would violate the ceiling rule. Therefore, the partnership allocates only the partnership's $688 of realized gain to the contributing partner.

  Note: If the partnership sold the security at 115 ($11,500), the partnership would realize a $11,500 – $10,312 = $1,188 gain. The partnership would allocate the $688 of built-in gain to the contributing partner, and the remaining $500 of realized gain to all of the partners.

The following graph illustrates this example.

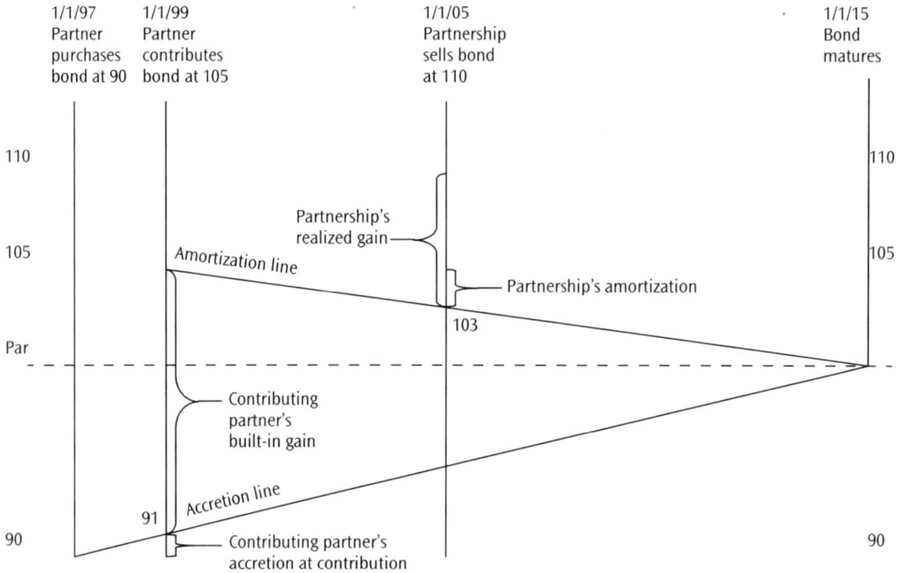

Partner's Amortization/Accretion Continues After Contribution: An Example

On 1/1/1997, a partner purchases a $10,000 bond that matures on 1/1/2015 (6,574 days to maturity) at 90 ($9,000, a $1,000 discount).

1 On 1/1/1999 (5,844 days to maturity), the partner contributes the bond to the partnership. The bond's fair market value at the time of contribution is 105 ($10,500), for a $500 premium.

- ❖ The partner has recorded (730 days since purchase / 6,574 days from purchase to maturity) × $1000 discount = $111 of accretion, so the partner's adjusted cost for the bond is $9,000 + $111 = $9,111.
- ❖ The contributing partner's built-in gain is $10,500 (the bond's market value) – $9,111 (the partner's adjusted cost basis) = $1,389.

2 On 1/1/2005 (3,652 days to maturity), the partnership sells the bond at 110 ($11,000).

- ❖ The partnership has recorded (2,192 days from contribution to sale / 5,844 days from contribution to maturity) × $500 premium = $188 of amortization for the partnership, and allocated it to the partners. Therefore, the partnership's adjusted cost for the bond is $10,500 – $188 = $10,312.

  Note: The partnership has the option of whether to allocate this to the contributing partner, or to all of the partners.

- ❖ The partnership has recorded (2,192 days from contribution to sale / 6,574 days from purchase to maturity) × $1000 discount = $333 of accretion for the contributing partner. Therefore, the contributing partner's adjusted cost for the bond is $9,111 + $333 = $9,444.

- ❖ The partnership's realized gain is $11,000 (the proceeds from the sale) – $10,312 (the partnership's adjusted cost basis) = $688.

- ❖ The contributing partner's built-in gain $10,312 (the partnership's adjusted cost basis, that is, the bond's market value at contribution amortized to the sale date) – $9,444 (the partner's adjusted cost basis at the sale date) is $868. Because the built in gain exceeds the partnership's realized gain of $688, allocating it to the contributing partner would require allocating a $180 loss to all of the partners in the partnership, which would violate the ceiling rule. Therefore, the partnership allocates only the $688 of realized gain to the contributing partner.

Note: If the partnership sold the security at 115 ($11,500), the partnership would realize a $11,500 – $10,312 = $1,188 gain. The partnership would allocate the $868 of built-in gain to the contributing partner, and the remaining $320 of realized gain to all of the partners.

Important: Notice that the contributing partner's built-in gain using this method ($868) is less that the partner's built-in gain using the method described in the section "Partner's Amortization/Accretion Ends at Contribution: An Example" on page 197 ($1,389). If the partnership amortizes or accretes both the partner's original cost, and the security's contribution cost, this reduces the contributing partner's built-in gains.

The following graph illustrates this example.

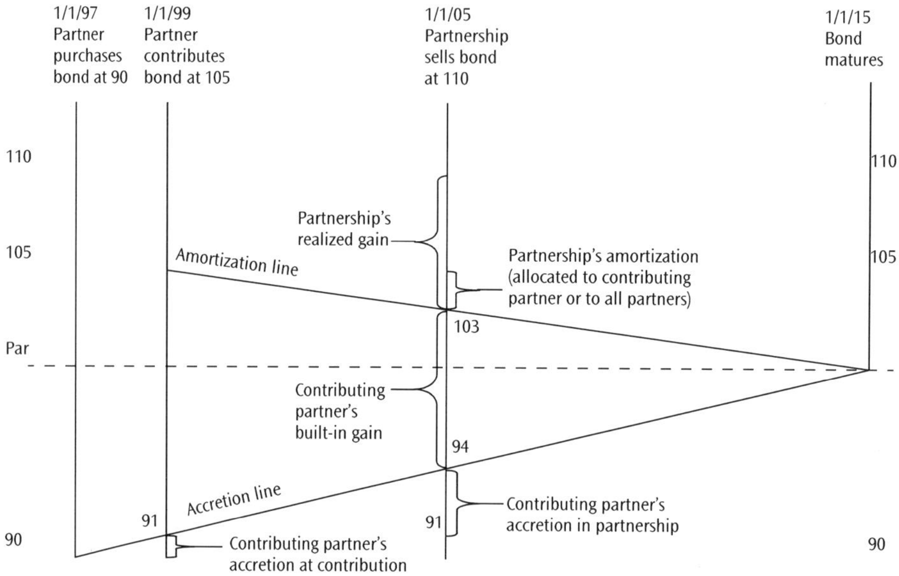

Understanding Built-In Accrued Interest

If the partnership uses accrual basis accounting, bonds that pay a coupon will have a certain amount of interest accrued when the partner contributes them (unless the partner contributes them on a coupon date). When the partner contributes the bond, the partnership must calculate the amount of interest that has accrued on the bond from the last coupon date to the contribution date, and allocates this amount to the contributing partner. The partnership allocates the interest accrued after the contribution date to all of the partners.

Example: A partner purchases a bond that pays a coupon on January 15 and July 15. On 1/1/1999, the partner contributes the bond to the partnership, which has monthly break periods. When the break period ends on 1/31/1999, the partnership allocates:

❖ The interest accrued on the bond from 7/16/1998 to 1/1/1999 to the contributing partner.

- The remainder of the coupon (the interest accrued from 1/1/1999 to 1/15/1999) to all of the partners.
- The accrual towards the next coupon (from 1/16/1999 to 1/31/1999) to all of the partners.

Note: If the partnership uses cash basis accounting, when it books its first coupon, it allocates the partner's built-in interest from the last coupon payment to the contribution date, and allocates the remainder to all of the partners according to their current capital percentages. If a coupon period spans several break periods, however, the coupon's allocation to the partners in the current period may not match their interests in the partnership over the coupon period.

10 Understanding Distributions and Redemptions

If a partner withdraws capital in excess of its tax basis from a partnership, both the withdrawing partner and the remaining partners are ultimately taxed on the withdrawn unrealized gains. This chapter describes the three ways partnerships can counteract this effect.

In This Chapter

Understanding Distributions and Redemptions

A partner's capital account comprises the net of its contributions, withdrawals, and allocations of the partnership's appreciation/depreciation. The total of a partner's contributions and allocations of taxable income (generally, all items except unrealized gain), less withdrawals, represents the partner's *tax basis* in the partnership.

When a partner makes a cash withdrawal from its capital account, the withdrawal comes first from the partner's tax basis, that is, from contributions (on which it has already been taxed), or on previous allocations of taxable income from the partnership. The partner is not taxed on such withdrawals. If the partner's withdrawal exceeds its tax basis, however, the amount of the withdrawal in excess of its tax basis comes primarily from the partner's share of the partnership's unrealized gains. This income is taxed as capital gains.

Example: A partner contributes $100 to a partnership. In the first period, the partnership allocates the partner $50 of taxable income, and $50 of unrealized gain. The partner's capital account balance is now $200, and its tax basis (contribution + allocation of taxable income) is $150.

- *If the partner withdraws $50*, the entire withdrawal comes from the partner's tax basis (contribution, or taxable income reported on the partner's Schedule K-1), and is not taxed.
- *If the partner completely withdraws ($200)*:
  - $150 of the withdrawal comes from the partner's tax basis, and is not taxed.
  - $50 of the withdrawal comes from the partner's unrealized gains in the partnership. The partner must report this $50 on its tax return as capital gains.

In addition, the partnership must have the cash to pay out the partner's withdrawal of unrealized gains. If the partnership:

- Does *not* have cash on hand to pay the withdrawal, it must sell open positions (and realize gains) to generate the required cash. The partners are taxed on their allocable share of the realized gains, *and* the withdrawing partner pays tax on its receipt of the cash. Both the remaining partners and the withdrawing partner are taxed.

- Has cash on hand to pay the withdrawal, the withdrawing partner is taxed on the cash that it receives in excess of its tax basis. When the partnership ultimately closes the positions in which the withdrawing partner had an interest, the remaining partners are allocated, and pay tax on, that realized gain, including the amounts that would have been allocated to the withdrawing partner.

In both cases, both the partner and the partnership are taxed on the withdrawn unrealized gains. This chapter describes the three ways partnerships can counteract this effect.

For Information About	See
Distributing appreciated securities to withdrawing partners for the unrealized gains, in lieu of cash.	"Distributing Securities" on page 205.
Electing IRC Section 754 to adjust the tax basis of security positions by the withdrawing partner's interest in them.	"Electing Section 754" on page 209.
Directing realized gains to the partner, as though the partnership realized the partner's interest in open positions.	"Directing Gains" on page 212.

Note: If a partnership elects IRC Section 754, it cannot distribute securities or direct gains.

Distributing Securities

Partnerships can distribute appreciated securities to fully liquidating partners in lieu of cash. The partnership gives the withdrawing partner securities with:

- A market value equal to the partner's capital balance.
- Unrealized gains (market value – original cost) equal to or exceeding the partner's share of the partnership's unrealized gains.

The Internal Revenue Code specifies that a partner receiving securities in liquidation of its partnership interest does not recognize gain or loss until it liquidates the positions. When the partner receives the securities, it assigns its tax basis in the partnership to those securities. When the partner ultimately sells the securities, the gain it recognizes equals the proceeds less its tax basis in the securities (its tax basis in the partnership).

Example: A partner has a capital account balance of $200, with a tax basis of $150, and $50 of unrealized gain. When the partner withdraws, the partnership distributes a security with an original cost of $100, and a market value of $200, to the partner. If the partner:

- Sells the security immediately, it recognizes $50 of gain ($200 market value – the partner's $150 tax basis in the partnership).
- Sells the security at a later date, it recognizes the proceeds of the sale – $150 tax basis as realized gain/loss.

Distributing securities in lieu of cash allows both the partner and the partnership to defer their tax liability from the withdrawal.

- The partner is not immediately better or worse off than if it had received cash, although if it holds the security, it may gain a tax advantage from a longer holding period, but also exposes itself to changes in the security's market value.

  Note: If the partnership distributes a security that it has held for longer than one year, the partner gains the advantage of automatically realizing long-term capital gains when it sells the security.

- The partnership's remaining partners are not taxed on the distribution of securities in liquidation of the withdrawing partner's interest, whereas they would be taxed if they had to sell positions to generate the required cash. The remaining partners' interests in the distributed security "leave" the partnership, but their interests in the partnership's remaining securities are realigned (to allocate the interests that the withdrawing partner "left behind"), so that their total unrealized gain remains unchanged (assuming that the unrealized gain in the distributed securities equals or exceeds the unrealized gain in the withdrawing partner's capital account). The remaining partners are not taxed on this unrealized gain until they ultimately withdraw or the partnership sells the securities.

Example: Three partners begin a partnership by each contributing $100. The partnership opens three security positions, which appreciate in the first period as follows.

Position	Cost/Tax Basis	Market Value at Period End	Unrealized Gain
1	$100	$500	$400
2	$150	$500	$350
3	$50	$500	$450
Total	**$300**	**$1,500**	**$1,200**

1 At the end of the first period, the partnership allocates the $1,200 to the partners according to their capital percentages ($400 each). This changes the partners' capital accounts as follows.

Tax Basis (from contribution)	$100
Unrealized gain allocation	$400
Capital account balance	$500

2 One of the partners withdraws from the partnership. The partnership must liquidate the $500 in that partner's capital account. If the partnership:

- Pays out the partner's account in cash, the partner realizes $400 in taxable gains. In addition, when the partnership closes security positions (which it may have to do in the next period to raise the cash for the withdrawal), the remaining partners will be responsible for the entire $1,200 of realized gains, even though the withdrawn partner held a one-third interest in those securities.
- Distributes position 1 to the withdrawing partner instead of cash, the tax basis ($100) and unrealized gains ($400) of the position cover the tax basis and unrealized gain in the partner's capital account.
- Distributes position 2 to the withdrawing partner instead of cash, it distributes a smaller amount of unrealized gains ($350) than the partner had in the partnership ($400). When the partnership sells the

other positions, the remaining partners will have a larger tax liability for the realized gains ($850 instead of $800).

- Distributes position 3 to the withdrawing partner instead of cash, the partner receives a greater amount of unrealized security gain ($450) than the partner had in the partnership ($400). Because the withdrawing partner's tax basis of $100 becomes its basis in the security, it is only taxed on $400 of the unrealized gain it withdraws. When the partnership sells the other positions, the remaining partners will have a smaller tax liability for realized gains ($750 instead of $800).

Partnerships' distributions of property are subject to certain limitations, including:

- The "anti-abuse" regulations in Treasury Regulations Sections 1.701-2. These ensure that partnerships are formed for substantive business purposes, and that the partners' tax consequences properly reflect the partnership's economic activity.
- Partnerships cannot distribute securities if they have elected IRC Section 754.
- Partners must recognize gain upon the distribution of appreciated securities that qualify under IRC Section 731(c) or Section 751(b).

For more information on these concepts, consult your tax advisor.

Note: If a partner withdraws completely from the partnership, the partnership must adjust the remaining partners' layers in the remaining securities, or aggregate accounts, by the withdrawing partner's interest in them, as described in the following sections.

If the Partnership Uses	See
Aggregate methodology	"How Total Withdrawals Affect Aggregate Accounts" on page 133.
Tax lot layering methodology	"How Withdrawals Affect Layered Gains" on page 147.

Electing Section 754

Section 754 of the Internal Revenue Code allows a partnership to elect to adjust the tax basis of securities it holds by an amount equal to a withdrawing partner's share in the partnership's unrealized gains at the time of the withdrawal. When the partnership ultimately sells the security, it only allocates the gains attributable to the remaining partners in the partnership. IRC Section 734(b) describes how to perform these adjustments.

Important: Once a partnership elects Section 754, it is binding for all subsequent periods.

Example: A partnership has three partners, A, B, and C, with equal interests.

1 In period 1, the partnership purchases 10 shares of a security at $10 per share.

2 Partner A withdraws completely from the partnership at the end of period 2. The security's price is $19 per share, for an unrealized gain of ($19 price – $10 cost) × 10 shares = $90.

Partner A's withdrawal includes $30 of unrealized gain for this security. Under Section 754, the partnership increases the security's tax basis by $3 / share × 10 shares = $30 to compensate for the withdrawn unrealized gain. The security's adjusted cost is $10 original cost + $3 adjustment = $13. The security's unrealized gain is now ($19 price – $13 cost) × 10 shares = $60: $30 for each partner, which matches their pre-withdrawal allocations.

The following table shows the partner's unrealized gain from the security before and after Partner A's withdrawal, and after the Section 754 adjustment.

	Before Withdrawal		After Withdrawal		After Section 754 Adjustment	
Partner	**Capital Percent**	**Unreal. Gain**	**Capital Percent**	**Unreal. Gain**	**Capital Percent**	**Unreal. Gain**
A	33%	$30	Withdrawn		Withdrawn	
B	33%	$30	50%	$45	50%	$30
C	33%	$30	50%	$45	50%	$30
Total		**$90**		**$90**		**$60**

3 In period 2, the partnership sells the security at $22 per share, for a realized gain of ($22 price – $13 adjusted cost) × 10 shares = $90 ($60 from period 1; $30 from period 2). The partnership allocates each remaining partner $45 of realized gain.

Note: If the partnership had not elected Section 754, it would have realized ($22 price – $10 cost) × 10 shares = $120 of gain ($90 from period 1; $30 from period 2), and allocated each remaining partner $60 of realized gain. The $30 of unrealized gain withdrawn by Partner A would have been taxed again as realized gains allocated to partners B and C.

Implementing Section 754 with Tax Lot Layering

If the partnership allocates gains using tax lot layering, it can implement Section 754 election by not realigning the remaining partners' historical capital percentages for the periods when the withdrawn partner was in the partnership. When the partnership allocates realized gains from a security in which the withdrawn partner had an interest, it does so according to these unrealigned percentages. It allocates the remaining gain from the security (that is, the withdrawn partner's share) as *non-taxable* realized gain according to the remaining partners' realigned percentages, using a special allocation item.

Example: A partnership has three partners, A, B, and C, with equal interests. At the end of period 3, Partner C withdraws. When the partnership sells any securities it held in periods 1, 2, or 3, it allocates the layers of gain for those periods 33.3% to Partner A, and 33.3% to Partner B. The partnership allocates the remaining 33.3% (Partner C's share) equally to partners A and B as non-taxable realized gain.

ADVENT PARTNER

Advent Partner uses this method to handle Section 754 elections in partnerships that use tax lot layering allocation. When the partnership closes a position in which the withdrawn partner had an interest, Advent Partner allocates the following items to the remaining partners according to their realigned tax percentages in each layer. (These items do not flow through to the partners' Schedule K-1s or reports.)

Advent Partner Allocates This Amount to	Item Name	Item Code
Non-taxable realized gain	Sec. 754 Adjustment for Realized Gain (Layering)	RG754L
Change in unrealized gain attributable to the withdrawn partner's interest in the security	Sec. 754 Adjustment for Unrealized Gain (Layering)	UG754L

Example: A partnership has three partners, A, B, and C, with equal interests.

1 In period 1, the partnership purchases ten shares of a security at $10 per share. The security's price is $19 per share, for an unrealized gain of ($19 price / share – $10 cost / share) × 10 shares = $90.

At the end of period 1, Partner A withdraws completely from the partnership, taking with it its $30 of unrealized gain in this security. The following table shows the partners' unrealized gain from the security immediately before and after Partner A's withdrawal.

	Before Withdrawal		After Withdrawal	
Partner	**Percentage**	**Unrealized Gain**	**Percentage**	**Unrealized Gain**
A	33%	$30	Withdrawn	
B	33%	$30	50%	$45
C	33%	$30	50%	$45
Total		**$90**		**$90**

2 In period 2, the partnership sells the security at $22 per share, for a realized gain of ($22 price / share – $10 cost / share) × 10 shares = $120 ($90 from period 1; $30 from period 2). The partnership allocates:

- Layer 1 of realized gains (in which Partner A had an interest) to the partners according to their unrealigned percentages.
- The remaining realized gains in layer 1 (Partner A's interest) to the partners according to their realigned percentages, as non-taxable realized gains.
- Layer 2 of realized gains (in which Partner A had no interest) to the partners according to their current percentages

- The security's change in unrealized gains (-$90) in the same way that it allocated layer 1 of the realized gains: -$60 for the remaining partners' unrealigned shares, and -$30 (Partner A's withdrawn unrealized gains) as a Section 754 adjustment item.

The partnership realizes $120 from the security, but only allocates $90 to the remaining partners ($45 to each partner) as taxable realized gain. This matches the remaining partners' pre-withdrawal layers of gain from period 1 ($60) plus their layers of gain from period 2 ($30).

Partner	Layer	Change in Unrealized Gain	Sec. 754 Unreal. Gain Adj.	Taxable Realized Gain	Sec. 754 Non-taxable Realized Gain	Total Realized Gain
B	1	$45		$30	$15	
	2	-$30	-$15	$15		
			Partner B Total	$45	$15	$60
C	1	$45		$30	$15	
	2	-$30	-$15	$15		
			Partner C Total	$45	$15	$60
					Total	**$120**

Directing Gains

A *directed gains* provision (sometimes called a "fill-up," "fill-down," or "stuffing" provision) in a partnership's limited partnership agreement allows the partnership to allocate realized gains to a withdrawing partner in place of unrealized gains that the partner would otherwise withdraw. The partnership reallocates realized gain equal to the amount of unrealized gain that the partner would withdraw from the remaining partners to the withdrawing partner. The partnership then:

- Credits the withdrawing partner's unrealized gains to the remaining partners' capital accounts according to their current realigned tax percentages.

- Allocates the withdrawn partner's interest in the partnership's historical unrealized gains to the remaining partners as follows.

If the Partnership Uses	It Allocates the Withdrawn Partner's Unrealized Gains by
Tax lot layering	Realigning the remaining partners' historical tax percentages when it allocates realized gains from securities in which the withdrawing partner had an interest.
Aggregate methodology	Distributing the withdrawn partner's aggregate account balance to the remaining partners, according to their current realigned tax percentages.

Note: A "fill-up" provision allows the partnership to allocate realized gains to a withdrawing partner with net unrealized gain, and a "fill-down" provision allows the partnership to allocate realized losses to a partner with net unrealized loss. Partnership agreements can implement these provisions separately.

Caution: It is currently unclear whether directed gains satisfy the "substantial economic effect" test required of allocations by Internal Revenue Code Section 704(b). Partnerships should exercise caution and consult their tax advisors before implementing a directed gains agreement.

Important: The partnership cannot direct gains if it has elected Section 754.

When setting up its directed gains provision, a partnership should consider:

- ✔ **Timing:** If a partner withdraws at year end (12/31), it typically does not receive the cash from its withdrawal until the following year. The partnership agreement, however, can specify that it must report the partner's withdrawal of taxable income in the previous year.

- ✔ **Character of Gains:** The partnership must consider whether the realized gains it allocates to the withdrawing partner carry a long- or short-term capital gains tax burden, and whether the withdrawing partner's tax burden differs substantially from what it would have been if the partner had stayed in the partnership, or not received the directed gains.

✔ **Reallocating Unrealized Gain:** Directing gains generally credits the withdrawing partner's unrealized gains to the remaining partners according to their current realigned tax percentages. If the partnership uses:

- *Tax lot layering methodology,* it allocates realized gains from securities in which the withdrawn partner had an interest according to the remaining partners' realigned historical percentages. Therefore, the realized gains allocated to a partner may not reflect the unrealized gains credited to its capital account.

- *Aggregate methodology,* it credits both the withdrawing partner's unrealized gain and its aggregate account balance to the remaining partners according to their realigned current tax percentages. Therefore, the realized gain allocated to a partner will match the unrealized gain in its capital account, but that unrealized gain may not reflect its historical interest in the partnership.

✔ **Insufficient Realized Gains:** If the unrealized gain a partner withdraws exceeds the partnership's realized gain in the period when the withdrawal occurs, the partnership must allocate a realized loss to the remaining partners in order to direct enough realized gains to the withdrawing partner.

Example: A partner with $500 of unrealized gain in its capital account withdraws from the partnership in a period when the partnership recognizes $400 of realized gain. In order to direct $500 of realized gain to the withdrawing partner, the partnership must allocate a $100 loss to the remaining partners in the current period.

Important: Partnerships must consider whether this violates the ceiling rule. For details, see "Ceiling Rule: Aggregate Allocation" on page 142 and "Ceiling Rule: Tax Lot Layering Allocation" on page 154.

The following sections show examples for implementing directed gains agreements with tax lot layering and aggregate allocation methodologies.

Directed Gains with Tax Lot Layering: An Example

A partnership has three partners, A, B, and C, who each contribute $1,000 to the partnership. In period 1, the partnership purchases securities 1, 2, and 3. In period 3, the partnership sells security 3, and Partner C withdraws from the partnership. Each partner has the following layers in each security.

Layer	Security 1 (Unrealized)	Security 2 (Unrealized)	Security 3 (Realized)
1	$30	$20	$10
2	$20	-$10	$20
3	-$10	$10	$10
Total for each partner	$40	$20	$40
Total for partnership	$120	$60	$120

The following table shows the partners' capital accounts after the partnership allocates period 3, but before Partner C withdraws:

Partner	Contribution	Realized Gain (Security 3)	Unrealized Gain (Securities 1 & 2)	Capital Balance
A	$1,000	$40	$40 + $20 = $60	$1,100
B	$1,000	$40	$40 + $20 = $60	$1,100
C	$1,000	$40	$40 + $20 = $60	$1,100
Total	**$3,000**	**$120**	**$180**	**$3,300**

Rather than allowing Partner C to withdraw $60 of unrealized gains from the partnership, the partnership directs $60 of realized gain to Partner C.

The following table shows the partners' capital accounts after the partnership directs gains.

Partner	Contribution	Realized Gain (Security 3)	Unrealized Gain* (Securities 1 & 2)	Capital Balance
A	$1,000	$10	$60 + $30 = $90	$1,100
B	$1,000	$10	$60 + $30 = $90	$1,100
C	$1,000	$100		$1,100
Total	**$3,000**	**$120**	**$180**	**$3,300**

*Because the partners' realigned current and historical percentages are identical, the amount of unrealized gains credited to Partner A's and B's capital accounts is the same as their realigned layers of security 1's and 2's unrealized gains.

Note: If the holding period for security 3 is less than one year, but the holding period for securities 1 or 2 (when the partnership sells them) is greater than one year, directing gains effectively reduces Partner A and B's tax burdens by directing short-term capital gain to Partner C while directing long-term realized gain to B and C.

Directed Gains with Aggregate Allocation: An Example

A partnership has three partners, A, B, and C, who each contribute $1,000 to the partnership. In period 1, the partnership purchases securities 1, 2, and 3. In period 3, the partnership sells security 3 for a realized gain of $120 ($40 per partner), and Partner C withdraws from the partnership. The following table shows the partners' capital and aggregate accounts after the partnership allocates period 3, but before Partner C withdraws.

Partner	Contribution	Realized Gain	Unrealized Gain	Aggregate Acct. Balance	Capital Balance
A	$1,000	$40	$60	$60	$1,100
B	$1,000	$40	$60	$60	$1,100
C	$1,000	$40	$60	$60	$1,100
Total	**$3,000**	**$120**	**$180**	**$180**	**$3,300**

Rather than allowing Partner C to withdraw $60 of unrealized gains from the partnership, the partnership directs $60 of realized gain to Partner C. This reduces Partner C's aggregate account balance from $60 to $0. The partnership credits Partner C's unrealized gains to Partner A and B's capital accounts, and to their aggregate accounts, according to their current realigned tax percentages. The following table shows the partners' capital accounts after the partnership directs gains.

Partner	Contribution	Realized Gain	Unrealized Gain	Aggregate Acct. Balance	Capital Balance
A	$1,000	$10	$90	$90	$1,100
B	$1,000	$10	$90	$90	$1,100
C	$1,000	$100		$0	$1,100
Total	**$3,000**	**$120**	**$180**	**$180**	**$3,300**

*Because the partners' realigned current and historical percentages are identical, the amount of unrealized gains credited to Partner A's and B's capital accounts is the same as their realigned layers of security 1's and 2's unrealized gains.

Note: If the holding period for security 3 is less than one year, but the holding period for securities 1 or 2 (when the partnership sells them) is greater than one year, directing gains effectively reduces Partner A and B's tax burdens by directing short-term capital gain to Partner C while directing long-term realized gain to B and C.

Understanding Tax Issues

This chapter discusses general tax issues relevant to partnership accounting. For detailed information on these issues, consult the appropriate professionals.

In This Chapter

Understanding Book To Tax Differences

Partnerships record certain events differently in the economic ("book") allocation than in the tax allocation, usually because of differences between accrual basis (GAAP) accounting practices and IRS regulations. Examples of this include:

- Accrued interest and dividends, which record income on record date, but for tax purposes are recorded as of payment date.
- Prepaid expenses, which record the expense on the prepayment date, but for tax purposes are recorded as of the actual payment date (that is, when they are fully amortized).

In addition, IRS regulations require taxpayers to adjust how they recognize gains and losses from certain securities or positions for tax purposes. This can involve:

- Recognizing certain unrealized gains as realized.
- Deferring recognition of certain expenses or realized losses.
- Reclassifying certain long-term gains or losses as short-term, or short-term as long-term.

ADVENT PARTNER

When book to tax differences occur, Advent Partner records and allocates a *tax adjustment*. This is an item amount that only affects the tax allocation.

Example: A partnership records $100 of unrealized gain for a Section 1256 contract that it holds. For tax purposes, however, the partnership records the following tax adjustments to mark the contract to market and allocate its gain 60% long-term, 40% short-term, as if realized.

Item	Amount
Unrealized gain	-$100
Short-term realized gain	$40
Long-term realized gain	$60

In cases where the partnership defers an expense or loss, in the subsequent year, the partnership must also enter a *reversal* to correctly allocate the deferred amount.

Example: A partnership receives a $100 dividend with a record-date of 12/5/1998 and a payment date of 1/5/1999. For book purposes, it records the dividend on 12/5/1998. For tax purposes, however, it must record the following adjustments to defer the dividend until 1/5/1999.

Item	Date	Amount
Dividend income	12/5/98	-$100
Dividend income	1/5/99	$100

Several of the tax issues described in this chapter and elsewhere require partnerships to enter tax adjustments or reversals. The following table identifies these sections.

Adjustment	See
Section 754 election	"Electing Section 754" on page 209.
Section 1091 wash sales	"Understanding Wash Sales" on page 223.
Section 1092 straddles	"Deferring Loss to Offsetting Positions" on page 229.
Section 1233 short positions covered but not settled at year end	"Covered Shorts Not Settled At Year End" on page 231.
Section 1256 mark-to-market securities	"Allocating Aggregate Section 1256 Gains" on page 136 and "Allocating Layered Section 1256 Gains" on page 150.
Section 1259 constructive sales	"Understanding Constructive Sales" on page 233.

For more information about tax allocations, see "How Do Tax and Economic Allocations Differ?" on page 93.

Recording Tax Adjustments and Reversals

Partnerships can record book to tax differences caused by deferrals in one of two ways.

- Record all deferrals and reversals "as you go" throughout the year.
- Record only those deferrals that it has not reversed at year end and which therefore affect its tax returns. Reversals for these deferrals occur in the subsequent year.

Example: For accrual basis accounting purposes, partnerships record book income from a dividend on the ex-dividend date. For tax purposes, however, partnerships must record it on payment date. Stock XYZ pays four $100 dividends per year as follows.

Ex-Dividend Date	Payment Date
December 5, 1998	January 1, 1999
March 5, 1999	April 1, 1999
June 5, 1999	July 1, 1999
September 5, 1999	October 1, 1999
December 5, 1999	January 1, 2000

If the partnership records deferrals and reversals as it goes throughout the year, it must record the following tax adjustment transactions for its dividend income allocation item.

Date	Amount
January 1, 1998*	$100
March 5, 1998	-$100
April 1, 1998	$100
June 5, 1998	-$100
July 1, 1998	$100

Date	Amount
September 5, 1998	-$100
October 1, 1998	$100
December 5, 1998	-$100
January 1, 1999	$100

*Reversal for December 5, 1997, deferral

Notice that, when the partnership closes final for the year on 12/31, only the 12/5 deferral remains in effect: it has already reversed all of the other deferrals. If the partnership only records those deferrals that affect its tax returns (that is, are still open at year end), it would record the following tax adjustment transactions for its dividend income allocation item.

Date	Amount
January 1, 1998*	$100
December 5, 1998	-$100
January 1, 1999	$100

*Reversal for December 5, 1997 deferral

Important: A partnership must decide whether it allocates reversals to its partners according to the same percentages it used to allocate the original deferral. This may require that it use separate items to allocate reversals. For details, consult your tax advisor.

Understanding Wash Sales

According to the IRS, a wash sale occurs when you sell or trade a security at a loss, and during the continuous period of 30 days *before* and 30 days *after* that transaction (61 days total), you purchase a "substantially identical" security. When the purchase transaction takes place, it causes the sell transaction to be defined as a wash sale.

The Internal Revenue Code Section 1091 requires that if a wash sale occurs, the investor must defer recognizing the loss from the sell transaction. This requirement is known as the "wash sale rule," and it is designed to prevent the investor from recognizing a loss for tax purposes while remaining in the same economic (usually long or short) position.

When the partnership identifies a wash sale, it adds the amount of the disallowed loss to the cost basis of the open position. Additionally, the partnership treats the new position as though it were opened on the opening date of the original position. This effectively defers the loss until the partnership closes the open position that created the wash sale, and stays out of that position for 30 days before or after the sale.

Identifying Wash Sales

A wash sale generally only occurs when the open position has the same character (long or short) as the position that realized the loss. A buy/sell/buy (or a short/cover/short) set of transactions could create a wash sale, but not a buy/sell/short.

Example: The following set of transactions shows the deferral of loss on a long position.

Date	Trans.	Book		Tax		Deferred Loss (Wash Sale)
		Cost/ Proceeds	Gain/ Loss	Cost/ Proceeds	Gain/ Loss	
01/01/99	buy 100	$1,000		$1,000		
02/10/99	sell 100	$0	-$1,000	$0	-$1,000	
02/03/99	buy 100	$1,000	$0	$2,000*		-$1,000
1999 Total		**$1,000**	**-$1,000**	**$2,000**	**$0**	**-$1,000**
06/15/00	sell 100	**$2,000**	**$1,000**	**$2,000**	**$0**	**$0**

*Tax cost basis is increased by the amount of the disallowed loss, and its holding period begins on 01/01/99.

Notice that:

- Without a wash sale, this investor would have recognized a $1,000 loss in 1999, but still held the same position at year end. The investor has the same economic position as one who held the position, but has a tax advantage of recognizing a loss in 1999.

- With the wash sale, the investor must "wash" the loss into the next year's gains, effectively recognizing the loss in the following year. In this case, the investor recognizes no loss in 1999, and no gain (because of the loss "deferral" in 2000). The result is the same as if the investor had held the position, and it deters the investor from realizing the loss in 1999 purely for tax purposes.

ADVENT PARTNER

Advent Partner's Wash Sale Wizard is a tool that can automatically identify wash sales involving the same security, and allows partnerships to manually identify "substantially identical" securities. After you identify the wash sales, Advent Partner automatically creates the necessary tax adjustments. For details, look up **Wash Sale Wizard** in Advent Partner's Help index.

How Much Can Be Washed?

Wash sales are typically "share-driven": the number of shares in the transaction that creates the wash sale determines how much of the loss must be washed. Divide the number of opened shares by the number of shares realized at a loss to determine the percentage of the loss to wash into the new shares' cost basis.

Example: In the following example, opening one new share creates a wash sale. This represents 1 open share / 1 closed share = 100% of the shares that create the wash sale. The entire $90 loss must be washed into the cost of the open position, giving it a $100 cost for tax purposes, even though its book cost is only $10.

Trans.	Book		Tax
	Cost/ Proceeds	Gain/Loss	Cost/ Proceeds
buy 1	$100		
sell 1	$10	-$90	
buy 1	$10		$100

Example: In the following example, opening one new share creates a wash sale. This represents 1 open share / 100 closed shares = 1% of the shares that create the wash sale. In this case, 1% × \$100 = \$1 of the loss must be washed into the cost of the open position, giving it a \$2 cost for tax purposes, even though its book cost is only \$1.

Trans.	Book		Tax
	Cost/ Proceeds	Gain/Loss	Cost/ Proceeds
buy 100	\$100		
sell 100	\$0	-\$100	
buy 1	\$1		\$2

Carrying Forward Losses, Rolling Positions

When a wash sale occurs, the investor must consider future activity. The realized loss washes into the cost basis of the next opening position on a FIFO (first in, first out) basis. But what happens if this second lot closes at a loss? Or at a gain? And if the investor opens a third position within 30 days of that loss? The following examples illustrate these situations.

Example: This example shows several losses washed in sequence.

Date	Trans.	Book		Tax		Deferred Loss (Wash Sale)
		Cost/ Proceeds	Gain/ Loss	Cost/ Proceeds	Gain/ Loss	
01/01/99	buy 100	\$1,000		\$1,000		
02/10/99	sell 100	\$0	-\$1,000	\$0	-\$1,000	
02/03/99	buy 100	\$1,000		\$2,000		-\$1,000
02/26/99	sell 100	\$0	-\$1,000	\$0	-\$2,000	
03/06/99	buy 100	\$1,000		\$3,000		-\$2,000
03/22/99	sell 100	\$500	-\$500	\$500	-\$2,500	
04/06/99	buy 100	\$5,000		\$7,500		-\$2,500
1999 Total			**-\$2,500**		**\$0**	**-\$2,500**
03/31/00	sell 100	**\$10,000**	**\$5,000**	**\$10,000**	**\$2,500**	

Each deferred loss increases the cost basis of the next opening position on a FIFO basis. When the investor closes the final lot, the realized book gain is \$10,000 – \$5,000 = \$5,000 (short-term).

For tax purposes, however, the realized gain is \$10,000 – \$7,500 = \$2,500 (long-term).

The difference is the \$2,500 of deferred loss recognized in the current year.

Example: The following example shows a loss followed by a gain, followed by a loss.

Date	Trans.	Book		Tax		Deferred Loss (Wash Sale)
		Cost/ Proceeds	Gain/ Loss	Cost/ Proceeds	Gain/ Loss	
01/01/99	buy 100	\$1,000		\$1,000		
02/10/99	sell 100	\$0	-\$1,000	\$0	-\$1,000	
02/03/99	buy 100	\$1,000		\$2,000		-\$1,000
02/26/99	sell 100	\$5,000	\$4,000	\$5,000	\$3,000	
03/06/99	buy 100	\$1,000		\$1,000		\$0
03/22/99	sell 100	\$500	-\$500	\$500	-\$500	
04/06/99	buy 100	\$5,000		\$5,500		-\$500
1999 Total			**-\$2,500**		**-\$2,000**	**-\$500**
03/31/00	sell 100	**\$10,000**	**\$5,000**	**\$\$10,000**	**\$4,500**	

The first sale, which creates a wash sale of \$1,000 is absorbed into the gain on the second sale (which exceeds the original loss). Consequently, only the buy on 04/06/1999 creates a wash sale.

Example: The following example shows a loss followed by a gain.

Date	Trans.	Book		Tax			Deferred Loss (Wash Sale)
		Cost/ Proceeds	Gain/ Loss	Cost/ Proceeds	Cost/ Proceeds	Gain/ Loss	
01/01/99	buy 100	$1,000		$1,000	$1,000		
02/10/99	sell 100	$0	-$1,000	$0		-$1,000	
02/03/99	buy 100	$1,000		$1,000	$2,000		-$1,000
02/26/99	sell 100	$5,000	$4,000	$5000		$3,000	
03/06/99	buy 100	$5,000		$5,000	$5,000		$0
1999 Total			**$3,000**			**$3,000**	**$0**

Even though the first sell creates a wash sale, the second sell's gains more than offset it, so that the final buy does not create a wash sale.

Contributed Securities

The wash sale rules follow the security, not the entity that holds it. Therefore, if a partnership receives a tax-free contribution of a security, it must:

- Consider that security's original cost basis (rather than its contributed cost) when it closes the security, to determine whether it realizes a loss on the security, and possibly triggers a wash sale when it opens another position in the security.
- Count the contributed security among its open positions for determining wash sales when it closes another position in the same security at a loss.

If the contribution is taxable, however, the contributing partner recognizes any loss on the security, so if the partnership opens a position in the security, it does not trigger a wash sale. The partnership must still count the contributed security among its open positions if it closes another position at a loss within 30 days before or after the contribution.

Important: Issues arising from wash sales involving contributed securities are complex, and partnerships should consult the appropriate professionals.

Understanding Straddles

Internal Revenue Code Section 1092 defines a straddle as holding offsetting positions in actively traded personal property. An "offsetting" position is one that substantially reduces the investor's risk of loss in another position. The following is a list of some of the more common types of straddle positions.

Position	Offsetting Position
Equity	Deep in-the-money call or put option
Equity portfolio	Short position on an index option comprising the stocks
Convertible bond	Related equity (depending on the amount of the conversion premium)
Long equity swap	Long put option and short call option on the same equity

Deferring Loss to Offsetting Positions

If the investor realizes a loss on a position that is part of the straddle, it can only deduct the amount by which the loss exceeds the unrealized gain at year end on the offsetting position. The investor must defer the remaining loss.

Example: On 12/15/1998, a partnership sells a position that is part of a straddle, and realizes a loss of $100. On 12/31/1998, the unrealized gain on the other position in the straddle is $80. The partnership sells the other position on 3/15/1999. The partnership records the following tax adjustments.

- On 12/15/1998, the day the partnership closes the offsetting position:
  - $80 to realized gain (so that the partnership only realizes a $20 loss)
  - -$80 to unrealized gain
- On 3/15/1999, the day the partnership closes the position:
  - -$80 to realized gain (to realize the remainder of the loss)
  - $80 to unrealized gain

Terminating Holding Period

When an investor enters a straddle position, the holding period on the long positions is terminated. The long position does not age until the investor no longer holds the offsetting position. Exceptions include:

- ❖ If the investor held the long position longer than one year before opening the offsetting position. In this case, the position has matured into long-term status, and does not lose that status when the investor enters the straddle.
- ❖ If the offsetting position is a qualified covered call, the holding period of the long position is *suspended*, not terminated, for the period that the investor holds the qualified covered call.

Example: A partnership opens a long position on 3/15/1998. On 4/15/1998, the partnership opens an offsetting position, which it closes on 7/15/1998. The holding period for the long position begins on 7/16/1998.

Capitalizing Interest Expenses

The investor cannot deduct interest expenses incurred in opening or maintaining a position in a straddle. The investor must treat these expenses as negative adjustments to the capital gain or loss on the position.

Example: A partnership opens a short position to offset a long position, creating a straddle. The partnership pays $100 interest on the margin account that funds the short position. The partnership must record the $100 as an adjustment to capital gain, rather than an interest expense.

Understanding Short Sales

Internal Revenue Code Section 1233 provides the following rules regarding short sales.

Covered Shorts Not Settled At Year End

Generally, for tax purposes, partnerships record security transactions on a trade date basis, that is, when they enter into the transaction. For closing a short position, however, a taxable event does not occur until securities are delivered, that is, until the covering transaction settles (settlement date). If a partnership enters a cover short transaction prior to year end, but that transaction does not settle until after year end, the partnership must defer any loss on those positions to the subsequent year for tax purposes. Any gain on those positions, however, is taxable in the current year due to the constructive sale rules, as described in the section "Understanding Constructive Sales" on page 233.

ADVENT PARTNER

Advent Partner automatically creates tax adjustments for unsettled covered short positions that it imports from Axys.

Example: A partnership covers a short position on 12/30/1999, and realizes a $300 loss. The transaction has a 3-day settlement lag, so it does not settle until 1/5/1999. Advent Partner generates the following tax adjustments.

- On 12/30/1998, the day the short position closes:
  - $300 to realized gain.
  - -$300 to unrealized gain.
- On 1/5/1999, the day the short position settles:
  - -$300 to realized gain.
  - $300 to unrealized gain.

Holding Period For Short Positions

If an investor sells a security short, and has either:

- Held a long position in the same or a "substantially identical" security for a period of one year or less, or
- Opened a long position in the same or a "substantially identical" security while the short position is open

the holding periods of both positions are affected as follows.

- The short position is considered to be held for one year or less at the time it is closed, regardless of how long the position has been open.
- The holding period for the long position begins when the investor closes the short position.

Any *gain* the investor realizes when it closes the short position is short-term capital gain, even if the investor closes the short with a long position that has aged to long-term status. In addition, the holding period for the long position (or for the number of shares in the long position equal to the number of shares in the short position) does not begin until the investor closes the short position.

Any *loss* the investor realizes when it closes the short position is long-term capital loss *if* it held the long position for more than one year before it opened the short position (regardless of whether it uses the long position to close the short position).

Short Dividend Payments

When the investor borrows securities in order to sell them short, it must make dividend payments if:

- The dividend paid exceeds the rebate income (interest on the cash received from the short sale) received by the lender.

  and

- The short position is open over an ex-dividend date.

The partnership's treatment of the dividend payment depends on how long the short position has been open.

- *Less than 46 days,* and the short position:
  - Has been sold in the current period, the partnership treats the dividend payment as a realized loss on the short position.
  - Is still held at the end of the period, the partnership treats the dividend payment as a reduction in the sales proceeds.
- *More than 45 days,* the partnership treats the dividend payment as an interest expense.

Understanding Constructive Sales

Internal Revenue Code Section 1259 requires that partnerships recognize gain on certain "constructive sales" of positions of stock, certain debt instruments (bonds), or partnership interests. A constructive sale is defined as entering into one of the following offsetting positions.

If the Partnership Holds a(n)	A Constructive Sale is
Long equity	A short sale of the same or a "substantially identical" equity, offsetting equity swap, forward to sell stock.
Bond	An offsetting notional principal contract relating to the same or "substantially identical" property.
Commodity	A futures or forward contract to deliver the same or "substantially identical" property.
Short position, offsetting notional principal contract, or futures or forward contract	Purchase of the same or "substantially identical" property, offsetting equity swap, forward to buy stock.

The partnership treats the original position as if it had sold it at its fair market value on the date it entered the offsetting position, that is, it recognizes the realized gain at its fair market value at that time. When the partnership closes the position, it reduces its gain (or increases its loss) by the amount it has already realized.

Example: On 10/15/1998, a partnership opens a long equity position. On 11/15/1998, the partnership opens a short position of the same security. The market value of the long position on 11/15/1998 has increased $100 from the partnership's original cost (that is, the position has $100 of unrealized gain). On 12/15/1998, the partnership sells the long position at $120 over its original cost (that is, it realizes a $120 gain on the position). The partnership must enter the following tax adjustments.

- On 11/15/1998, when the partnership opens the offsetting position:
  - $100 to realized gain (to the increase in market value at the time of the constructive sale)
  - -$100 to unrealized gain
- On 12/15/1999, when the partnership closes the original position:
  - -$100 to realized gain (so that the partnership does not count the gain recognized from the constructive sale)
  - $100 to unrealized gain

Note: A partnership does not need to record a constructive sale if it:

- Closes the offsetting position within 30 days after the end of the taxable year.

  and
- Holds the original position "naked" (without holding an offsetting position) for 60 days after closing the offsetting position.

Selling Short Against the Box

Prior to the 1997 Act, an investor could protect an appreciated long position from market risk but postpone gain recognition for tax purposes by selling short the exact number of shares in the appreciated position. This strategy is commonly known as "selling short against the box." The investor can similarly defer a gain on a short position by buying long an exact number of shares. The clearing broker statement shows the position long *and* short, and the clearing broker must not have delivered the long against the short. For accounting purposes, the positions are reflected "broad," that is, as long and short. Recognition occurs when the long shares are delivered against the short position and the positions are deleted from the broker statements.

The 1997 Act limits using the short against the box technique for tax purposes by identifying some of these opposite transactions as "constructive sales," triggering gain recognition as previously described. The constructive sales rules further complicate the accounting and tax work for the fund. Therefore, the partnership should consult an appropriate professional.

Note: A "safe harbor" exists for boxed positions entered before June 9, 1997 (commonly called "grandfather boxes"). Because these positions were entered prior to the enactment of the 1997 Act, constructive sale rules do not apply to them.

Understanding Unrelated Business Taxable Income

Under Internal Revenue Code Section 511(a), an otherwise tax-exempt organization is subject to tax on its income from any trade or business that it regularly carries on but is not substantially related to its tax-exempt purpose (called "unrelated business taxable income" or UBTI). For this rule, tax-exempt organizations include pension, profit-sharing, Keogh, and IRA plans, as well as public and private charities and foundations. A tax-exempt organization's need to generate funds to carry on its activities to support its tax-exempt purpose does *not* constitute an activity that is substantially related to such purpose.

IRC Section 512 contains exemptions for items of income that are not considered UBTI because of their inherent passive nature. These items are excepted even if generated by a tax-exempt entity that is otherwise subject to UBTI.

- Interest
- Dividends
- Royalties

- Gains and losses from the sale of securities, as long as:
  - The tax-exempt organization is not a dealer.
  - The securities do not constitute inventory.

Section 512(c) provides that, if a partnership carries on a trade or business, any tax-exempt entities that are partners in the partnership are deemed to be carrying on the trade or business of the partnership. The tax-exempt partner must therefore consider its share of the partnership's UBTI when calculating its own UBTI. The regulations state, however, that income excepted from UBTI (such as dividends) received by the partnership remains exempted from UBTI to the tax-exempt partner.

The IRC specifies another exception from relief of UBTI treatment on investment type income. Under Section 514, income items such as interest, dividends, and capital gains may be included in UBTI to the extent that they are derived from "debt-financed" property, defined as any property held to produce income for which there is acquisition indebtedness at any time during the tax year (or twelve months before the disposition date of the property). Partnership's holding of securities create "acquisition indebtedness" whenever indebtedness:

- Is incurred by the partnership in acquiring such securities

  or

- Would not have been incurred by the partnership "but for" the partnership's acquisition of those securities.

In general, the amount of unrelated debt-financed income allocated to any tax-exempt partner, that is attributable to the partnership's debt-financed securities, is based on the average amount of indebtedness outstanding during the taxable year (of the exempt organization), in which dividend or interest income is generated by those securities. If the partnership sells debt-financed securities, however, the portion of a tax-exempt partner's share of the partnership's gain treated as unrelated debt-financed income is based on the highest amount of acquisition indebtedness that existed with respect to those securities during the twelve month period before the partnership sold them.

Under these rules, if a partnership borrows part of the funds necessary to acquire securities that pay dividends, its tax exempt partners are treated as having borrowed their proportionate shares of those funds. For example, if the partnership borrows half of the funds necessary to acquire such securities, half of the dividend income (net of half of the interest and other expenses attributable to the loan) constitutes UBTI when allocated to tax-exempt partners.

Important: These rules are complex, and partnerships should consult their tax advisors when dealing with this issue.

12

Understanding Partnership Performance

This chapter explains how partnerships calculate performance, including reporting requirements, annualization, and the effects of expenses, management fees, and performance incentive reallocations.

ADVENT PARTNER

Note: Many of the sections in this chapter are specific to Advent Partner, or show methods that Advent Office products use to calculate performance.

In This Chapter

Calculating Partnership Performance

Partnerships usually report performance at both the fund and the investor level. The cash flows associated with contributions and withdrawals, and timing of those flows, can make the partnership's performance calculations very complex. The manager must report performance at least yearly to partners, and generally reports performance at least quarterly. The limited partnership agreement (LPA) may require the manager to report performance monthly, as well.

Calculating Returns Within Break Periods

ADVENT PARTNER

Advent Partner uses a simple rate of return (SRR) calculation to calculate returns for break periods. The SRR figures for break periods are linked together (as in an index) to calculate time-weighted return (TWR), as explained below.

These are the characteristics of the SRR calculation.

- SRR answers the question: "If my money had been invested in a money market account instead of an investment partnership, what interest rate would give me the same ending capital?"
- Because there are no cash flows associated with an index, a simple rate of return is the the best calculation for index performance.

The formula for SRR is:

SRR = ((Ending Capital – Beginning Capital) / Beginning Capital) × 100.

Simple Rate of Return Calculation: An Example

Suppose you want to measure performance for a monthly break period, such as September 1 through September 30. The partner's beginning capital is $500,000.00 and its ending capital is $520,000.00.

Applying the SRR formula gives you: (($520,000 – 500,000) / 500,000) × 100 = 4%.

Calculating Returns Across Multiple Break Periods

Advent Partner can calculate performance returns across multiple break periods using either Time Weighted Return (TWR) or Internal Rate of Return (IRR) calculations, and both of these returns can be annualized. This section explains the calculations.

How Advent Partner Calculates Time Weighted Rate of Return

If you calculate a partner's performance over several break periods, the partner's base capital balance can differ each period, due to contributions, withdrawals, and profit allocations. To account for these changes, Advent Partner can calculate time weighted rates of return (TWRs) to report partners' performance over multiple break periods.

These are the characteristics of the TWR calculation.

- TWR gives the same weight to time periods, regardless of the amount of money invested.
- Because TWR eliminates the effect of cash flows on a partner's capital account, it is a useful factor for comparing the performance of one money manger to another manager or an index.
- TWR answers this question: "If my entire capital account had been invested on the start date and then left alone (with no contributions or withdrawals), what would its performance be?"

The TWR is determined by calculating the capital account's SRR between cash flows, and linking these SRRs. Here is the formula.

$$TWR = (((1 + SRR1 / 100) \times (1 + SRR2 / 100) \times \ldots) - 1) \times 100$$

where each SRR is divided by 100 then added to 1 to produce a multiplier. Subtracting 1 and multiplying by 100 converts the number into a percentage.

Time-Weighted Rate of Return Calculation: An Example

Let's look at three periods: January 1 through 31; February 1 through 28; and March 1 through 31.

For the first period, the account's SRR is 2.75%; for the second period, the account's SRR is 1.25%; for the third period, the account's SRR is –2%.

Applying the TWR formula gives you: TWR = $((1.0275 \times 1.0125 \times .98) - 1) \times 100 = 1.95\%$.

Period	SRR	SRR Multiplier	TWR for Periods 1 – 3
1	2.75%	1.0275	
2	1.25%	1.0125	1.95%
3	(2%)	.98	

How Advent Partner Calculates Internal Rate of Return

ADVENT PARTNER

Advent Partner uses average capital base (ACB) in the calculation that determines the internal rate of return (IRR) for a partner's capital account.

These are the characteristics of the IRR calculation:

- IRR measures the performance of a partner's capital account between two dates.
- IRR gives a greater weight to those time periods when more money was invested in the partner's capital account.
- IRR answers the question "If my entire capital account had been invested in a money market account instead of an investment partnership (but I made the same contributions and withdrawals), what interest rate would give me the same ending market value?"
- IRR shows the performance of an actual capital account. Results can be very different for two identically managed accounts due to the timing of cash flows.

The formula that Advent Partner uses to determine ACB is:

ACB = Beginning Capital + sum of (each change in Capital × (Days Left in Period / Total Days in Period)).

The formula that Advent Partner uses to determine ACB IRR is:

ACB IRR = Total Profit / Average Capital Base × 100.

Average Capital Base IRR Calculation: An Example

Let's look at two periods: January 1 through June 30; and July 1 through December 31. At the start of the first period, the partner's beginning capital is $100. There is no change in capital for this period, so the partner's ACB is $100. It earns $20 profit, so its ending capital is $120.

At the start of the second period, the partner contributes $100,000 to the partnership, so its beginning capital for that period is $100,120. The partner's ACB for this period is $100,120 and its ending capital is $100,120.

Period	Date	Capital Changes	ACB IRR
1	1/1	$100.00 beginning capital	
		$20.00 profit	
	6/30	$120.00 ending capital	
2	7/1	$100,000.00 contribution	
	7/1	$100,120.00 beginning capital	
		$0.00 profit	
	12/31	$100,120.00 ending capital	
Year	12/31		.0398%

For the first period, the capital account had $20 profit; for the second period, the account had $0 profit, so the total profit for the two periods is $20.

The account's ACB for the year is: 100 + (100,000 × (183 / 365)) = 50,237 ($50,237.00).

The account's ACB IRR for the year is: $20 / 50,237 × 100 = .0398%.

Compare a TWR calculation for the same year: the account's SRR for the first period is 20%, and reduced to a multiplier of 1.2. The SRR for the second period is 0%, reduced to a multiplier of 1.0. Therefore, the calculation is: ((1.2 × 1.0) – 1) × 100 = 20%.

Period	Date	Capital Changes	SRR	SRR Multiplier	TWR
1	1/1	$100.00 beginning capital	20%	1.2	
		$20.00 profit			
	6/30	$120.00 ending capital			
2	7/1	$100,000.00 contribution	0%	1.0	
	7/1	$100,120.00 beginning capital			
		$0.00 profit			
	12/31	$100,120.00 ending capital			
Year	12/31				20%

Note: This example uses extreme contributions (impermissible by SEC standards) in order to highlight the differences between dollar-weighted (ACB) rate of return versus time-weighted (TWR) rate of return.

ACB IRR Calculation Net of Performance Fees: An Example

An account's ACB IRR is different before and after performance incentive fees (PIFs) are charged. The previous ACB IRR calculation shows amounts calculated gross of performance fees. The following example shows amounts that take performance fees into account (net of fees).

Let's look at the same two periods: January 1 through June 30; and July 1 through December 31. At the start of the first period, the partner's beginning capital is $100. There is no change in capital for this period, so the partner's ACB is $100. It earns $20 profit, so its ending capital is $120.

At the start of the second period, the partner contributes $100,000 to the partnership, so its beginning capital for that period is $100,120. The partner's ACB for this period is $100,120; and its ending capital is $100,120.

At the end of the two periods, the partner is charged a 20% performance incentive fee on the $20 profit: 20% × $20.00 = $4.00.

Period	Date	Capital Changes	ACB IRR Net of Fees
1	1/1	$100.00 beginning capital	
		$20.00 profit	
	6/30	$120.00 ending capital	
2	7/1	$100,000.00 contribution	
	7/1	$100,120.00 beginning capital	
		$0.00 profit	
	12/31	$100,120.00 ending capital	
	12/31	$4.00 performance incentive fee	
Year	12/31		.0318%

The account's ACB for the year is: 100 + (100,000 × (183 / 365)) = $50,237.

The account's ACB IRR (gross of fees) for the year is: $20 / 50,237 × 100 = .0398%.

For a "net of fees" calculation, the performance fee is subtracted from the partner's profit. Therefore: $20 × .20 = $16.

and the account's ACB IRR (net of fees) for the year is: $16 / 50,237 × 100 = .0318%.

How Advent Partner Calculates Annualized Return

Annualized return is the annual percentage rate of return that a partner's capital balance achieves in a period of one year or more. It is calculated based on the capital's TWR or IRR and the periods per year.

Periods Per Year is the number of the given period that makes up one year. For example, the number of one-year periods per year is 1 (1 / 1); the number of two-year periods per year is .5 (1 / 2); the number of three-year periods per year is .33 (1 / 3), and so on.

The TWR formula for Annualized Return is:

$$ARR = ((1 + TWR / 100) \text{ Periods Per Year} - 1) \times 100$$

and the IRR formula for Annualized Return is:

$$ARR = ((1 + IRR / 100) \text{ Periods Per Year} - 1) \times 100$$

where the TWR or IRR is divided by 100 then added to 1 to produce a multiplier. That multiplier is raised to the power of Periods Per Year. Subtracting 1 and multiplying by 100 converts the number into a percentage.

Annualized Return Calculation: An Example

Suppose you want to calculate the annualized return for a partner's capital account for a two-year period. The account's TWR for the two-year period is 36%, which produces a multiplier of 1.36. The annualized return is calculated as: $((1 + 36 / 100) .5 - 1) \times 100 = 16.6\%$.

How Expenses and Fee Reallocations Affect Performance

Expenses such as management fees, and allocations such as performance incentive fees, can affect a partner's performance. This section explains the considerations and differences gross and net of expenses and allocations.

How Expenses Affect Performance

Expenses, such as management fees, reduce the net appreciation allocated to a partner. Therefore, expense items affect a partner's performance, unless the partnership specifically excludes them from the partnership's profit for performance calculations.

Example: A partner begins a break period with a capital balance of $250,000. The partnership allocates the partner $11,000 in gross appreciation, and $1,000 of expenses, for a net appreciation of $10,000. The partner's rate of return for the period:

- *Gross of fees* is $11,000 / $250,000 = 4.4%.
- *Net of fees* is $10,000 / $250,000 = 4%.

Note: Within Advent Partner, all expenses reduce profit in performance calculations.

How Performance Fee Estimations and Reallocations Affect Performance

ADVENT PARTNER

Advent Partner offers two strategies for handling performance incentive fees: it can reallocate performance incentives or estimate them. Performance incentive reallocations reduce the amount of profit allocated to a partner. When performance fees are estimated (but not charged) both the partner's tax appreciation (net appreciation – estimated performance fee); and its tax capital balance (capital balance + tax appreciation) are affected in the subsequent period. These practices affect the ways Advent Partner calculates performance.

For periods when the partnership estimates (but does not charge) a performance fee, Advent Partner can calculate either:

- *Economic performance:* the partner's capital balance, divided into the partner's economic (book) appreciation; or

  Note: Because no performance fee has been charged, economic performance is the same both gross and net of performance fees.

- *Tax performance:* The partner's capital balance, divided into the partner's tax appreciation.

For periods when the partnership charges a performance fee, Advent Partner can calculate either:

- *Economic performance (gross of performance fees):* The partner's capital balance, divided into the partner's economic (book) appreciation;

- *Economic performance (net of performance fees):* The partner's capital balance, divided into the partner's economic (book) appreciation – *all* performance fees *since the last charge*; or

  Note: If the partnership has not charged in previous periods, the performance fee for all of those periods impacts the current period.

- *Tax performance (net of performance fees only):* The partner's tax capital balance, divided into the partner's tax appreciation (book appreciation – estimated performance fee) *in the current period.*

  Note: Regardless of whether performance incentive fees were charged in previous periods, the current year's tax performance only reflects the performance reallocation for the current period. This is because performance incentive fees are charged incrementally on the tax side.

Example: A partner begins period 1 with a capital balance of $250,000. The partnership allocates the partner $10,000 of appreciation. The partnership estimates the partner a 20% performance fee, so the partner's tax appreciation is $8,000. The partner's rates of return for period 1 are shown in this table.

	Beg. Capital	Allocation	Performance	End. Capital
Economic	$250,000	$10,000	4%	$260,000
Tax	$250,000	$8,000	3.2%	$258,000

The partner begins period 2 with an economic capital balance of $260,000, and a tax capital balance (net of performance fees) of $258,000. The partnership allocates the partner $10,000 in appreciation. The partnership:

- Charges the partner a 20% performance fee on its $20,000 of appreciation since last charge ($10,000 from period 1, and $10,000 from period 2), so the partner's net economic allocation is $6,000.

- Charges the partner a 20% performance fee on its $10,000 of appreciation in period 2, so the partner's net tax appreciation is $8,000.

The partner's rates of return for period 2 are shown in this table.

	Beg. Capital	Allocation	Performance	End. Capital
Economic (gross)	$260,000	$10,000	3.85%	$270,000
Economic (net)	$260,000	$6,000	2.3%	$266,000
Tax	$258,000	$8,000	3.1%	$266,000

Note: The partner's economic and tax TWRs for the two periods match.

- *Economic:* $(((1 + .04) \times (1 + .023)) - 1) = .0639\%$.
- *Tax:* $(((1 + .032) \times (1 + .031)) - 1) = .0639\%$.

Differences in Tax Performance Between Partners

In Advent Partner, performance net of performance incentive reallocations can vary between partners for one of two reasons: capital changes and performance fee charge dates.

Tax Performances Differences Due to Capital Changes

Capital changes (contributions, withdrawals, and assignments) affect both tax and economic performance on a gross basis; that is, they are not reduced by estimated performance fees. These cash flows impact economic and tax performance differently because:

- A capital change has the same effect on both economic and tax capital balances;

  but

- An allocation of appreciation affects economic and tax capital balances differently due to estimated performance fees.

Therefore, cash flows have a disproportionate impact on the partner's tax capital base compared to allocations. Charging the performance fee realigns the partner's economic and tax capital.

Example: A partnership allocates $10,000 of appreciation to a partner with a capital balance of $100,000. The partnership estimates a performance fee of $2,000 from this appreciation. The partner ends the period with an economic capital balance of $110,000, and a tax capital balance of $108,000. A $10,000 contribution by the partner would constitute a 9.09% change in the partner's economic capital, but a 9.25% change in the partner's tax capital.

Tax Performances Differences Due to Performance Fee Charge Dates

Charging partners performance fees on different dates reduces some partners' capital relative to others. This in turn affects the partners' economic percentages, and the allocation of profit in subsequent periods.

Differences in Tax Performance: Examples

The following examples illustrate the differences between the economic and tax performance of two limited partners, A and B. The examples assume that:

- Both partners are charged a performance fee.
- All allocations are *pro rata* (no hot issue or other non-*pro rata* allocations).

In both examples, notice that:

- The partners have identical *economic* performance.
- When you charge partners a performance fee:
  - Their tax performance is 1% of their *economic* performance.
  - In the next period, their beginning tax capital balances equal their beginning economic capital balances.

- When Partner A's beginning tax balance equals its beginning economic balance, and Partner B's beginning tax balance is less than its economic balance, all other factors being equal, Partner B's tax performance is higher than Partner A's.
- If partners A and B have identical capital changes since their last performance fee charge, their tax performance matches.

Note: The performance fee is high (99%), to make the tax performance differences clear.

How Capital Changes Affect Tax Performance: An Example

1 Partners A and B each contribute $1 to the partnership. The partnership earns $18 profit the first period. The following tables show the economic and tax allocations and performance for the first period.

Economic Allocation and Performance: Period 1

Partner	Prev. Ending Capital	Contrib.	Beginning Capital		Allocated Profit	Performance (IRR)*	Ending Capital	
			Balance	Percent			Balance	Percent
A	$0	$1	$1	50%	$9	900%	$10	50%
B	$0	$1	$1	50%	$9	900%	$10	50%
Total	**$0**	**$2**	**$2**	**100%**	**$18**		**$20**	**100%**

*Allocated Profit / Beginning Economic Capital

Tax Allocation and Performance: Period 1

Partner	Prev. Ending Capital	Contrib.	Beginning Capital		Allocated Profit*	Performance (IRR)**	Ending Capital	
			Balance	Percent*			Balance	Percent
A	$0	$1	$1	.5%	$.09	9%	$1.09	50%
B	$0	$1	$1	.5%	$.09	9%	$1.09	50%
Total	**$0**	**$2**	**$2**	1%	**$.18**		**$2.18**	**100%**

*Reduced for the estimated 99% performance fee

**Allocated (After PerfFee) Profit / Beginning Tax Capital

2 At the beginning of the second period, Partner A contributes $80. The partnership then earns $100 profit during the period. The following tables show the economic and tax allocation and performance for the second period.

Economic Allocation and Performance: Period 2

Partner	Prev. Ending Capital	Contrib.	Beginning Capital		Allocated Profit	Performance (IRR)*	Ending Capital	
			Balance	Percent			Balance	Percent
A	$10	$80	$90	90%	$90	100%	$180	90%
B	$10	$0	$10	10%	$10	100%	$20	10%
Total	**$20**	**$80**	**$100**	**100%**	**$100**		**$200**	**100%**

*Allocated Profit / Beginning Economic Capital

Tax Allocation and Performance: Period 2

Partner	Prev. Ending Capital	Contrib.	Beginning Capital		Allocated Profit*	Performance (IRR)**	Ending Capital	
			Balance	Percent*			Balance	Percent
A	$1.09	$80	$81.09	.9%	$.90	1.1%	$81.99	98.6%
B	$1.09	$0	$1.09	.1%	$.10	9.1%	$1.19	1.4%
Total	**$2.18**	**$80**	**$82.18**	1%	**$1**		**$83.18**	**100%**

*Reduced for the estimated 99% performance fee

**Allocated (After PerfFee) Profit / Beginning Tax Capital

Notice that, even though the partners' capital percentages change, their economic performance remains the same (100%). Partner A's contribution, however, causes its profit to be divided into a larger tax capital base. This lowers its performance (relative to Partner B, who made no contribution) until the partnership next charges the performance fee, at which time Partner A's economic and tax capital again match.

How Different Performance Fee Charge Dates Affect Tax Performance: An Example

1 Partners A and B each contribute $1 to the partnership. The partnership earns $18 profit during the first period. The partnership charges Partner A a performance fee at the end of the period. The following tables show the economic and tax allocation and performance for the first period.

Economic Allocation and Performance: Period 1

Partner	Prev. Ending Capital	Contrib.	Beginning Capital		Allocated Profit	Performance (IRR)*	Ending Capital	
			Balance	Percent			Balance	Percent
A	$0	$1	$1	50%	$9	900%	$1.09**	9.8%
B	$0	$1	$1	50%	$9	900%	$10	90.2%
Total	**$0**	**$2**	**$2**	**100%**	**$18**		**$11.09**	**100%**

*Allocated Profit / Beginning Economic Capital

**Reduced for the charged 99% performance fee

Tax Allocation and Performance: Period 1

Partner	Prev. Ending Capital	Contrib.	Beginning Capital		Allocated Profit*	Performance (IRR)**	Ending Capital	
			Balance	Percent*			Balance	Percent
A	$0	$1	$1	.5%	$.09	9%	$1.09	50%
B	$0	$1	$1	.5%	$.09	9%	$1.09	50%
Total	**$0**	**$2**	**$2**	**1%**	**$.18**		**$2.18**	**100%**

*Reduced for the estimated 99% performance fee

**Allocated (After PerfFee) Profit / Beginning Tax Capital

Charging Partner A a performance fee reduces its economic profit allocation by the fee when the partnership calculates its ending capital. This also affects both partners' ending percentages, which in turn affects their profit allocations in period 2.

In the tax allocation, although the partnership only charges Partner A a performance fee, it estimates Partner B's fee. The partners' ending capital and performance match.

2 The partnership earns $10 profit during the second period. The partnership charges both partners A and B performance fees at the end of this period. The following tables show the economic and tax allocation and performance for the second period.

Economic Allocation and Performance: Period 2

Partner	Prev. Ending Capital	Contrib.	Beginning Capital		Allocated Profit	Performance (IRR)*	Ending Capital	
			Balance	Percent			Balance	Percent
A	$1.09	$0	$1.09	9.8%	$.98	90%	$1.10**	90%
B	$10	$0	$10	90.2%	$9.02	90%	$1.18**	10%
Total	**$11.09**	**$0**	**$11.09**	**100%**	**$10**		**$2.28**	**100%**

*Allocated Profit / Beginning Economic Capital

**Reduced for the charged 99% performance fee

Tax Allocation and Performance: Period 2

Partner	Prev. Ending Capital	Contrib.	Beginning Capital		Allocated Profit*	Performance (IRR)**	Ending Capital	
			Balance	Percent*			Balance	Percent
A	$1.09	$0	$1.09	.5%	$.01	1%	$1.10	48.2%
B	$1.09	$0	$1.09	.5%	$.09	8%	$1.18	51.8%
Total	**$2.18**	**$80**	**$2.18**	**1%**	**$.10**		**$2.28**	**100%**

*Reduced for the estimated 99% performance fee

**Allocated (After PerfFee) Profit / Beginning Tax Capital

Charging performance fees to both partners A and B reduces their economic profit allocations by the fee for calculating their ending capital. Partner B's ending capital reflects its performance fee covering both period 1 and period 2.

Notice that, even though the partners' capital percentages change, their economic performance remains the same (90%). Because the partnership charges Partner A a performance fee in period 1, however, its allocated profit, and therefore its ending capital, is reduced.

Because the partnership charges each partner a performance fee this period, each partner's ending tax capital matches its ending economic capital. The difference between Partner A's and Partner B's ending capital balances reflects the fact that the partnership charged Partner A at the end of each period, whereas it charged Partner B only at the end of period 2.

Disclosures and Issues to Consider When Reporting Performance

Advisory fees, brokerage and other commissions, and any other expenses should be deducted from gross performance. The following items should also be disclosed.

- The effect of any material market or economic conditions on the results. (*Example:* If the fund and the market moved in lockstep, this may be relevant information to an investor.)
- How the market performed during the period by presenting an appropriate index (if relevant), including any facts bearing on the fairness of the comparison. (*Example:* The nature of the index, whether the figures for the index assume reinvestment of dividends, and so on.)
- All material differences between the fund's results and any index used for comparison. (*Example:* If the volatility of the index is greater than that of the fund's portfolio.)
- Material conditions, objectives, or investment strategies used to obtain the fund's results. (*Example:* Specific types of equity securities, hedging techniques, and the like.)
- The size of the fund during the periods presented. (*Example:* Disclosing that the fund appreciated 50 percent for the year without saying whether the fund consisted of $100,000 or $100 million in assets fails to provide material information to an investor.)

Glossary

accredited investor	An individual having either a net worth in excess of $1,000,000, or income in excess of $200,000 (or $300,000 joint with spouse), in each of the two most recent years. Rule 506 of the Securities Act of 1933 also provides qualifications for employee benefit plans, corporations, trusts, and other institutional investors. At least 65% of an investment partnership's investors must be accredited investors for the partnership to qualify as a Section 3(c)(1) fund.
adjusted book gain	A partner's economic allocation of book gain, adjusted for performance fees. Investment partnerships use adjusted book gain in aggregate methodology.
Advent Partner	Advent Software's partnership accounting system. Advent Partner imports transaction information from Axys, and allocates the results of the partnership's activities to the partners according to their capital contributions to the partnership. Advent Partner also reallocates performance fees, performs tax lot layering or aggregate gains allocation, accounts for a variety of book-to-tax issues (such as Section 1256 gains and wash sales), and helps users prepare IRS Form 1065 and Schedule K-1s.
aggregate account	The account that an investment partnership must maintain for each partner in order to track the partner's share of aggregate unrealized gain or loss in the partnership. Each period, the partnership adds the partner's share of book gain, less the partner's share of taxable gain (and certain book-tax adjustments), to the partner's aggregate account balance.
aggregate assumption	The conditions that determine whether an investment partnership allocates aggregate realized gains according to aggregate percentages, tax percentages, or both.

aggregate methodology	A method of allocating realized gains and losses. Unlike tax lot layering methodology, aggregate methodology looks at a partner's share of unrealized appreciation in the partnership's portfolio as a whole. Realized gains and losses are aggregated, and then allocated to the partners according to the aggregate unrealized gain or loss that has been allocated to their aggregate accounts.
aggregate percentage	A given partner's percentage of an investment partnership's total aggregate account balance. Partnerships use aggregate percentages in certain aggregate assumptions.
allocation item	An investment partnership's items of profit and loss. Partnerships can use a different allocation methodology for each item, or break items out on reports or Schedule K-1s.
allocation methodology	The method an investment partnership uses to allocate a profit item to its partners. *See also* aggregate methodology; even methodology; manual methodology; side pocket methodology; system methodology; tax lot layering methodology.
anniversary date	The date on which a limited partner joins an investment partnership. A general partner registered under the Investment Advisors Act of 1940 must wait 12 months before charging a performance fee. Partnerships can interpret how to apply this anniversary date in several ways.
assignment of interest	The act of one partner transferring some or all of its interest in an investment partnership to another partner. This assignment includes a proportionate amount of the assigning partner's capital account balance, tax basis, and aggregate account balance or layers of unrealized gains.
assumption	*See* aggregate assumption.
benchmark	*See* hurdle rate.
book allocation	*See* economic allocation.

book gain	The total of an investment partnership's realized and unrealized gains in a given period. Partnerships that use an aggregate methodology allocate book gains economically, adjusted for performance fees, to calculate partners' aggregate account balances and tax allocations of realized and unrealized gains.
break period	A period during which there are no cash flows into or out of an investment partnership. The partnership allocates its profits during the break period according to the partners' capital percentages during that period.
built-in gain	A security's unrealized gain at the time the partner contributes it. The contributing partner's allocation of realized gain is said to be "built into" the security at the time of contribution. When the contributing partner sells the security, the built-in gain is allocated to the partner, and the remaining gain is allocated to the partnership as a whole.
capital account	An account established for each partner that tracks capital changes (such as contributions and withdrawals), as well as allocations of profit to each partner.
capital percentage	A given partner's percentage of an investment partnership's capital. This capital percentage is the partner's capital account balance.
carve-out	The portion of the performance fee a partner receives if the partnership has more than one general partner, or if any limited partners receive part of the fee.
ceiling rule	According to Internal Revenue Code Section 704-3(b)(1), the rule which states that no individual partner may receive gain or loss greater than that recognized by the overall investment partnership. In theory, tax lot layering methodology and allocation methodology can produce violations of the ceiling rule.
"check-the-box"	An offshore corporation can elect to be taxed as a partnership for U.S. tax purposes. By investing in an offshore master-feeder fund, taxed as a U.S. partnership, the limited partners will receive "pass-through" treatment for their share of the feeder's income from the master.

clawback provision	A provision in a limited partnership agreement stating that the general partner must refund all or part of the performance fee if the partnership's profits fall below a certain level.
class	A group of investors with the same attributes. Profit and loss are divided equally among all members of the class.
commodity pool operator	If an investment partnership trades any commodity options or futures, the general partner(s) must register as a commodity pool operator (CPO) with the Commodity Futures Trading Commission (CFTC), unless they receive an exemption from the CFTC.
constructive sale	According to the Internal Revenue Code Section 1259, a taxable event in which an investor must recognize gain on an open position of stock, certain debt instruments, or partnership interests at the time the investor opens an offsetting security position.
contributed securities	*See* contribution, in-kind.
contribution, cash	Money, contributed by a partner to the partnership, that increases the partner's capital account and tax basis interest in the partnership.
contribution, in-kind	A property contribution, usually in the form of stocks or securities, by a partner to a partnership that increases the partner's capital account and tax basis interest in the partnership. *Also called* contributed securities.
designated capital	Capital, contributed by a partner, to fund a side pocket investment.
designated percentage	A partner's capital contribution to a side pocket investment, divided by the total of all partners' contributions. Designated percentages are used to allocate the investment's profits.
directed gains	The realized gains allocated to a withdrawing partner, and the unrealized gains (equivalent to the realized gains allocated to the withdrawing partner) allocated to the remaining partners. A partnership that allows its general partner to direct gains must include a directed gains provision in its partnership agreement.

distribution, cash	Cash distributed to a partner in order to partially or completely liquidate the partner's interest in an investment partnership.
distribution, property	Stocks or securities distributed to a partner in order to partially or completely liquidate the partner's interest in an investment partnership.
economic allocation	An allocation of an investment partnership's economic results (profit or appreciation) to the partners' capital accounts. Partnerships usually perform an economic allocation in proportion to the partners' economic percentages.
economic capital	A partner's capital in an investment partnership, not counting performance fee estimates or other tax adjustments.
economic percentage	A partner's economic capital account balance as a percentage of the investment partnership's total capital.
ERISA	(Advent Partner) The Employee Retirement Income Security Act of 1974. ERISA establishes a comprehensive federal regulatory framework for employee benefit plans sponsored by private employers in the United States. If more than 25% of an investment partnership's capital comes from retirement funds regulated by ERISA, the partnership's manager has additional duties, requirements, and restrictions.
even methodology	Allocation pro rata according to partners' capital percentages.
fill up/fill down provision	*See* directed gains.
fund of funds	An investment fund (such as an investment partnership) that invests its capital in a number of other partnerships or money management vehicles. Some funds of funds retain a portion of their capital to invest directly for their own accounts.
general partner	A member of an investment partnership who manages the business of the partnership, and is personally liable for the fund's debts. A limited partnership must have at least one general partner.

gross net asset value (GNAV)	The total assets of a fund, class, or series minus its total liabilities *excluding* performance fee. This amount may be compared to the partner's highwater mark to determine whether a performance fee should be charged.
GNAV per share	The GNAV of a fund, class, or series divided by the number of outstanding shares.
hedge fund	An investment fund that reduces risk by following a defensive investment strategy, such as arbitrage, leveraging, short-selling, or investing in derivatives. *See also* investment partnership.
highwater mark	An amount equal to the greatest value of a partner's capital account, adjusted for contributions and withdrawals. An investment partnership uses the highwater mark to calculate a limited partner's target capital for performance fee charges.
highwater net asset value (HNAV)	The net asset value that the gross net asset value (GNAV) of a class or series must exceed before a performance fee can be charged.
HNAV per share	The HNAV of a fund, class, or series divided by the number of outstanding shares.
hot issue	Securities that are part of a public distribution (such as an initial public offering) that trades at a premium in the secondary market immediately after the distribution begins. Members of the National Association of Securities Dealers, Inc. (NASD) cannot sell hot issue securities to an account in which a member or person affiliated with, or related to, a member of the NASD has an interest ("restricted" members or affiliates). Investment partnerships cannot allocate gains from hot issue securities to restricted partners. (NASD Rules of Fair Practice)
hub and spoke fund	*See* master-feeder fund.

hurdle rate	The amount a limited partner's capital account must appreciate before it is subject to a performance fee charge. Hurdle rates are defined as an annual percentage of the partner's highwater mark (or beginning capital account balance for the performance fee charge period). *See also* target capital.
incentive allocation, incentive fee	*See* performance fee.
investee fund	A fund that a fund of funds invests in. An investee fund views the fund of funds ("investor fund") as a partner.
investment partnership	A limited partnership formed as an investment vehicle for high net worth individuals and institutions. This is typically done to avoid the limitations and regulations of mutual funds and other investing structures. *See also* hedge fund.
investor fund	A fund of funds in relationship to an investee fund. Compare "investee fund".
item	*See* allocation item.
knowledgeable employee	An executive officer, or other manager, of an investment fund. All of an investment partnership's investors must be either knowledgeable employees or qualified funds purchasers for the partnership to qualify as a Section 3(c)(7) fund. (Investment Company Act of 1940, amended.)
layering	*See* tax lot layering methodology.
limited liability company (LLC)	An entity that combines certain characteristics of corporation law with certain characteristics of partnership law. LLCs offer their owners limited liability, full management capability, and flow-through gains and losses similar to a limited partnership. They are considered partnerships for tax purposes, thereby avoiding two layers of taxation. Many investment partnerships structure their general partner as an LLC.

limited partner	A member of a limited partnership, who contributes capital without liability for the fund's debts beyond the loss of its investment. A limited partnership must have at least one limited partner.
limited partnership	A type of partnership that incorporates limited liability characteristics of a corporation, but retains the pass-through characteristics of a partnership. A limited partnership must have at least one general partner, who is liable for the partnership's debts, and one limited partner, who is liable only for its capital investment.
limited partnership agreement	The legal agreement between the limited partner(s) and general partner(s) in a limited partnership. The agreement usually includes performance fee and management fee structures, powers of the general partners, descriptions of allocation formulas, and other legal considerations.
lock-up	A fund that includes only the original partners that joined at the time the fund was formed. These partners do not have withdrawal rights.
loss carry-forward	*See* highwater mark.
management fee	A fee used to fund the operating expenses of an investment partnership, such as rent, salaries, and office supplies. Partnerships usually calculate management fees as a percentage of the net asset value of the partnership at a certain time, usually quarterly. A typical management fee structure is 1% of the partnership's net asset value, paid quarterly in advance (that is, .25% of net asset value at the beginning of each quarter).
manual methodology	An allocation methodology that allows the general partner to determine the amount of an item allocated to each partner.
mark-to-market	To adjust the valuation of securities or portfolios to reflect current market values. Investment partnerships mark Section 1256 securities to market at the end of each year or reporting period, and allocate the gains as if they had sold the securities, 60% long-term and 40% short-term gain, regardless of the actual holding period.

master-feeder fund	A two-tiered investment system in which investors invest their capital in a "feeder" fund, which invests in the securities held in a "master" fund operated by the same investment company.
memo account	*See* aggregate account.
methodology	*See* allocation methodology.
Net Asset Value	The total assets of a fund, class, or series minus its total liabilities *including* the impact of the performance fee.
NAV per share	The NAV of a fund, class, or series divided by the number of outstanding shares.
offering document	The legal document that documents the understanding between an offshore fund's investment advisor and shareholders. Compare "private placement memorandum" in U.S. investment partnerships.
partnership	A legal relationship created by the voluntary association of two or more persons to act as co-owners of a business for profit. The IRS stipulates that a partnership must possess no more than two of the following characteristics of a corporation: continuity of life, centralization of management, limited liability, and free transferability of interest. Partnerships are not taxed as entities. Instead, the partnership "passes through" its taxable income (interest income, realized gains and losses, operating expenses, etc.) to the partners.
partnership agreement	*See* limited partnership agreement.
pass-through income	Income that, in general, is only taxed once, and that retains the tax attributes as it flows from the investment entity to the ultimate taxable entity. For example, gains and losses that a limited partnership create are not taxed at the partnership level, but rather, they "pass-through" to the individual limited partners, while retaining the character (for example, long-term capital gains, dividend income, and so on). Contrast this with a corporation, which, as it earns income, is taxed at the corporation level, then, as income is distributed, is taxed again at the investor level. The tax attributes of the income are *not* maintained at the investor level.

payout percentage	The percentage of a limited partner's appreciation that an investment partnership reallocates to the general partner as a performance fee. Partnerships can also charge performance fees "above the hurdle," in which case the payout represents the percentage of the limited partner's appreciation above its target capital that the partnership reallocates.
performance fee	Compensation to the general partner of an investment partnership for investment advisory services rendered. In U.S. partnerships, this "fee" actually reallocates a percentage (usually 20%) of the partnership's profit for the year from the limited partners to the general partner. In offshore funds, performance fee is usually charged to the limited partners as an expense.
period	*See* break period.
qualified eligible participant	An individual with a net worth of $1 million, or an income greater than $200,000 ($300,000 with their spouse) in each of the last two years, and at least $2 million in investments or $200,000 on deposit with a futures commission merchant. Investment partnerships registered with the Commodity Futures Trading Commission (CFTC) do not require any special disclosure if all of the partners are qualified eligible participants.
qualified purchaser	An individual or family of companies with $5 million in investments, or an entity that holds and controls $25 million in investments. All of an investment partnership's investors must be either qualified funds purchasers or knowledgeable employees in order for the partnership to qualify as a Section 3(c)(7) fund. (Investment Company Act of 1940, amended)
reallocation	*See* tax reallocation/tax allocation.
redemption	A withdrawal of cash or securities from an offshore fund. Compare "withdrawal" in U.S. investment partnerships.

registered investment advisor (RIA)	An investment advisor registered with the Securities and Exchange Commission (SEC), and subject to certain restrictions. The Investment Advisers Act of 1940 requires managers who have more than $30 million under management to register with the SEC, although they can seek an exemption.
restricted partner	A member of an investment partnership who is affiliated with, or related to, a member of the National Association of Securities Dealers, Inc. (NASD). Under the NASD Rules of Fair Practice, members of the NASD cannot sell hot issue securities to the accounts of restricted investors.
revalue account	*See* aggregate account.
RIA	*See* registered investment advisor (RIA).
Schedule K-1	A schedule of IRS Form 1065 (Partner's Share of Income, Credits, Deductions, etc.) used to report to a partner its share of an investment partnership's income, deductions, gains, and losses.
Section 1256	The section of the Internal Revenue Code that specifies that lots of regulated futures contracts, foreign currency contracts, non-equity options, and dealer equity options must be marked-to-market at the end of the year or other reporting period, and allocated as if sold, 60% long-term and 40% short-term gain, without regard to actual holding period.
Section 3(c)(1) fund	A type of fund that can avoid registration as a mutual fund with the Securities and Exchange Commission (SEC) under the Investment Company Act of 1940. A Section 3(c)(1) fund must have no more than 100 investors, at least 65% of whom are accredited investors.
Section 3(c)(7) fund	A type of fund that can avoid registration as a mutual fund with the Securities and Exchange Commission (SEC) under the Investment Company Act of 1940. All Section 3(c)(7) fund investors must be either qualified funds purchasers or knowledgeable employees.

Section 754 election	The section of the Internal Revenue Code that allows investment partnerships to adjust the tax basis of securities they hold by the difference between the economic (book) basis and the tax basis (that is, unrealized gain) of partners who have withdrawn 100% of their capital account balance from the partnership.
Section 988	The section of the Internal Revenue Code that defines gains and losses from foreign currency movement as ordinary income. Section 988 overlaps with Section 1256, however, regarding regulated futures contracts in a foreign currency, foreign currency contracts, and non-equity options on foreign currencies. Investment partnerships can elect to treat these instruments as either ordinary income, or as 60% long-term and 40% short-term capital gain.
series	A group of shares issued when an offshore fund receives a new or additional subscription. All subscriptions that occur at the same time belong to the same series. All shareholders in the same series pay performance fee on those shares at the same time.
shareholder	An investor in an offshore fund. Compare "limited partner" in U.S. investment partnerships.
side pocket investment	An investment to which only some of the partners contribute designated capital. Partnerships allocate profits from the investments according to the partners' designated percentages in the investment.
side pocket methodology	The allocation methodology used for proceeds from side pocket investments. The partnership allocates profits from the investment to the partners, according to their designated percentages.
straddle	A position in actively trading property that substantially reduces the risk of loss on an offsetting position. Internal Revenue Code Section 1091 limits the amount of loss an investor can recognize on a position in a straddle, defines holding period rules for long positions in a straddle, and sets rules for deducting interest expenses incurred in opening or maintaining a position in a straddle.
stuffing	*See* directed gains.

subscription	A contribution of cash or securities to an offshore fund. Compare "contribution" in U.S. investment partnerships.
system methodology	Allocation instructions for specific items built into Advent Partner. Examples include the tax lot layering and aggregate gain reallocations of multiple historical periods.
target capital	The amount that a limited partner's capital account balance must exceed for the partner to be subject to a performance fee charge. A partner's target capital is the partner's highwater mark (or beginning capital account balance), plus the partner's hurdle rate.
tax basis	The net amount of a partner's contributions to and withdrawals from an investment partnership, plus all taxable and tax-free profit that the partnership has allocated to the partner.
tax capital	A partner's capital in an investment partnership, including performance fee charges or estimates and other tax adjustments.
tax lot layering methodology	A method of allocating realized gains and losses that specifically tracks a partner's share of unrealized gains and losses in each security tax lot in a partnership's portfolio. When the partnership sells a security, it allocates realized gain and loss to the partners based on their historic unrealized gain or loss.
tax percentage	A partner's economic percentage, adjusted for performance fees.
tax reallocation/ tax allocation	A restatement of one or more economic allocations for tax purposes. Tax allocations include adjustments for tax lot layering or aggregate allocations of gains, wash sales and other gain deferrals or holding period adjustments, Section 1256 and other mark-to-market securities, and directed gains. These allocations typically include the performance fee in the item amounts allocated to each partner.
underwater	A term used to describe a partner whose highwater mark exceeds his or her capital account balance.

uneven methodology	An allocation methodology that allocates items of profit and loss unevenly, yet according to a set formula. Advent Partner supports off-the-top literal, off-the-top realigned, and off-the-bottom uneven methodologies.
unrealized memo account	*See* aggregate account.
unrelated business taxable income (UBTI)	Income earned by a tax-exempt organization that is derived, either directly or through a partnership, from any trade or business regularly carried on that is substantially unrelated to the exercise or performance of the organization's exempt purpose or function. Internal Revenue Code Section 511 states that tax-exempt organizations are subject to tax on this income. The trade or business unrelated to its tax-exempt purpose can also lead to revocation of the organization's exempt status.
wash sale	A realized loss, within 30 days of which (prior to or after the loss) the investor opens a position in a substantially identical security. Internal Revenue Code Section 1091 states that investors must defer such losses for tax purposes.
withdrawals	A decrease in the amount of money, or appreciated securities, in a partner's capital account in an investment partnership. The partner's tax basis in the partnership also decreases by the amount of the withdrawal, though never below zero.

Index

Numerics

A

B

C

D

E

H

I

J

K

L

M

N

O

P

T

U

V

W

Y

Comment Form

Please use this form to give us constructive comments on this guide. We'll consider your comments carefully and try to incorporate the appropriate changes in future editions.

Guide and version:______________________________ **Date:**__________

Comments: *Please describe any changes or enhancements you'd like to see in this guide. If you find any errors, list the page number(s) and error(s). Add additional pages if necessary.*

Optional: It would be helpful if we could contact you if we have any questions about your comments.

Your name/Job title:____

Company name: ____

Address:____

City, state, zip:____

Phone number:________________________Email:____________________________

Would you like a response?______ Yes______ No

Mail or fax this form to Director, Learning Products, Advent Software, 301 Brannan St., San Francisco, CA 94107. Fax 415-543-0466. You can also send your comments via email to *documentation@advent.com,* or send feedback through Advent's client-only Web site at *http://connection.advent.com/feedback/*. We appreciate your comments.